T0382791

BEST PRACTICES SERIES

Winning the Outsourcing Game

Making the Best Deals and Making Them Work

THE AUERBACH

BEST PRACTICES SERIES

Broadband Networking, James Trulove, Editor,
ISBN: 0-8493-9821-5

Electronic Messaging, Nancy Cox, Editor,
ISBN: 0-8493-9825-8

Enterprise Systems Integration, John Wyzalek, Editor,
ISBN: 0-8493-9837-1

Financial Services Information Systems, Jessica Keyes, Editor,
ISBN: 0-8493-9834-7

Healthcare Information Systems, Phillip L. Davidson, Editor,
ISBN: 0-8493-9963-7

Internet Management, Jessica Keyes, Editor,
ISBN: 0-8493-9987-4

Multi-Operating System Networking: Living with UNIX, NetWare, and NT, Raj Rajagopal, Editor,
ISBN: 0-8493-9831-2

Network Design, Gilbert Held, Editor,
ISBN: 0-8493-0859-3

Network Manager's Handbook, John Lusa, Editor,
ISBN: 0-8493-9841-X

Project Management, Paul C. Tinnirello, Editor,
ISBN: 0-8493-9998-X

Server Management, Gilbert Held, Editor,
ISBN: 0-8493-9823-1

Web-to-Host Connectivity, Lisa Lindgren and Anura Guruge, Editors
ISBN: 0-8493-0835-6

Winning the Outsourcing Game: Making the Best Deals and Making Them Work, Janet Butler, Editor
ISBN: 0-8493-0875-5

AUERBACH PUBLICATIONS

www.auerbach-publications.com
TO ORDER: Call: 1-800-272-7737 • Fax: 1-800-374-3401
E-mail: orders@crcpress.com

BEST PRACTICES SERIES

Winning the Outsourcing Game

Making the Best Deals and Making Them Work

Editor

JANET BUTLER

AUERBACH

Boca Raton   London   New York   Washington, D.C.

Library of Congress Cataloging-in-Publication Data

Winning the outsourcing game : making the best deals and making them work / Janet Butler, editor.
    p. cm.
Includes bibliographical references and index.
ISBN 0-8493-0875-5
    1. Electronic data processing departments—Contracting out. 2. Information resources management. I. Butler, Janet G. II. Best practices series (Boca Raton, Fla.)
HF5548.2 .W4765   2000
658′.05—dc21   00-030630

Visit the Auerbach Publications Web site at www.auerbach-publications.com

© 2000 by CRC Press LLC
Auerbach is an imprint of CRC Press LLC

No claim to original U.S. Government works
International Standard Book Number 0-8493-0875-5
Library of Congress Card Number 00-030630
Printed in the United States of America   2 3 4 5 6 7 8 9 0
Printed on acid-free paper

Contributors

LEILANI ALLEN, *Partner, Summer Point Consulting, Mundelein, Illinois*

MARIE ALNER, *Information Security Consultant, Integrated Systems Technologies, Inc.*

WILLIAM J. BEAUMONT, *Vice President, Marketing, DecisionOne Corporation, Frazer, Pennsyslvania*

KEN DOUGHTY, *ASA, CISA, Principal Consultant, O'Driscoll & Doughty Audit Services, Ormistron, Australia*

RAOUL J. FREEMAN, *Professor and Chair, Computer Information Systems, California State University–Dominguez Hills, California*

FRANKE GRIECO, *Manager, Information Systems' Audit, Brisbane City Council, Brisbane, Australia*

FRITZ H. GRUPE, *Professor, CIS, University of Nevada, Reno, Nevada*

RICHARD D. HAYS, *President, Hays Consulting, Sarasota, Florida*

DOUGLAS B. HOYT, *Consultant and Writer, Hartsdale, New York*

JOSEPH JUDENBERG, *Manager of Outsourcing, PricewaterhouseCoopers*

BRIAN KEANE, *Information Services Division and Healthcare Services Division, Keane, Inc.*

WILLIAM R. KING, *Professor of Business Administration, University of Pittsburgh, Pennsyslvania*

RALPH L. KLIEM, *Principal, Practical Creative Solutions, Inc., Redmond, Washington*

IRWIN S. LUDIN, *Principal, Practical Creative Solutions, Inc., Redmond, Washington*

DAVID MASSEY, *Technical Market Development Manager, Productivity Point International, Seattle, Washington*

N. DEAN MEYER, *Consultant, NDMA, Inc., Ridgefield, Connecticut*

NATHAN J. MULLER, *Independent Consultant, Oxford, Connecticut*

JOHN P. MURRAY, *Senior Management System Consultant, Viking Insurance Co., Madison, Wisconsin*

HOWARD A. RUBIN, *Professor and Chair, Department of Computer Science, Hunter College, City University of New York, New York, New York*

S. YVONNE SCOTT, *IS Audit Manager, GATX Corp., Chicago, Illinois*

JOHN R. VACCA, *Information Technology Consultant, Pomeroy, Ohio*

WIM VAN GREMBERGEN, *Professor, Business Faculty, UFSIA, Antwerp, Belgium*

DANIEL VANDER BORGHT, *Corporate Internal Auditor, Belgian Multinational Corporation*

Table of Contents

Table of Contents

Introduction

"DO WHAT YOU DO BEST AND OUTSOURCE THE REST," advises author Tom Peters, and chief information officers (CIOs) are listening closely, as they try to keep pace in a competitive marketplace, maintain flexibility in a rapidly changing business/technology climate, control costs under the ever-closer scrutiny of upper management, and shore up their skills gap, by which some 350,000 information technology (IT) positions go unfilled nationwide. Outsourcing is already the rule rather than the exception when companies seek application service providers, Web hosting, and integration of their legacy and ERP systems. In fact, more than 90 percent of all multinational companies now outsource some of their business, and total revenues from outsourcing are estimated to exceed $300 billion in 2001. More specific to information systems, industry analysts predict that 60 percent of all IT work will be outsourced by 2003.

All outsourcing deals are not created equal, however. While some succeed, far too many fail. The effects of failure can be disastrous, ranging from poor morale of permanent employees, heavy dependence on outside suppliers, and negative relationships with vendors, to lost control of mission-critical functions.

This intensely practical book stacks the odds in favor of success, in light of the numerous, potentially fatal outsourcing risks. It does so by providing a background and framework by which IT managers can develop a sound outsourcing strategy, choose which IT functions to outsource, and effectively manage the risks of using third-party contractors to carry out their companies' IT functions.

It should come as no surprise to IT managers that good management requires well-thought-out delegation of responsibility, whether it relates to individuals or companies; and be it in-house or supplied from outside. However, while outsourcers generally win contracts by presenting a good business case for their services, senior management has despaired of obtaining the same from IT. This book seeks to correct that situation.

To gain the advantages and avoid the pitfalls of outsourcing, CIOs must learn to approach it from a business-case perspective, weighing outsourcing against in-sourcing and right-sourcing. The approach requires gauging the current situation against long-term goals, balancing advantages against risks, measuring return on investment, and monitoring outsourcing relationships and contracts.

From the outset, in determining whether or not to outsource, IT professionals can foster success by making the right business decision, based on guidelines found in this book. If a company judges IT to be better and cheaper than an outsourcer, it might decide to keep the function in-house.

In fact, some IT departments that took this proactive approach when their organizations first considered outsourcing managed to thereby stave off the use of outside services. They retained IT functions in-house, gained the respect of upper management, and saved their companies money in the process.

If the organization does decide to outsource, it can use the IT assessment to negotiate a beneficial outsourcing contract. The book can help immeasurably in vendor negotiations, by providing detailed checklists for drafting requests for proposal (RFPs) and contracts, as well as determining policies and procedures for on-site contractors.

A business approach also works well with selective outsourcing, whereby an IT organization outsources only particular functions rather than the entire department, such as application development, software maintenance, or computer operations. This book discusses these scenarios, providing case studies of outsourcing success.

Once the outsourcing contract begins, the book offers guidelines for ongoing control via project management and monitoring. It also provides suggestions for handling conflicts or problems, and advice on terminating a contract, where necessary.

Section I, entitled "Rules of the Outsourcing Game," recommends that organizations consider the outsourcing decision as a business issue. Rather than abdicating responsibility for IT, savvy enterprises should first determine the fundamentals of their internal IT operations. They might avoid a disappointing outsourcing experience by investing time and energy to improve its performance, ending up with better and cheaper services from a cost-effective, service-sensitive internal IT unit.

At the very least, improving the internal IT organization can be the basis for negotiating a successful outsourcing contract, or helping organizations determine which specific functions to selectively outsource. Furthermore, knowledgeable IT organizations can become far more aggressive in managing ongoing outsourcing engagements by measuring the relationship, and adding penalty clauses to contracts for nonperformance.

Organizations can find tips for IT outsourcing success, as well as advice for avoiding pitfalls in Section II, entitled "Outsourcing to Win." For example, a cooperative partnership between an organization and the outsourcing vendor can prove far more beneficial than an adversarial relationship, and success is fostered by complete, specific contracts; an infrastructure that supports the relationship; and good communications. Authors also offer recommendations for negotiating contracts, making the transition to an outsourcer, monitoring the vendor's work, handling employees when downsizing, addressing security, and terminating an outsourcing contract. In addition, organizations are urged to quickly resolve conflicts and obstacles, monitor performance and demand contracted-for results, and retain current copies of computer data and software in-house.

With Section III, the book turns to several aspects of "Outsourcing and Process." Rather than simply providing contingent staffing, the book suggests that IT managers optimize outsourcing relationships by developing partnerships with service providers. This requires skill in project management, systems analysis and design, contracting, and strategic management.

Furthermore, most organizations that outsource computer work use several vendors. This section therefore offers advice on selecting the best outsourcing vendors, and negotiating favorable terms. Finally, the section shows how outsourcing can be used as a process improvement approach to improve productivity and lower the costs of application development.

As a means of avoiding some outsourcing pitfalls, many organizations have decided to outsource selective functions to third parties, rather than the entire IT department. Section IV recommends that in so doing, companies should target activities with little strategic implication as the most likely outsourcing candidates, while retaining strategic activities in-house.

For example, given the skyrocketing costs of desktop assets, organizations might outsource service and support for PCs and LANs, thereby enabling scarce, expensive employees to concentrate more attention on strategic activities. And, because software maintenance is often perceived as boring, outsourcing this function can improve internal staff morale, and free up existing maintenance staff to work on new development, utilizing new technology.

Section V addresses the most important aspect of outsourcing; that is, management. Organizations cannot ensure successful outsourcing experiences merely via good intentions, a 600-page contract, or penalties for failure. Rather, outsourcing agreements must specify expected results and outcomes in basic business terms, and continuously assess the relationship for performance and value.

Furthermore, organizations should practice risk management in their outsourcing relationships and agreements. This requires performing meaningful risk assessment, which can be used as a negotiation tool, and placing controls in place that minimize the negative consequences of a bad outsourcing agreement. In this way, organizations can minimize the outsourcing risks and maximize the return on investment.

Finally, Section VI deals with long-term effects and implications of outsourcing. At a time when quality and customer service are paramount, organizations should beware of outsourcing functions that can adversely affect either. In addition, before embarking on an outsourcing relationship, organizations should appraise their core competencies, project future needs, try to determine new problems that may stem from outsourcing itself, and consider alternatives. They should also gauge the dangers posed by a long-term loss of expertise, and assess the security implications of outsourcing.

Although IT outsourcing is not an entirely new concept, the era of IT outsourcing really began in 1989, when Eastman Kodak entered into a 10-year, $100 million agreement to outsource its entire IT function. Now, outsourcing is no longer an all or nothing proposition; instead, selective outsourcing has become most popular. This strategy lets organizations cost effectively tap highly skilled and specialized personnel for non-core functions, while allowing them to focus on core business competencies. Therefore the strategic decision is no longer when or whether to outsource, but to what extent.

Savvy IT managers will use the book's many practical ideas, guidelines, and tips to realize outsourcing advantages, while minimizing the risks. When offloading nonessential IT functions, they will thereby cut the best deal and make the outsourcing relationship work.

Section I
Rules of the Outsourcing Game

Chapter 1
Making the Decision to Outsource IT

John R. Vacca

WHILE OUTSOURCING SOME OR ALL of information technology (IT) operations has been around since computers were first introduced into enterprises, IT managers are eyeing more current, compelling reasons to completely switch to an outsourcer. The purported advantages, including system flexibility, keeping current with technology, eliminating costly employee issues, and capital cost savings, point to what might be considered a self-evident decision. However, it is not as simple as that. This article explores several essential components of the decision to guide enterprise IT managers in gaining the advantages of outsourcing and avoiding the pitfalls.

OUTSOURCING DEFINED

Looked at from its most basic level, having a third party take over some or all of an enterprise's IT operations is nothing new.

Many can recall the beginnings of the computer age, when enterprises turned to third-party technology firms to obtain contracted automated support. Known then as service bureaus, user enterprises were linked across town into their giant and very expensive computer. The enterprise's employees accessed (or time-shared) their applications through *dumb* terminals. In many instances, operational and management reports were delivered the next day after overnight processing, and the service bureau generally dictated the technology the enterprise used and its pace of change. Pricing by the transaction served to escalate enterprise costs as the enterprise grew.

The fact that computer hardware costs spiraled steadily downward made enterprise purchases of mainframe (and subsequently mid-range and micro-) computers affordable. More critical, the need for immediate, less-expensive, and onsite IT management support forced computer ownership (or leasing) to be a requirement of operating for most enterprises. Many service bureaus were replaced by a commercial product marketplace that has expanded today to license highly flexible and industry-specific software at a more affordable price using less-expensive computers.

The advent of networks, the push for application integration, an ever-increasing chip capability and speed, and the advancement of data communications technologies now places the IT executive in a very complex and fast-changing world. Words and acronyms like 4GL, token ring topologies, multiplexers, hubs, concentrators, and T1 lines have become a part of the everyday lexicon for the IT community. However, keeping up at the IT management level can be frustrating and costly. These otherwise highly capable IT executives can be forgiven if an outsourcer promises relief from dealing with another area of complexity.

WHY ENTERPRISES SHOULD CONSIDER OUTSOURCING

Every day there is a new announcement of an IT product or IT service that someone in an enterprise believes is absolutely necessary for long-term (or short-term) success. Staffing and retaining the personnel to provide the needed support is a difficult and costly effort, especially when the needs are for just a few days per month for a dozen or more specialties.

Somewhat like legal or financial services, IT services are best provided through a custom blend of internal and external professionals. This chapter gives some guidelines on how to plan and develop the right mix for an enterprise through outsourcing, as well as the reasons for doing so.

Outsourcing Reasons

Private industry and the federal government have numerous reasons for outsourcing. In descending order of importance, the following are reasons for outsourcing IT services:

- focus in-house resources on core functions
- personnel cost savings
- improved quality of IT systems services
- increased flexibility
- increased access to new technology
- provide alternatives to in-house costs
- stabilize IT costs
- technology cost savings
- reengineer process
- reduce technological obsolescence risk

IT managers have similar reasons for outsourcing. These reasons can be combined and categorized as follows:

- budget realities
- cost reduction

- access to skilled personnel
- improved IT responsiveness
- help with legacy systems
- improved enterprise and customer service
- implement new architecture

Budget Realities and Cost Reduction. Budget realities and reducing costs are clearly a significant concern for both the federal government and private industry. Four of the seventeen preceding reasons dealt with cost savings of one type or another. Budget restrictions are the controlling factors in the federal government and private environment and have a key impact on deciding which functions to perform in-house versus which to outsource.

Federal government and private sources have determined that outsourcing is an excellent method to produce savings. The Heritage Foundation has estimated potential savings at 20 to 30 percent. The Congressional Budget Office estimated in 1998 that between 50 and 70 percent cost-savings could be achieved through outsourcing. The potential savings make it feasible to consider outsourcing as a means of providing IT services.

Access to Skilled Personnel. Federal agencies and private enterprises need to consider access to skilled personnel. Federal IT agencies are experiencing a shortage of highly skilled and experienced personnel brought about by continued buy-outs and early retirements. In addition, hiring freezes, loss of funding, buy-outs, and early retirement authorizations have prevented restaffing. Remaining employees may not always have the specialized skills or training to keep pace with the rapidly evolving technology. Additionally, technicians and programmers skilled in the most current technology and programming languages (C++, etc.) are often hired by commercial enterprises at salaries significantly higher than the government can offer.

Improved IT Responsiveness and Enterprise and Customer Service. Outsourcing is a means of improving IT responsiveness and enterprise/customer service. Federal agencies and private enterprises are taking a closer look at their core competencies and how these services can be provided to the customer in a more efficient and effective manner. Federal agencies and private enterprises are also focusing their resources on the core functions that they do best — their mission. Outsourcing some functions provides federal agencies and private enterprises with the flexibility to strategically redirect those resources to mission-critical activities.

Outsourcing also enables a federal agency and private enterprise to potentially improve the quality of information systems services by obtaining those services from an enterprise whose primary mission is IT. An example is the current industry move to obtain certification using Carnegie Mellon University's Software Engineering Institute (SEI) Capability Maturity

Model (CMM). The SEI CMM rating validates that an agency or enterprise has put repeatable software development and program management processes in place in its projects/programs and in various levels of its enterprise. Few federal activities have the resources or funds to obtain the knowledge and skills required, implement the repeatable processes, and go through the certification process. However, these capabilities can be obtained from vendors whose core competency is to provide high-quality software development. Agencies and enterprises are finding that outsourcing gives them access to CMM that which they otherwise could not afford to develop in-house.

Help with Legacy Systems. Federal agencies and private enterprises are currently looking to outsource functions related to legacy systems. Many agencies and enterprises have large systems written in earlier computer languages such as COBOL. These programs are full of *spaghetti code* — the result of years of modifications to the code, some without adequate documentation. The programming challenges resulting from these undocumented programs are intensified by a lack of programmers skilled in the earlier languages. Although the number of legacy system programmers is limited, private industry has better access to people with these skills.

The year 2000 (Y2K) is an excellent example of federal agencies and private enterprises having to make major modifications to legacy systems. Contractors have developed tools and management processes to handle much of this reprogramming and reengineering effort. When Y2K was coming to the forefront, programmers with skills in the older languages were in high demand. Accordingly, they were demanding and getting higher compensation than the government could provide. Outsourcing Y2K projects provided federal agencies with access to the specialized tools, management processes, and personnel that private industry had available.

Implement New Architectures. Federal agencies and private enterprises are also looking at outsourcing as a solution and source to keep up with the increasing changes in technology. Private enterprises are seen to have more leverage to acquire and maintain new computing/telecommunications resources at a significantly reduced cost than the federal agency can have directly. Private enterprises are also seen to be able to implement the new technology better and more quickly because of their focus on continuous technology refreshment.

Most large enterprises already have the vendor agreements in place — and the revenue volume necessary to take advantage of them — to provide continuously updated technology. The enterprise can spread the cost of this technology over several customers so that one customer does not bear the brunt of the entire technology upgrade.

THE BENEFITS OF OUTSOURCING

Along with eliminating time-consuming and sometimes costly employee issues like recruitment, retention, and other employee relations concerns, turning over an enterprise's computer operations to a third party can also transfer the worries of:

- trying to avoid major computer failures, especially during critical database updates
- deciding among competing software products, which often become obsolete right after emerging from a lengthy, enterprisewide selection and contracting process
- staying abreast of the latest equipment and communications technology, which often requires frequent return trips to the enterprise's finance committee
- overtaxing the IT budget due to unforeseen human resource or technology demands

Is the promise of outsourcing a guarantee? Not by any means. Yet many enterprises within commercial, public, and not-for-profit industries are considering, and indeed shifting to, outsourcing arrangements. Does the future hold this in store for your enterprise? If so, how does one go about evaluating and implementing the option? What are the risks?

OUTSOURCING RISKS

Still, while the trend is turning back once again toward outright outsourcing of the entire IT function, it is causing many IT executives to wonder: Are we returning to the service bureau arrangement? Their concern is valid because the old service bureau arrangement was rightly branded as too expensive and too technologically rigid. So is it a return? In a sense, yes and no.

Yes in the fact that outsourcers are third parties and are providing IT support under a contracted arrangement. *No* in the aspect that the association is not limited by an inflexible outsourcer marketplace providing only certain technological options at a certain price. Therein lies the key to making an outsourcing arrangement work for an enterprise — the customized contract that reflects the enterprise's most appropriate technological needs and grows with the enterprise in a controlled manner.

Outsourcing Risks Concerns

Private and federal IT managers historically have been resistant to the idea of outsourcing, citing concerns for security, control, corporate knowledge, and reversibility once a function has been outsourced. While these are legitimate issues that must be addressed, a well-organized and differentiated approach to IT outsourcing can overcome these concerns and ultimately enhance the IT decision-maker's position.

Control. Critics of IT outsourcing argue that an outside vendor cannot match the responsiveness and service levels as that done by an in-house IT function because the outsider is not subjected to the same management direction and control as federal or private enterprise employees. The major reason for this concern may be that federal and private enterprise IT managers historically have not been required to apply success metrics to vendors or to internal operations. IT managers will now be required to benchmark the performance of their systems against commercial activities and develop metrics for their internal operations. Once developed, these metrics can easily be used to measure and control an outside vendor's performance.

Similarly, there was little pressure to, or knowledge about how to, write performance-based statements of work. In addition to becoming more adept at measuring and benchmarking their internal activities, federal agencies and private enterprises will become more comfortable at managing performance-based contracts instead of simply managing people and activities. As this experience and knowledge grows, *loss of control* will diminish as an objection to outsourcing.

Security. Federal agency and private enterprise concerns regarding the security and confidentiality of data and other information are important. Both Congress and the Office of Management and Budget (OMB) consider information security to be an overall concern and are working on issues for federal agency implementation. However, the OMB also recognizes that activities that may require access to secure and sensitive information may be contracted out.

Outsourcing has been in effect in private industry for a number of years. Commercial enterprises such as banks, brokerage houses, insurance enterprises, and enterprises with extensive research and development activities have designed processes by which their most closely held information is often processed in an outsourced environment.

Contractors have long operated in the most secure environments in government and industry. The language in secure environment contracts requires contractors to take the necessary precautions. In addition, contractors working in such situations are often required to establish and promulgate security procedures with the appropriate federal agency and private enterprise auditing compliance by the contractor and the contractor's personnel.

Enterprise Knowledge. Another concern of outsourcing critics is that outside vendors' lack of enterprise knowledge will prevent them from performing as well as insiders who are familiar with the agency or enterprise, its customers, its reporting requirements, and its idiosyncrasies.

Many agencies and enterprises are facing a loss of enterprise knowledge from their workforces. Personnel buy-outs and hiring freezes have taken their toll on enterprise knowledge as knowledgeable and experienced staff have taken advantage of the many downsizing opportunities offered by the agencies and enterprises. At the same time, there have been no new staff hired and trained to take their places due to hiring freezes. Thus, agency and enterprise knowledge is being drained. Agencies and enterprises increasingly have to rely on the skills of service providers who are new to the arena, regardless of whether they reassign internal resources, receive authority for new staff hires, or outsource to contractor personnel.

If enterprise knowledge is a specific concern, then agencies and enterprises can base the evaluation and selection of outsourcing vendors on their past record of working closely with a customer in the customer's environment. Additionally, close communication and cooperation between the contractor and the agency will facilitate contractors becoming knowledgeable in the critical areas.

Reversibility. Critics of outsourcing express concern that once IT functions have been turned over to a contractor, it will be too costly to reverse the situation and return them in-house. This concern is based on the assumption that once functions have been outsourced, the agency or enterprise will lose all of its critical skills and resources (hardware, software, etc.), will become locked-in to a particular vendor's proprietary hardware or software, or will have difficulty recompeting contracts if problems arise with service quality.

Although these are valid concerns, agencies and enterprises can use contractual requirements to address many of their concerns. As an example, a key person provision might be included in the contract requiring the contractor to keep certain, specifically named individuals assigned to the project. In other instances, federal agencies have included language in Request for Proposals (RFPs) that require the successful vendor to provide *knowledge transfer* back to the government. The use of award or incentive fee contracts is a good technique to avoid prematurely recompeting a contract or bringing it back in-house.

Concerns with a vendor's proprietary hardware or software, or of not having title to, and the use of data generated under the contract should be addressed during the requirement's analysis phase of the outsourcing effort. Appropriate language can be drafted assuring the agency or enterprise of interoperability of equipment/software and of the retention of all necessary intellectual property (escrow of source code, conversion of data to any follow-on system, etc.).

Finally, *big bang* or *grand design* contracts probably work no better for outsourcing situations than they did for large system development projects. If the IT functions being outsourced are of a critical enough nature to the agency's or enterprise's mission, then the agency or enterprise should seriously consider awarding several small contracts for various, severable functions. Likewise, such an incremental or modular approach can be effectively used where the agency or enterprise lacks outsourcing experience.

HUMAN RESOURCE (HR) CONCERNS

A key element of any outsourcing/acquisition effort is cooperation and participation by the human resources (HR) staff. An enterprise must get its HR staff on board as part of the outsourcing/acquisition team from the very beginning. With HR involvement, the status of any discussions concerning outsourcing should be communicated with the employees and with the union(s).

HR helps an outsourcing study team to ensure that all relevant issues have been raised and considered, and that information is prepared and available for employees. The study team needs to have information on issues such as the number of affected employees, transition costs, retraining opportunities and obligations, termination costs, relocation requirements, etc. Employees will want information on issues such as job status, benefits, timing of any outsourcing and how it affects retirement possibilities, potential buy-outs, etc.

CHALLENGES TO OUTSOURCING

Once the decision to pursue outsourcing has been made, IT management and the outsourcing study team will be faced with numerous challenges. Political opposition to the potential outsourcing may come from internal sources, unions, community leaders, and possibly other contractors, who may be affected by the outsourcing decision. Senior IT management should communicate with internal or external groups. This communication should begin as early in the process as possible and continue periodically.

WHAT TO EXPECT FROM AN OUTSOURCING VENDOR

Outsourcers today are very flexible in their service arrangements. They will:

- take over and occupy an enterprise's data center
- move the enterprise operation into their data center
- manage enterprise software in their data center or the enterprise's data center
- develop new applications

- purchase the enterprise's hardware and software
- employ some or all of the enterprise's employees
- allow the enterprise to manage or not manage their employees

There are, of course, many variations on the preceding and other themes.

KEYS TO SUCCESSFUL OUTSOURCING

No one wants to fail nor sets out to do so. Keeping in mind a couple of guideposts helps avoid the potential problems. First, *know thyself.* What software components are potential outsourcing candidates? What shape are they in? What are the documented requirements for these applications in terms of operating demands, reporting, and processing? How much do applications now cost in terms of staff and nonpayroll components? What advantages (cost- and operations-wise) would one expect to achieve from their conversion to an outsourcing arrangement? The answers to these questions will help point the way to evaluating whether or not outsourcing is a viable option.

If so, convert these factors into contractual requirements. Let enterprise expectations be known and seek out reputable outsourcing enterprises to address these requirements in a competitive and formal manner.

Next, *go slow.* For some enterprises, this will represent a cultural change that takes some getting used to. A slower introduction might be the best way.

Finally, *find that key employee or consultant* who can be dedicated to the conversion process to oversee that the change meets the expectations that are in the contract. In the long run, this type of investment is worthwhile for the future survival of the enterprise.

FUTURE OUTSOURCING TRENDS

The outsourcing industry has changed much over the past decade. These changes are reflected in the trends that now shape the next 10 years of outsourcing.

Business Process Outsourcing

The IDC estimates that business process outsourcing (BPO) services currently claims 70 percent (or nearly $70 billion) of all outsourcing spending worldwide, and non-IT executives throughout the industry are quickly waking up to the idea of outsourcing non-core functions. The next iteration is electronic BPO, as small to midsize enterprises that do not have the wherewithal to launch their own E-commerce ventures present a hot new marketplace for IT vendors that do.

The Fall of the Outsourcing Broker

As enterprises gain outsourcing experience, they are reluctant to hire middlemen to broker their deals. Customers do not want to spend $360,000 to $2 million for third-party negotiation. And they shouldn't!

However, outsourcing deals are bigger and more complex than ever and require a specialist's expertise. The real future, therefore, for outsourcing middlemen, is in relationship management during the life of the deal.

Global Growth

According to the IDC, outsourcing will top $262 billion by 2004. This trend signifies both a greater market share to be grabbed by outsourcing vendors, as well as an opportunity for remote enterprises to boost their IT/enterprise capabilities and become world-class competitors. With one swipe of a pen, a small enterprise will have access to the same global resources as a big enterprise. It will be difficult to tell the smaller enterprises from the larger ones.

CONCLUSION AND SUMMARY

Outsourcing is emerging once again as a way to manage the technology necessary to serve today's IT requirements. Enterprises look to their systems to manage IT to the benefit of the enterprise's purposes; and, there is a constant search taking place to enhance the speed and quality of the systems. Each enterprise must answer for itself how it will structure these systems to optimize their assistance to the enterprise, and to do so in a cost-effective manner. It is advisable for enterprise IT executives to look closely at the outsourcing option.

Furthermore, the popularity of outsourcing continues to gain momentum in both the private and public sectors. Private enterprises are turning to outsourcing for a wide range of functions — from logistics to human resources to purchasing. The government is being forced to seriously consider reliance on outsourcing as well. At one time, government outsourcing was primarily applied to contracts for blue collar-oriented functions such as maintenance, security, and food services. However, the government is finding it necessary to follow the commercial trend to outsource white collar-type functions as well, including IT functions.

The outsourcing trend has accelerated as U.S. enterprises have endeavored to become or remain competitive in the global economy. To do so, enterprises are focusing on their core competencies.

This drive to focus on core competencies is fueled by a desire for private enterprises to provide better customer service, while at the same time increase profit margins. While government agencies are not concerned with profit motives, *per se,* they are increasingly driven to focus on delivering responsive service to the customer within shrinking budgets. Outsourcing represents one way for federal government IT managers to perform the seemingly impossible task of improving service in the face of declining funding and staffing.

Aside from focusing on core competencies, the reasons for benefits being obtained from improved efficiencies are many. It appears that enterprises that outsource for long-term strategic reasons are often more satisfied with the outsourcing results than those that outsource for short-term tactical reasons. As an example, outsourcing benefits those enterprises that have the foresight to take the time to "benchmark" the services required and place measurable, performance-based requirements into a Performance Work Statement rather than rely on a Statement of Work, which describes the exact steps a contractor is to follow. Additionally, building flexibility into the contract is beginning to be seen as a basic tenet of outsourcing — especially in the IT world, where requirements change quickly.

Finally, in the private sector, outsourcing can usually be accomplished quickly once the decision to do so has been made. In the public sector, federal officials must maneuver through what often appears to be a quagmire of rules and regulations, although Congress has passed several pieces of legislation to facilitate and promote outsourcing in the IT arena. The most notable of these, the Information Technology Management Reform Act (ITMRA), requires agency heads to determine the appropriate sources of goods and services for new IT systems. On the other hand, agencies and enterprises must remain mindful of the political considerations of making outsourcing decisions.

Companies Cited in this Chapter

1. The Heritage Foundation, 214 Massachusetts Ave. NE, Washington, D.C. 20002-4999.
2. Congressional Budget Office, Ford House Office Building, Room 410, Washington, D.C. 20515.
3. Software Engineering Institute, 4500 Fifth Avenue, Pittsburgh, PA 15213-3890.
4. IDC Corporate Headquarters, 5 Speen Street, Framingham, MA 01701.

Chapter 2
The Outsourcing Alternative

John P. Murray

MANY ORGANIZATIONS HAVE BEGUN TO TAKE AN INTEREST, ranging from mild to enthusiastic, in outsourcing. The need to reduce expenses, coupled with the opportunity to rid the organization of at least some aspects of the IS function, can be a powerful incentive to company executives to seriously consider outsourcing. The increased interest in the topic among clients and vendors ensures that IS managers can expect to spend more time dealing with the issue in some form in the future.

In some instances, outsourcing may improve the inadequate performance of certain IS functions, or it may offer opportunities to cut expenses. For example, the current marketing efforts of many of the leading outsourcing vendors are focused on the data center because the data center expense is a large and highly visible item. The data center is, however, by no means the only candidate for outsourcing. Systems development and integration work is outsourced by some organizations.

Correctly managed, outsourcing may improve IS operations, customer service, and credibility. However, the organization considering outsourcing should think about the potential long-term effects that can result from turning over control of the business's various IS functions — or even the entire function — to outside managers.

An organization's sudden interest in outsourcing may, in some cases, be indicative of a more basic problem or set of problems in the organization. Whatever the issues are that prompt management to look at the outsourcing alternative, an objective analysis of the source of the problem is in order. Pinpointing the problem source may present opportunities to make improvements in the organization and, in the process, perhaps eliminate the need for outsourcing.

THE LONG-TERM EFFECTS OF OUTSOURCING

A typical justification for outsourcing is that a particular IS function does not appear to be an integral part of the business. Management questions the efficacy of devoting scarce resources and management effort to a function that can be fulfilled more effectively and less expensively by an outside vendor.

Although this promise of more efficient service at reduced cost is appealing, outsourcing is more complex than is readily apparent. Organizations frequently enter outsourcing agreements without proper analysis and thought.

In some situations, outsourcing is at best a short-term solution to a long-term problem. If an organization begins to outsource for the wrong reasons, its mistake may not be realized for several years. Even if the mistake does become apparent relatively early, the customer probably has little recourse other than to abide by the outsourcing contract. The option of disputing the contract is likely to be an expensive proposition.

The long-term effects of any outsourcing agreement — no matter how appealing — must be carefully considered. The organization should examine the realistic business implications of removing the functions from its direct control. Again, these effects may not be immediately apparent and may not even surface for some time; however, the possible long-term implications of outsourcing, including all the disadvantages, must be acknowledged. Exhibit 2-1 summarizes the pros and cons of outsourcing that must be fully explored before the contract is signed.

One pitfall for many organizations is that a smooth marketing effort aimed at the highest level of the organization can create a climate in which decisions are made without an understanding of their practical ramifications. To forge an effective and appropriate outsourcing arrangement or to find alternative solutions for organizational problems, the decision-making process must involve those directly affected by the outsourcing. Toward this end, the IS staff must contribute actively to the solution of the problem at hand, whether or not the final scheme involves outsourcing.

THE MANAGEMENT ISSUES

Although outsourcing may seem the logical solution for cost-related problems, other measures to resolve problems can be taken before outsourcing becomes a necessity. For example, facing up to the issue of poor management in the data center (or any other IS function) and taking the appropriate action to strengthen management may be a much better solution in the long term than outsourcing. Outsourcing should not be undertaken as a reaction to poor management in the IS department.

Furthermore, sometimes the problems associated with the performance of the IS function have more to do with factors outside the department than within it. There may be a lack of interest in and attention to the function at the senior management level. The difficulty may stem from strong resistance

Exhibit 2-1. Outsourcing pros and cons.

Pros

- The organization is relieved of the responsibility for management of those IS functions that are taken over by the outsourcing vendor.
- The outsourcing agreement should reduce expenses for the organization, at least in the near future.
- If carried out selectively, the outsourcing arrangement allows the IS department to concentrate on the most critical issues in the organization. The sections requiring less high-level expertise (e.g., technical support and the data center) can be relegated to the outsourcing vendor, allowing the in-house IS staff to focus on applications development concerns.
- The outsourcing contract can generate some revenue for the organization indirectly, through the sale of data center assets (e.g., disk drives and the mainframe).
- The contract provides an opportunity to reduce the IS department head count.

Cons

- Outsourcing removes some control of the information processing function from the IS department, which could seriously affect that department's mission-critical functions.
- The short-term savings provided by the outsourcing contract could be negated in the future, should the organization decide to reintegrate the outsourced function.
- The outsourcing vendor may not feel obligated to keep the outsourced function up to date and may use outdated technology to save money.
- Outsourcing can create morals problems in the IS department, particularly if in-house employees begin to fear that their function will be outsourced as well.
- Any contingency not addressed in the original agreement must be renegotiated. Post-contract negotiations are likely to be troublesome and costly for the client.
- Vendor stability cannot be guaranteed.
- Predicting the future of an organization is at best difficult, and predicting the effects of a current outsourcing contract on the basis of unknown future changes is even more difficult.
- Hidden agendas can create a disadvantageous situation for the unwary client. The organization should exercise extreme caution when examining an outsourcing contract, paying special attention to possible ulterior motives on the part of the vendor.

---

to change on the part of the departments the IS function is attempting to serve. In short, the causes of dissatisfaction with information processing may be beyond the control of IS management. If that is the case, it is questionable that the introduction of outsourcing will bring about much in the way of improvement.

Under certain conditions, however, outsourcing may prove to be the most efficient solution to an organization's information processing needs. For example, an organization may find itself with a growing backlog of requests to make enhancements to existing production systems. If the level of both technical and business knowledge is so low within the IS department that little or no progress can be made without a dramatic increase in staff, the organization may discover that the most it can do is move to a set of packages that would eventually replace the existing systems.

Managing both a greatly accelerated maintenance effort and the movement to a portfolio of new packaged systems to run a large portion of the business would require additional talent. In this example, outsourcing the enhancement backlog may clear the way for movement to the new systems with the existing staff. Therefore, IS managers should realize that outsourcing is not inherently detrimental to the IS department.

The Role of IS Management

Developing a knowledge of outsourcing issues sufficient to be able to present relevant issues to senior management in a businesslike manner is only part of the IS management team's responsibility. The team must also be able to formulate a plan to address those issues that an outsourcing contract proposes to solve. If IS management perceives that the improvements targeted by outsourcing can be addressed in-house, the team must be prepared to provide workable alternatives to the outsourcing contract.

The vendor, who wishes to capture an organization's outsourcing business, will likely talk about the issues of service levels and problem and change control. The members of the IS management team must also be able to address these issues.

Because many organizations may not view IS as a mainstream business function, IS managers must be prepared to counteract this attitude from senior management. The IS function is indisputably critical to the business; relinquishing control of the function, no matter how attractive it might appear to the organization's business managers, must be approached with caution.

Senior management may see the role of IS management, in light of the outsourcing decision, as a purely defensive stance. Although this may not be the case, objections raised by IS managers can appear to be protectionist. To overcome this hurdle, the IS group must build the strongest and most realistic case possible, which it should present in an unemotional manner. If outsourcing does not make sound business sense, that case should be developed and presented; conversely, if aspects of outsourcing are appropriate and in the best interests of the organization, they should be recognized.

Developing a Counterplan for Keeping IS In-House

When building a case against outsourcing, the marketing and business skills of IS managers will be tested to the extent that they find themselves dealing with experienced sales and marketing people who have probably negotiated contracts in the past. The IS department might, given the staff's relative inexperience, consider using an outside party to help present its case. A consultant to assist in the development of the case can bring a different perspective to the issues. In addition, someone with strong marketing skills could be particularly effective in convincing the organization's senior management to retain the work within the IS department.

It is in the best interest of IS management to develop a plan for those areas in which outsourcing seems inappropriate. Outsourcing may prove to be more beneficial in some sections of the department than in others, yet decisions about these areas should also be made by the installation's management, not by an outside party. This is particularly important when the outside party has a vested interest in the outcome.

Presenting the Alternatives to Outsourcing

A plan to improve efficiency by keeping IS work in-house should include a strategy to address the issues that have been identified. The scope of this effort must be stated in order to understand what needs to be accomplished on the part of senior management. Each component of the plan must be assigned a priority so that those pertaining to the business issues can be addressed immediately. Details must be provided about the required human resources and other expenses required to accomplish the plan's goals. A schedule that is based on the items identified and the priorities assigned in the plan should also be devised to lay out what is to be accomplished and when.

When this preliminary work has been completed, IS management should present its plan to senior management. The IS management team must assure senior management that it can deliver what is required and acknowledge that its performance is to be measured against what it has proposed in the plan. IS management must further commit to specific objectives developed as a result of the issues identified. Some examples of objectives might include:

- a reduction of information-processing expense (e.g., of 3 percent of the existing budget) without a reduction in current processing service levels to be implemented within six months of approval of the plan
- the establishment of a joint application development (JAD) process to improve the manner in which applications systems are developed and implemented to take effect within four months of the plan's approval.
- the establishment of a set of well-defined customer service levels for the data center operation; this could include:
  — network response time goals
  — a reduction of total production jobs rerun in a month to a certain percentage of all production jobs
  — improved response time to all help desk calls and the resolution of 95 percent of all calls within five working days

- the installation of a concise applications project management and reporting and control system to identify all approved projects, their completion dates, and current status

If, after examining the conditions that have created the need for improvement, outsourcing is judged to be the most effective solution, specific decision points should be developed so that a series of tests can be conducted throughout the vendor selection process, both to define how specific items are to be addressed and to determine whether the answers provided by the vendors are adequate and realistic. The success of the outsourcing venture depends more on the management and negotiation skills of the customer than those of the vendor. Everything must be in writing, clearly spelled out, and fully understood by all the parties to the agreement.

OUTSOURCING TECHNICAL SUPPORT

In many instances, a reasonably strong case can be built to support outsourcing IS technical support. Although this function is important to the continuing operation of the business, its operations do not have to be performed entirely by the organization's employees or conducted wholly onsite at the particular location. In addition, there is usually a limited business relationship to the function. The work is technical and is, with limited variation, the same in all organizations.

There are sound business reasons for considering outsourcing the technical support function. Technical support personnel, who are expensive, can be difficult to find and retain. Because of the common characteristics of the work within the structure of a particular operating system, the skills of the individuals are readily transferable. In addition, because much of the work can be accomplished from a remote location, having several people onsite may be unnecessary.

Three factors that should be considered when an organization contemplates outsourcing technical support are training, service, and control.

1. Training. Because effectively managing the technical support section is difficult for many organizations, transferring the function to an agency with the appropriate management skill and experience could prove to be a sound decision. Training is expensive and must be ongoing to remain current with the changing technology. Some organizations, unwilling to make the required training investment, allow the technical support function to lag behind; consequently, morale suffers because employees are not able to continually upgrade their skills.

2. Improved Service. In addition to the more obvious benefits of reduced cost and simplification of the associated personnel issues, outsourcing can improve service levels. If the chosen outsourcing vendor has a competent and experienced staff, these staff members will introduce new techniques and approaches. Extensive experience with several organizations is a factor that should recommend a vendor to an organization.

3. Assigning Control. If an organization decides to outsource its technical support function, it should consider the issue of ultimate control over the function's operations. Although technical support is not a mainstream business function, the decisions regarding the use of technology cannot be made outside the organization. The vendor should be encouraged to offer suggestions and present proposals, but final decision-making authority must remain with the IS staff. To meet this need, some members of the IS department must stay current with developments in the operating software world. As an alternative, an independent consultant could be engaged to periodically review the work plans of the technical support outsourcing vendor. Control, regardless of the function being outsourced, must be recognized as a prime consideration. Relinquishing control could pose serious problems for the organization.

If the vendor retains too much power, the consequences of the contract can be disastrous to the organization. Discovering that control resides in the inappropriate hands after an agreement has been reached will not help the organization much. If all power is held by the outsourcer, it may prove difficult and expensive to raise the levels of service provided by the vendor. Particularly in the context of data center outsourcing, which is discussed later in this article, the contract must be regarded as a long-term arrangement.

UNDERSTANDING THE OUTSOURCING AGREEMENT

If an organization decides to further explore an outsourcing arrangement with an outside vendor, it should take every precaution to safeguard its operations against all possible contingencies. Although most vendors want to render high levels of service to their outsourcing customers, they may hesitate to raise issues that might jeopardize their chances of obtaining a contract. In addition, they are not likely to raise issues that will make management of the contract more difficult after it has been signed. The customer therefore must be attentive, careful, and knowledgeable. The burden to protect the organization rests with the organization, not with the vendor.

Contract Negotiations

Members of the IS management team who may become involved in the negotiations with outsourcing vendors must perform the necessary detail work to develop the best contract. Nothing should be left to chance: anything that can affect the processes involved in the outsourcing contract must be analyzed, and the implications resulting from actions with regard to these processes must be clearly understood. After these areas have been identified, the contract should be written to preclude future problems. This can be an onerous task, but it is necessary.

Should a dispute arise, the vendor will rely on the language of the contract to settle the debate. IS managers cannot rely on a handshake or a verbal agreement to work out the details at a later date. Usually, after an agreement has been reached, the original vendor representatives are replaced by technical or operations managers. These managers have a different perspective and set of interests from those of the salesperson; as a result, the relationship between the organization and the vendor may change. During the negotiating stage, IS managers must consider all the details and ensure that all conditions are stated in writing.

All too often, organizations make decisions in response to strong sales pressure from vendors. There are many instances of sales made at some level above the IS department — these situations frequently become IS nightmares. Even sales made at the IS department level can ultimately deliver much less than the original agreement seemed to promise. Caution in these areas must be exercised by both business and IS management.

The organization should consider seeking assistance outside the managerial group when examining the outsourcing contract. Consulting legal counsel and seeking outside assistance from another organization are actions that can significantly help preclude contract problems.

Legal Expertise. To avoid disadvantageous situations caused by unclear wording or legal loopholes, the organization's attorneys should carefully review the outsourcing contract before proceeding with the agreement. IS managers should not ignore the legal expertise provided by these attorneys, which is to their benefit to follow.

Outside Assistance. The organization should ensure that the contract is formulated so that the vendor can deliver the services promised in the agreement and earn a profit. If the vendor, whether through inexperience or some other reason, has agreed to conditions that do not allow it to cover necessary costs, the vendor may renege on the stated services in the future. Organizations would be well advised to consider consulting someone with experience in outsourcing contracts to avoid creating this situation. Although every contingency cannot be anticipated, taking this precaution is a prudent approach.

OUTSOURCING THE DATA CENTER

When an organization seriously considers outsourcing its data center, one crucial aspect of the contract is the way in which service levels will be set and monitored. Another important point is determining what will occur in the event of a dramatic change in the workload or setup of the data center. The organization must also ensure that the contract addresses increases in outsourcing fees. These and other considerations are discussed in the following sections.

Setting and Monitoring Data Center Service Levels

The question of service levels to be rendered by the outsourcing contract has a decided impact on the efficacy of the data center. The organization should determine what penalties, if any, to charge if the outsourcing arrangement fails to meet the agreed-on service levels. An organization that has a set of service levels in place that it is working to strengthen may be managed well enough to determine its own service levels. By contrast, organizations without an adequate understanding of service levels may be at the mercy of the vendors in defining the data center's performance standards.

If an organization has not clearly defined its own service requirements, it may encounter difficulty in its dealings with the vendor. The vendor's presentations concerning service levels and the benefits the vendor can provide will likely sound appealing to senior-level executives of the business. When these promises of improvement are coupled with the ability to reduce data center expense, the interest of the business executives will be heightened. A vendor who presents a contract without defining service levels implies the absence of problem-tracking and change-control agreements. In this case, a business executive who is unfamiliar with data center operations may perceive such agreements as offering considerable savings in hardware maintenance charges. The organization should beware of such agreements, which are usually much more desirable in theory than in practice.

Anticipating Changes in Data Center Work Load

The organization should define the effects of a change in the workload of the data center on the outsourcing fee. The organization must determine whether (and by how much) the outsourcing fee will be affected by an increase or a decrease in the load.

Similarly, the organization should ask who will define the workload and the criteria for determining the change in fees. In addition, it is important to ascertain whether the appropriate fees have been clearly addressed in a schedule or left for later consideration. These factors must be clearly understood and discussed before the contract is signed because they may make the difference between the organization's receiving a fair amount of services for the fees charged and paying too much. Senior management must recognize the inherent risk connected with a dramatic workload increase in the data center processing schedules. Although an increased workload will most likely be accommodated by the outsourcer, it is not advisable to allow the vendor to determine the increases in the charges, especially on an ad hoc basis.

For example, an insurance company with an outsourcing agreement in place decides to expand to three new states in the following year. This change is estimated to increase the online processing load by 30 percent and the batch processing load by 15 percent. If such a situation has not been anticipated and adequately addressed in the contract, a difficult condition may arise — although the new states may be accommodated, the organization may have no choice but to process the work generated by these states through the outsourcing vendor.

Given this scenario, in which the circumstance has not been thought out in advance and covered in the contract, the vendor controls the important decisions concerning the organization's information processing operations. Even if the outcome is of no particular consequence, the inherent risk is too great to leave to chance.

Controlling Fee Increases

The organization should ensure that the contract contains a provision to cap annual increases in outsourcing fees. An organization cannot expect to retreat from any type of outsourcing agreement — and data center outsourcing in particular — without undertaking some expense. The vendor is going to take steps to protect itself against the effects of inflation; the organization must likewise guard against inordinate or inappropriate expenses that are left to the vendor's discretion.

Provisions for Downsizing the Data Center

Radical equipment changes and downsizing efforts can wreak havoc in an organization when plans are not made before the contract is signed. Downsizing deserves considerable thought.

Many people working in mainframe environments have strong feelings against downsizing, a sentiment that is based largely on the fear of losing their jobs. That concern, though perhaps unjustified, is understandable. Downsizing is nonetheless becoming increasingly popular, particularly as an expense-reduction strategy, and should be recognized as a possible eventuality. The organization should ask questions regarding the possible need to move to a new hardware platform and who makes the decisions about the equipment. The organization should question whether it will have the option to downsize and, if so, at what cost. The vendor's experience in downsizing should be determined as well as any possible ulterior motives. The vendor may be unenthusiastic about downsizing if the move is not in the vendor's best interest.

For the outsourcer, a downsizing effort is likely to be attractive as a means to reduce outsourcing costs. However, if the organization does not want the outsourced function to be downsized and the outsourcing vendor disagrees with the decision, the organization may find itself at the mercy of the vendor.

Senior management must be made aware that moving to a different hardware platform, whether a different vendor or smaller hardware, is by no means a small or risk-free task. If the outsourcer decides arbitrarily to make such a move, the consequences to the organization could be unfortunate. Unless the contract is very clear in this area, the majority of the risk is going to rest with the customer, not with the outsourcer. For example, a contract may state only that the vendor will provide information processing hardware sufficient to accommodate the processing requirements of the customer. Further, the contract may contain a clause stating that the customer is liable for any expense incurred by the vendor's decision to convert to different equipment. It is the responsibility of each organization to safeguard against such incidents by thoroughly examining its situation and the outsourcing contract.

Use of Old Technology

Should the vendor propose to use old equipment to cut costs, the client must be able to determine whether such a change will be advantageous to the organization. It can be argued that the outsourcer is seeking to fatten profits by continuing to use old technology well past its useful life. In such an event, the customer could end up having to depend on a collection of obsolete and inefficient equipment.

In addition, there are competitive considerations. The continued use of obsolete technology might preclude the organization from entering new business areas or being able to match competitors' new product or service offerings. The expense of upgrading the technology might turn out to be prohibitive, regardless of the benefits to be derived.

Another issue has to do with the particular vendor chosen for the process. Some hardware vendors who have entered the outsourcing business may require that clients use their products. Such a contract could require that any and all subsequent hardware (and software, if applicable) decisions about the course of growth or change be based on the vendor's products. This may or may not be acceptable to the organization; however, the ramifications must be carefully weighed.

REINTEGRATING OUTSOURCED RESOURCES

In some instances, an organization may need to bring an outsourced function back into the organization. This contingency should be acknowledged and planned for during the initial contract considerations. Because outsourcing is a service in which the vendors usually have more experience than their customers, IS departments that outsource often fall into difficult situations caused — at least partially — by their incomplete understanding of the implications of entering a contract. For example, the vendor, in an attempt to obtain business, might underbid a contract, which it later finds itself unable to honor, or a vendor may after some time decide to withdraw from the outsourcing business because it no longer seems practical.

In addition, an organization's circumstances change. What effect will the old contract have on the newly changed organization? The majority of outsourcing contracts being written today require long-term commitments, and it is difficult to predict changes in an organization's configuration in five or six years — not to mention in a decade or more.

A Lesson from the Past

Some years ago, several organizations found themselves facing unanticipated problems and loss when a large third-party vendor of mainframe hardware failed to support its product. In those instances, difficult as they may have been, the losses were limited to hardware expense and some legal fees. Prospective outsourcing clients should heed this example. Should a similar fate visit the customers of an outsourcing supplier, the resulting losses could be much more severe, depending on the extent of the particular arrangement. Rebuilding an entire data center function could be a monumental task, and rebuilding a large-scale IS function quickly enough to smoothly resume operations might be nearly impossible. Again, the short-term gains must be carefully weighed against the potential risk.

Protective Measures

Although the costs of keeping a function in-house may seem to outweigh the risk of an outsourcing vendor's default, the possibility always exists that an outsourcing vendor may be unable to support a contract. Some important issues must be thought out to protect the organization should the vendor renege on its agreement. For example, if the organization finds it necessary to bring the outsourced function back in-house, it should determine how the transition back to in-house processing, or to another outsourcing vendor, will be handled.

Before the contract is signed, a series of potential situations, or business contingency plans, should be drawn up to highlight for the organization the negative impact of a vendor default. The customer must carefully consider the issues involved and then protect the interests of the business to the greatest possible extent.

Necessary Expense. In the event of a default, the customer is certain to encounter additional expense. The organization should ensure that the contract obligates the vendor to cover such expense. Should the vendor default, obtaining compensation at that time will probably be impossible; therefore, the organization should ensure that some sort of protective provision exists in the contract — for example, protection might be provided by an escrow account.

CONCLUSION

Outsourcing can be regarded as either an onus or a challenge. Although outsourcing may be an inappropriate plan of action in certain cases, simply investigating this option can be advantageous to an organization by causing the organization's employees to examine their own effectiveness and productivity.

An outsourcing investigation can encourage managers of the IS department to look carefully at the way the function is being managed. This investigation, in highlighting areas for improvement, can help improve the organization's operations without the need for outsourcing. The investigation can, for example, identify those areas of operation that are redundant, unnecessary, or wasteful.

The investigation can also indicate those organizational functions that are performing efficiently. Turning the outsourcing investigation into a positive challenge should be an incentive to IS managers to approach the process with an open mind. Whether or not an organization decides to outsource a particular IS function, a well-conducted analysis of all aspects of outsourcing as it relates to the organization can produce positive results.

Chapter 3
Whether to Outsource and Downsize

Douglas B. Hoyt

IT HAS BEEN ESTIMATED that 73 percent of the leading companies contract out part of their information system (IS) functions, that $6 billion of client/server work was outsourced in 1996, and that 80 percent of information systems activities may be performed by contractors by 2000.

Organizations are finding that outsourcing can cut costs, sharpen management's focus, get access to expertise, and foster global expansion. Computer operations managers should help lead the way to finding improvement opportunities via outsourcing and downsizing and help to support exploratory studies initiated by the managements of their companies. This article reviews the ways to analyze and decide whether to and what to outsource and downsize.

Outsourcing Trend Statistics

Outsourcing and downsizing are being done with increasing frequency by large and small organizations to stay competitive and increase profitability. Global competition has added impetus to these steps, which are often tied to the reengineering movement whereby organizations redefine their goals and the processes for achieving them.

The Outsourcing Institute's studies have produced data which give measured perspective to outsourcing trends:

- ". . . over $40 million will be spent on IT [information technology] outsourcing in 1996. . . . IT outsourcing represents 40 percent of the $100 billion U.S. companies will spend on all types of outsourcing in 1996."
- "70 percent of companies that outsource IT, outsource less than 50 percent of their total IT budget."

- "Areas of outsourcing that are increasing the fastest are the desktop environment and networks, which now represent 40 percent of the total outsourcing expenditures."
- "On average, companies realize a 9 percent annual cost reduction through outsourcing."
- "Companies surveyed by the Institute report that improving their company's focus and gaining access to the provider's world-class capabilities are equally important reasons for outsourcing as are cost savings."

Need to Study and Weigh Issues

Because so many are using these tools to improve, it behooves each organization to ask itself whether to initiate outsourcing and downsizing steps to stay ahead in its field. Increasingly, service companies have grown that can provide many functions cheaper and more reliably than has been done at their client companies. (Downsizing is usually a by-product of outsourcing; however, downsizing is often done without outsourcing by eliminating "fat" that has grown from inattention, by designing simpler methods for doing the work, by eliminating an unwanted part of the business, or by reducing organizational levels.)

Computer Operations Manager's Role

Computer operations managers should play a leading role in deciding whether, and what, to outsource and downsize. By examining the options and the potential benefits from these actions, the managers who take the initiative in proposing improvements in these areas will be appreciated by their managements for pointing the way to accomplishing the organizations' goals. Also, those who propose outsourcing or downsizing are the persons most likely to be selected to manage the transition and be in charge of overseeing the work of the vendors who end up providing the services.

If senior management has initiated a study of whether and what computer operations to outsource or downsize, the computer operations manager should participate in that study, and this chapter should be helpful in pointing out the issues to consider in such an analysis.

Some computer operations managers may see the option of contracting out some of their work as a threat. However, when outsourcing can make for lower costs or other improvements, the managers can demonstrate their leadership by suggesting and promoting that option and should continue their control of the functions involved by being responsible for managing the contractors' work.

TRENDS IN OUTSOURCING

Several new trends in business structure and relationships with vendors have made some companies more effective and enabled significant cost reductions. One trend is for management to focus more heavily on the core businesses, contracting out less essential functions. Another is to establish more friendly relationships with other organizations, considering vendors and contractors as "partners" in alliances pursuing common goals. In seeking better ways, sometimes as part of reengineering processes, managements question traditional approaches, keeping an open mind in seeking alternatives that might improve their operations.

Although the organization's philosophy, goals, and strategic directions properly influence the decision whether to and what work to contract out, the organization should also apply the tried-and-true concepts relating to make-or-buy decisions. Outsourcing a computer function involves the same type of considerations that pertain to whether to make or buy a product part like spark plugs and transmissions, janitorial and guard services, legal work, and vehicle maintenance. In all these matters management must weigh the decision's effects on costs involved, control, flexibility, reliability, management's ability and time, and the product's or service's criticality to the business.

CONDITIONS THAT MAKE OUTSIDE COMPUTER WORK DESIRABLE

In this day and age of dynamic managements and changing conditions, the computer operations manager should review periodically the IS activities to evaluate which might be done to better advantage by an outside organization. In making such reviews, the computer operations manager should consider several factors as benefits that might be achieved by outsourcing.

Saving Money

Cost saving is a major purpose in many outsourcing decisions these days. Usually, savings can be easily demonstrated when a service provider invests in technology and hardware, the costs of which can be spread among a number of clients. Unless there is some such synergism opportunity, cost savings may be more difficult to prove, even considering all the overhead and administrative costs of doing the work internally, such as fringe benefits, office space, and phone and other services. If cost reduction is the objective, computer operations managers would do well to consider first whether internal costs might be cut before looking to outsourcing as the only way to achieve that objective.

In addition, many outsourcing arrangements provide for the vendors to purchase the computer hardware, giving the clients cash resources they can use more beneficially elsewhere.

Taking Advantage of Expertise: "Do Not Reinvent the Wheel"

A recent survey of chief information officers (CIOs) and chief executive officers (CEOs) at 365 companies showed that the need for expertise was the major reason for outsourcing decisions in their organizations.

American Airlines pioneered reservations systems and subsequently let other airlines use the system for a fee. Hyatt is doing the same with its hotel and motel reservation system. Many truckers have fought fiercely for competitive advantage with their computerized shipment tracking systems. These are all cases in which a competitor can benefit by not reinventing the wheel, rather buying a system from a vendor who has developed a practical system.

Free Management for More Critical Functions

For more than 10 years, Xerox Corp. has outsourced its information systems to Electronic Data Systems Corp. (EDS) for $4.1 billion to permit Xerox's management to direct its energies more fully to strategic matters, in addition to achieving more flexibility, gaining financial advantages, and benefitting from advanced technology.

The freeing up of management's attention is akin to the concept that some systems can be regarded as "commodities." A trucking company would not design and build trucks; it would buy them as commodities. Other companies regard common systems as commodities, such as payroll or even order processing. Rather than design and run a payroll system, for example, a company may prefer to buy its payroll system and operation from a supplier such as Automated Data Processing Corp. (ADP), which specializes in payroll, and free its management's time for more strategic activities related to the organization's prime product or service.

Job Is of Short Duration

Using outside sources for information systems work is clearly advantageous when the tasks at hand are of short duration, when the alternative would be to hire specialists for a short period and then release them.

No Security or Confidentiality Vulnerability

Using outside contractors is sensible only when there is no resulting significant danger likely from the lessening of security or revealing important trade secrets or information to the outsiders.

But Not when Internal IS Can Provide a Competitive Edge

If an organization is developing, or can create, a system that gives it an edge over its competitors, as did American Airlines with its Sabre reservation system, it is probably best not to subcontract the work to outsiders.

COMPUTER FUNCTIONS TO CONSIDER FOR OUTSOURCING

When evaluating what computer operations activities might be more advantageously contracted out, the computer operations managers should review the systems functions and applications and weigh the types of contractor services available that might be used beneficially.

Most major companies contract out portions of their information technology functions. However, an outsourcing pioneer, Kodak, outsourced its entire data center operations in 1988.

Systems Activities

The traditional systems activities involved started with an organization that had no computers, evaluating what could be computerized, designing the systems for doing so, selecting the equipment, programming the applications, testing, and training the users. These traditional activities continue with new organizations and new functions.

However, most organizations today have gone through the traditional systems development period. Their systems efforts are now directed to maintaining and improving the systems processes for these purposes: (1) to meet changing business plans, such as new products and new markets, and to meet competitive challenges; (2) to take advantage of new technologies such as client/servers, Windows 95, 98, and NT, and the Internet; and (3) to fulfill new management goals for reengineering and restructuring business processes, including cost reduction.

Each of these three current challenges to computer management requires evaluating what new approaches can be adopted, how the changes can be designed and implemented, what equipment should be secured, and where and how will it be operated. The use of outside expertise and services are options to be evaluated in each phase of the reevaluation and redesign process.

The following examples of outsourced systems activities give a picture of how some have worked well, to the advantage of the client and the contractor.

Programming. Programming assistance can be obtained from consultants, temporary help agencies, and brokers. Work can be done at the client's premises or the vendor's venue. A major trend has been to secure programming from India, the Philippines, Ireland, and other places at costs that can save up to and over one half the cost of using American programmers. These outsourcing sources can be worthwhile when the size and timing of a project make it feasible. An American retail company developed a warehousing program for $500,000 using offshore programmers, which would have cost three times that if done domestically.

Applications Development. Applications development is one of the most frequently outsourced activities. Southern Pacific and Air Canada are two companies that have sought applications development as a main part of their outsourcing plans. The Southern Pacific Lines has a $415 million 10-year contract with IBM's Integrated Systems Solutions Corp. (ISSC) to manage its information systems, including applications development, with the employment of new technologies. The development of applications with new technologies and client/servers was a major feature of Air Canada"s request for bids to take over its information systems, for $1 billion over 7 to 10 years.

PCs. PC contractors can provide a variety of services to ease the client's chores, including purchasing, installation, training, cabling, asset management, parts inventory, virus safeguards, and the help desk function. Chemical Bank had contracted its PC support activities to Unisys.

Legacy Systems. Developing new systems while maintaining legacy systems can create a manpower and management burden which can be overcome by outside services. Some have retained outsiders to maintain legacy systems while internal staff works on new systems. Others have contracted out new systems development and used existing personnel for legacy maintenance.

LAN and WAN Management. Organizations that cannot afford to keep a network expert at each location have found it beneficial to use local area network (LAN) and wide area network (WAN) outside management services. IBM, Digital Equipment Corp. (DEC), SHL Systemhouse, Inc., and EDS are among the firms that provide LAN management services. Netsolve Outsourcing Service provides remote WAN service in addition to selling related equipment.

Help Desk. A survey by the Help Desk Institute indicated that most of its 4,700 members outsourced the help desk function starting in 1994. Hewlett–Packard (H–P), Novell, and EDS are among those providing help desk services. Companies using help desk services find value in their vendors' staff's technical knowledge, phone capabilities, and documentation. Help desk services often involve substantial assistance to users, at widespread locations. Some organizations maintain an in-house help service and contract out certain types of questions and peak loads.

Applications, or Business Functions

Computer operations managers should consider applications and functions that can be and have been contracted out beneficially. The following examples of outsourced systems applications give a picture of how some have worked well, to the advantage of the client and the contractor.

Reengineering. Amtrak has outsourced much of its IS function to IBM's ISSC as part of the organization's reengineering program; ISSC is proposing new ways to perform accounting, reservations, and collection systems as well as help desk, network, and disaster recovery services. H–P, Computer Sciences Corp. (CSC), EDS, and Andersen Consulting all provide services in reengineering as well as outsourcing of IS. (Some IT outsourcing firms such as Andersen, EDS, PricewaterhouseCoopers, and KPMG Peat Marwick have been broadening their services to include business process outsourcing; that is, actually performing accounting, personnel, order processing, and such operating functions for their clients.)

Sales Effectiveness. Andersen Consulting has started a sales effectiveness service, launched in collaboration with Siebel Systems.

Payroll and Human Services. ADP has long been a leader in furnishing a full-service of payroll processing for its clients. ADP, which pays 17 million employees for more than 300,000 clients, has recently branched out to provide related human resources software developed by PeopleSoft, and client/service software with its payroll systems.

E-mail. The outsourcing of electronic mail systems has been increasing and is expected to continue further, to free up management's time for other activities and avoid switch installation difficulties. Also, e-mail is expected to change with the complexities of client/servers and the World Wide Web.

Traffic Functions. The systems for managing traffic departments, just-in-time material controls, and other logistics activities have similar requirements in varying industries, making it feasible to adopt or adapt a smooth-working system in one place at other organizations. Federal Express, Airborne Express, and others have established consulting services to help clients with their shipment and material control systems. Inchcape Shipping Services furnishes back-office services to shipping companies worldwide.

Electronic Data Interchange (EDI). Blue Cross/Blue Shield of Maryland has contracted with EDS to develop an EDI system for processing medical claims connecting patients, insurers, and medical services. The Association of American Railroads has requested bids for computer systems incorporating EDI and other features to improve delivery time, customer service, and transactions among the railroads, in an effort to compete better with the trucking industry. IBM's Health Care Network (HCN) connects clinical and benefits information among hospitals, pharmacies, insurers, and 30,000 doctors in eight states.

Health Care. Kaiser Permanente Health Plan, Inc. has contracted with ISSC for $70 million of services. Many feel that the health field is a ripe source of outsourcing, being in a dramatic period of change and increased competition, and without advanced information systems in place for many of the organizations in the industry.

Types of Contractors' Services

Outsourcing services are available to perform almost all computer functions that might otherwise be done internally — analysis of alternative approaches and recommendation of optimum new directions, equipment evaluation, systems design, programming, training, and running a help desk — and can include running the full range of computer operations and even managing the input and output, either at the vendors' venues or the clients'.

A few organizations have outsourced their computer work from soup to nuts, 0.3 percent per one survey. Several examples of outsourced systems work give a picture of how some have worked well, to the advantage of the client and the contractor.

Training. Andersen Consulting has added the training of users to the services it is prepared to furnish to its clients.

Transportation Joint Venture. In an unusual arrangement, Delta Airlines subcontracted important information services to AT&T Global Information Solutions. Delta and AT&T formed a company equally owned to manage Delta's communications and data processing, in a 10-year $2.8 billion deal which is expected to save Delta $400 million. AT&T has indicated its intention to become a leading information technology supplier in competition with major service vendors like EDS, CSC, and ISSC.

Disaster Recovery. Many firms provide disaster recovery services, such as backup facilities and housing of backup information. Assistance in planning disaster protection measures is a service these companies usually furnish, as do some consulting firms. Disaster protection may be bundled with other information outsourcing services. A recent survey indicated that disaster recovery was one of the functions most frequently contracted to outsiders.

Open Systems. When Northrop Grumman formed a commercial aircraft division, it decided to establish a computer system separate from that of the parent organization, based on open systems. Cambridge Technology Partners assisted the division in developing an Open Enterprise Plan, using packaged software tailored by its vendors to work with others through a communal database. In another situation, Telogy, a supplier of electronic test equipment, retained HCL America, a subsidiary of a company in India, to design and program Telogy's reengineering project; using many vendors' software, HCL and Telogy completed the open system reengineering project in half the time and cost compared to what could have been done by an American firm.

Business Processes via the Internet. Andersen Consulting has joined forces with BBN Corp. to provide a turnkey system structure for clients that do not wish to establish their own Internet operations. The joint venture furnishes business operations such as billing and order processing on an around-the-clock basis, using the Web and supported by Internet security.

PROS OF OUTSOURCING

In weighing whether or not to contract out any particular function or group of functions, the computer operations manager can analyze the advantages and disadvantages by listing the pros and cons, weighting their relative importance, and applying some numbers to indicate their relative value or disadvantage, The following summary of "pros" and "cons" should aid computer operations managers in making such an analysis. This type of methodical appraisal can also be used in preparing a recommendation to management, reinforcing the thoroughness and objectivity of the analysis and supporting information.

Availability of Expertise

An outsourcing service or consulting firm may have acquired experience and expertise in an area which a client may need. It is then often faster and cheaper to retain the firm than to develop the experience and expertise in-house. Using the outside service may be the best way to acquire state-of-the-art benefits quickly. For example, some colleges find that firms specializing in college systems can serve their needs better than by developing their systems from scratch.

Economies of Scale, and Shared Costs

The Association of American Railroads developed EDI and other systems to be used by its members more cheaply and effectively than for each member to create its own systems and coordinate them with other members with which it deals. When Hyatt sells its reservation system to other chains, in effect it spreads the development cost among its many customers. Similarly, when ADP furnishes payroll services to its hundreds of clients, it is sharing the costs of developing the common features of its complex and diverse payroll systems among its many customers.

Management Focus on Prime Strategies

When functions are not key to the competitive success of a company, management can often direct more of its time and energies to its essential tasks by contracting work to other organizations which can be depended on to perform those activities reliably and with a minimum of oversight from the client's management. For example, in a company that depends on its logistics systems for its success, the information management may contract out its payroll system to help devote more of its attention to the critical logistics procedures.

Cut Costs

Cost saving may be a prime reason for considering contracting out systems work. It is always one of the important issues to be analyzed. In making a cost comparison, it is important to weigh the full cost of outsourcing — including management's time in overseeing the work — and the full costs of doing the work internally (e.g., fringe benefits, office space, and overhead and administrative costs, including supervision, human resources, and similar costs). Offshore programming, which can save 50 percent or more of programming costs, is a prime example of cost-saving opportunities.

Save Cash

In situations in which an outsourcing service undertakes the operation and management of the computer operations, the service may buy the equipment from the client, providing the client with cash that can be used more advantageously elsewhere. Similarly, when a new function is outsourced rather than done internally, it saves the investment capital — cash — that would otherwise be spent on equipment and start-up costs. When cash availability is a problem, such outsourcing arrangements can be a significant benefit.

Avoid Internal Delays

Telephone companies are anxious to move rapidly to client/server billing and customer service systems. A major reason several telephone companies are outsourcing the design and development of those systems has been to avoid internal delays they would anticipate without the outside help.

Vendors Can Be Good Employers

Countering the disadvantage of disrupting employee morale by letting employees go when a function is contracted out, some have found that employees whom a contractor employs from its client's staff are often better off. With the trend to outsourcing today, outsourcing vendors are a growing industry, and relocated employees may end up with benefits and security superior to those they had before.

Easier to Terminate or Change

When it becomes necessary to discontinue or revise a function, it may be easier to accomplish if the work has been contracted out; then the necessity for dropping employees and equipment, hiring new specialists or retraining existing staff, and installing new gear may be avoided.

CONS OF OUTSOURCING

A checklist describes the potential disadvantages of contracting work out. These are matters a computer operations manager should evaluate as they apply to an outsourcing plan that is being considered.

Lessened Direct Control

Control is less direct. Information about outsourced functions is slower to get and less complete than it would be if the activities were done in-house. To make a change in the process involves working with people in another business entity and may require discussions about the terms of the agreement.

Higher Costs

Lower costs of outside work are likely if there are good reasons; for example, a vendor spreading development costs among many clients, or using overseas programmers at a fraction of domestic pay rates. However, without those saving potentials, it is likely to cost more outside because vendors must cover their advertising and selling costs, risks, and profit. Unless the contract pricing terms are fixed costs, which many are not, it is likely that the ultimate costs may be impossible to forecast with accuracy. Another danger is that a long-term contract may lock a client into current costs whereas technology improvements later allow the vendor to reduce its operating costs, with the savings not passed on to the client. Thus, the manager must give a great deal of care and thought to cost projection (e.g., by estimating the best possible outcome, worst possible outcome, and most likely outcome). This cost analysis may be the trickiest and most debated part of the thinking-through process.

Exposure of Confidential Information

Contracting work out can often, if not usually, let outsiders know about a client's business plans, customer lists, product plans, and other information that could benefit competitors. Though contract terms may forbid misuse of such information, leaks are more likely when processes are performed by outside organizations.

Dropping Employees Lowers Morale of Remaining Employees

Though openness and considerate termination arrangements can lessen morale damage, the effect of outsourcing on departing and remaining employees must be considered. Some downsized employees have sued and won. At one company, outsourced data capture annoyed its IT staff, which then caused the system to crash. These possible detrimental effects must be anticipated and evaluated in the decision-making process.

Limits a Company's Effectiveness

As one writer has put it, "Outsourcing can only make a company as functional and economically efficient as its competitors."

Inflexibility

Some vendors are unable or unwilling to tailor their services to a client's needs or desires. Also, when a contract is signed, the client is locked in to the arrangement and may be less able to maneuver as conditions change.

DOWNSIZING WITHOUT OUTSOURCING

Downsizing — eliminating employees — is usually one result and sometimes the primary objective of outsourcing. The outsourcing vendor performs a needed function previously done by the client's employees. Often the service vendor hires all or many of the employees let go by the client.

But downsizing can sometimes be effected without outsourcing in four ways: (1) identifying and cutting out "fat," (2) designing a more efficient system, (3) eliminating an unprofitable or unwanted part of the business, and (4) reducing the number of organizational levels.

Cutting Fat

Over time, without tight supervision, workers slow their pace, ineffective people are retained, and jobs that are not essential are perpetuated. The excess staffing is often reduced by arbitrary budget cuts, say 15 percent to 30 percent. Some work measurement studies can determine the time really necessary to do the work and identify the excess hours or people to eliminate.

Designing a More Efficient System

Creative imagination and analysis can often discover simpler ways to do a job. For example, a manually prepared interdepartment invoice system was replaced by a simple Lotus spreadsheet design, cutting the time from five to two days to perform. Or, in the programming area, work time can sometimes be reduced by using off-the-shelf software instead of tailor-made systems, or by applying techniques such as CASE (computer-aided software engineering).

Eliminating Less Essential Businesses

Many large banks provided payroll services to clients on the theory that they could run their expensive hardware on the idle shifts and thereby save by spreading their computer equipment costs. However, these banks discovered that doing payrolls for other companies also diverted their managements' efforts, and encountered other problems that drained their side-line profits, which led them to abandon their payroll service outside businesses.

Horizontal vs. Hierarchical Organization

Some organizations have reduced staffs considerably by eliminating several levels in their hierarchical organization structures. A major electric company is said to have reduced the number of levels by more than 50 percent, cutting thousands of middle-management positions. The simpler structures are made feasible by spreading decision-making powers to the lower levels and by making information available to remaining management staff through more open network systems.

SOURCES OF GUIDANCE AND SUPPORT

When making decisions about whether and what to outsource and to downsize, the computer operations manager may wish to seek guidance and advice from others experienced in these matters. Consulting assistance may be secured from:

- Independent Computer Consultants Association (ICCA), 11131 South Towne Square, Suite F, St. Louis, Missouri 63123; (800) 774-4222.
- Institute of Management Consultants (IMC), 521 Fifth Avenue, 35th floor, New York, NY 10175; (212) 697-8262.
- The Association of Management Consulting Firms (ACME), 521 Fifth Avenue, 35th floor, New York, NY 10175; (212) 697-9693.
- The Outsourcing Institute, 45 Rockefeller Plaza, Suite 2000, New York, NY 10111; (800) 421-6767.

The Outsourcing Institute has free membership which includes a quarterly newsletter and a buyer's guide to outsourcing services, sponsors training conferences and seminars, and provides advisory assistance for a fee.

When considering such issues, computer operations managers would do well to compare experiences and ideas with contacts at other organizations developed through meetings and activities of professional associations such as the Data Processing Management Association (DPMA) and the Association for Computing Machinery (ACM).

SUCCESSFULLY CONTRACTED COMPUTER OPERATIONS: HUGHES AIRCRAFT — COMPUTER SCIENCES CORP.

Hughes Aircraft achieved significant success in outsourcing its computer work. Hughes Aircraft outsourced many of its information systems functions to CSC, involving hundreds of employees, enabling Hughes to focus more of its energies on its primary missions as well as save money.

Hughes Aircraft completed a substantial move to outsourcing, as reported in the July 1996 issue of *Enterprise Reengineering*. Hughes had a wide range of goals from this major transition: (1) to reduce costs and improve performance, (2) to establish a consistent worldwide IT operating structure to help foster expansion into global markets, (3) to facilitate the move from legacy to client/server systems and apply resources to reengineering, and (4) to free up capital and enhance return on investment.

Hughes's CIO Mahvash Yazdi was the leader in planning and implementing the outsourcing process. One of her guiding principles was to be careful in selecting the proper functions to keep and to let go. She decided on retaining activities that are key to the company's primary activities, including the control of strategic information, the design of the information architecture's structure, and oversight of the activities contracted to the vendor.

Hughes selected CSC as its vendor, and CSC took over responsibility for Hughes's mainframe and network management, applications management, and desktop and help desk functions. The contract calls for a $1.5 billion expenditure over a seven-year period. CSC purchased from Hughes the computer hardware and operates the computer systems at Hughes's premises.

The procurement process, which took only three months, was performed by a team made up of human relations, legal, and purchasing specialists under Yazdi's leadership. Another key to the successful outcome was the team's insistence on making the outsourcing requirements absolutely clear in its request for proposals, so there could be no major misunderstanding on the part of Hughes's or CSC's management. However, a clause was built into the arrangement for arbitration of differences and difficulties that might arise. The arbitration group made up of representatives from the client and vendor have smoothly resolved the issues that needed to be resolved.

CSC hired the 1,023 employees that were cut to do the work. Hughes insisted that those transferred employees be provided benefits similar to what they had at Hughes.

The outsourcing operation has met Hughes' goals well, with the exception of a few residual problems in the area of distributed computing. The Hughes user community is sophisticated, with high expectations in terms of quality of service. They will not be done until they meet their expectations. Some employee anxiety is considered inevitable after any major organizational change, and the Hughes management is on balance delighted with the way the new arrangement has worked out. The difficulties were a result, in part, of the speed with which the company made its changes, a speed that was an intentional part of management's plan and which the management considered important to the plan's success.

CONCLUSION

What author Tom Peters has said, "Do what you do best and outsource the rest," expresses the general terms of the concept of why and how organizations should decide what work should be contracted. Outsourcing has become fashionable, almost a fad, in recent years, tied in to the trend to reengineer.

Outsourcing is contrary to the traditional instincts of many leaders in business and elsewhere. The leadership type of person enjoys increasing power and control, usually measured by numbers of employees and sizes of buildings and plants. Those instincts of late have been tempered by examples of organizations that have found that smaller can often be better in terms of meeting goals, profits, and global competition. An extreme example is a successful $20 million consumer product concern which operates with only three employees; all other workers perform as outside contracted services.

Computer operations managers should seek out and support outsourcing and downsizing projects that can help their organizations to reach their goals. Tempering normal tendencies to "build empires," the managers should make thorough analyses and evaluations of the multitude of issues involved, many of them old-fashioned make-or-buy considerations, such as the effect on costs, employees, control, reliability, and flexibility.

Chapter 4
A Sensible Approach to Outsourcing
N. Dean Meyer

IN MANY CASES AN IS ORGANIZATION'S INTEREST IN OUTSOURCING — that is, paying other firms to perform all or part of the IS function — originates with pressure from top executives who use outsourcing as a threat to force change. Outsourcing vendors promise dramatic savings and enhanced flexibility so that line executives have more time to focus on their core businesses. On the surface, these claims seem plausible, but they do not hold up well under close scrutiny.

CLAIMS VERSUS REALITY

For each of the claimed benefits of outsourcing, there are underlying assumptions, which are explained in the following sections.

Cost Savings

It may appear that economies of scale reduce costs. The vendor, however, must earn a profit at its customer's expense. Furthermore, external contracting brings added sales and transaction costs.

Most of the savings from outsourcing generally come from data center consolidation. Once a firm has consolidated its data centers on its own, outsourcing is generally more expensive. The only lasting cost savings occur where there are true economies of scale across corporate boundaries — for example, in long-distance communications. There are some cases in which interorganizational sharing is possible, but such cases must be examined carefully. Hardware no longer presents economies of scale, and many software licenses are corporation specific.

In a few cases, outsourcing has been viewed as a source of near-term cash, because IS assets may be sold to the outsourcing vendor. Selling a strategic resource is an extreme way to save a sinking firm. Furthermore, selling off IS cripples all remaining business units and increases long-term costs.

Increased Flexibility

Some people say that outsourcing converts fixed costs (or such relatively fixed costs as people) into variable costs, giving the firm greater financial flexibility. In fact, most outsourcing vendors require long-term contracts that provide them with stable revenues over time. Renegotiating these contracts may be more expensive than changing internal commitments.

If flexibility is the goal, the contract must be carefully negotiated to allow variability in demand and cost. Demanding this flexibility comes at a relatively high price.

Downsizing

In organizations that must downsize, it may seem that the outsourcing vendor can move surplus people to other jobs serving other companies. If those other jobs exist, surplus staff can compete for them on the open market with or without the outsourcing deal. If they have the qualifications for those other positions, they will get them — whether or not the firm pursues outsourcing. If they are not qualified enough to win other jobs on their own merits, it is unlikely that a highly competitive outsourcing vendor will retain them in these positions for long. Ultimately, then, outsourcing does little to change the employment picture for surplus IS professionals.

Better Access to Technology

Equipment vendors suggest they can provide customers with better access to new technologies. In practice, vendor sales representatives are quick to bring new products to the attention of internal IS staff in any case. The firm must judge for itself when to adopt a new vendor offering than leave that decision to a vendor that has a vested interest in selling new products. Vendor-owned outsourcing services are also less likely to tap opportunities presented by competitive vendors (e.g., more cost-effective, plug-compatible products).

More Time for Business Issues

Another argument is that when a firm outsources IS, business managers have more time to focus on the corporation's main lines of business. This is only true if IS managers are transferred into other business functions. If the IS managers are fired or transferred to the outsourcing vendor, there are not likely to be more business managers to focus on the organization's business issue than there were before outsourcing. In other words, the business only gets more attention if line management is expanded (and costs are increased). Of course, line managers can be added regardless of whether IS is outsourced.

Some organizations are attracted to outsourcing because it relieves senior management of having to worry about managing its IS function. The argument is that outsourcing reduces the demand on senior management because a contract is substituted for direct authority. This rarely proves to be the case. In fact, managing an outsourcing vendor is no easier (and is often more difficult) than managing an internal IS executive.

If senior management becomes less involved in managing IS, outsourcing may actually be counterproductive. Those who understand the strategic value of IS argue that management should spend more, not less, time thinking about IS. Without management involvement, the danger is that the IS function does no more than it has done in the past. That is, it may continue to invest in administrative systems but fail to find breakthroughs in strategic applications.

Greater Competence

It can be argued that vendors are more experienced than internal staff at running an IS function. This can be remedied by hiring competent IS managers as readily as by hiring an outsourcing vendor.

In some cases, outsourcing is simply a matter of paying someone else to experience the pain of managing a dysfunctional IS function, rather than trying to figure out how to make the function healthy again. This is a costly form of escapism that sacrifices a valuable component of business strategy for a short-term convenience.

INSIDERS' ADVANTAGE

There are two key reasons why some insiders have an advantage over outsourcing vendors for some key functions within the department: continuity and vested interests. For both of these reasons, insiders are more likely to be invited to clients' key meetings and will be in a better position to play a role in the strategic imperatives of the firm.

Continuity

Internal staff members have a history and an expectation of continuity with the organization that may pay off in a better understanding of the business and improved partnerships with clients. By contrast, outsourcing vendors may rotate their staff more easily, because individuals develop loyalties to the outsourcing vendor rather than one customer organization. The insiders' improved partnership advantage pays off in client satisfaction and strategic alignment. Long-term employees better understand the clients' culture, strategies, and politics; they also know they will be around to deal with the consequences of their actions.

Vested Interests

Outsourcing vendors may be sincere about partnership, but ultimately they work for different shareholders and ethically must (and will) place their shareholders' interests first. For example, what would happen if, in a needs assessment interview with a client, the IS consultant sees an opportunity for either a $200,000 administrative application that could save clerical time, or a $200 end-user computing tool that could significantly impact the client's personal effectiveness? Although the latter choice may provide a higher payoff and more strategic value, the outsourcing vendor has a strong incentive to recommend the more lucrative administrative system because it generates more revenues, which are added costs rather than cost savings.

In one extreme case, an automobile rental company wanted to acquire software that would help it make better use of its fleet. An expert in the industry offered to license a state-of-the-art yield management package, but because the company had outsourced its IS function, the outsourced IS department saw no profit in this arrangement. Instead, the outsourced IS department spent hundreds of thousands of dollars — nearly the price of the package — on a study of alternative, and then even more money replicating the package to ensure that it had a role in both development and support.

Insourcing

The insiders' advantage may also be used to bring in new revenue. *Insourcing* is a term that refers to sales made by a staff function to clients outside the corporation. A staff function may sell directly to external clients if two conditions are met

- The staff function has a distinctive competence in a particular area that ensures success in a well-defined niche, in spite of competition.
- Insourcing will improve internal client satisfaction, at a minimum by building a critical mass of specialists in an area that otherwise might not warrant permanent headcount. (Size permits a higher degree of specialization, which in turn reduces costs, improves quality, speeds time to market, and accelerates the pace of innovation.)

Before insourcing is considered, the IS function must be sure that internal clients are completely satisfied with its work. Unless the corporation is pursuing a strategy that takes it into the IS business, it is more important that the IS function help internal clients to succeed than that it makes more money on its own.

In general, it is preferable to sell products and services to internal clients, who in turn may add value and sell them outside the corporation. This ensures consistency and coordination with line management's customer-oriented strategies. It also keeps the focus of the staff function on its primary mission — serving internal clients.

WHEN OUTSOURCING MAKES SENSE

Upon scrutiny, outsourcing is usually found to carry with it certain risks. After investigation, many firms have shied away from outsourcing all or major portions of an IS function. Instead, these organizations are pursuing a selective outsourcing strategy.

Outsourcing selected functions can be quite valuable, especially in the case of functions where an insiders' advantage — continuity and appropriate vested interests — are not so important. Indeed, the use of contractors and consultants is hardly new and generally represents a healthy form of outsourcing.

The goals of selective outsourcing include

- Minimizing fluctuations in staffing that could result from rising and falling demand.
- Maximizing the development of employees by outsourcing less interesting work.
- Minimizing costs by using relatively less expensive employees whenever possible or sharing costs with other corporations.

For this discussion, the term *external consultants* refers to those people who are hired to transfer their skills and methods and improve employees' effectiveness. These consultants are distinct from contractors who do work in place of employees.

Generally, consultants may be used by anyone whenever justifiable. Contractors are considered extensions of the staff of employees. Employees should decide when and whom to hire, supervise all contractors, and be accountable for their work.

GUIDELINES ON OUTSOURCING, FUNCTION BY FUNCTION

At a more detailed level, the pros and cons of outsourcing vary by function within the IS department. The five basic functions found in any IS department are:

1. Machine-based service bureaus that own and operate systems for use by others (e.g., computer and network operations)
2. People-based service bureaus providing routine services that are produced by people (e.g., client support, training, and administration)
3. Technologists who design, build, maintain, and support systems (e.g., applications developers, platform experts, information engineers, and end-user computing specialists)

4. The architects who coordinate agreements on standards and guide-lines that constrain design choices for the sake of integration
5. The consultancy that works with clients to define requirements, set priorities, measure benefits, and coordinate relations with the rest of the IS department

The issues of outsourcing can be examined within each of these functional elements.

Machine-Based Service Bureaus

Outsourcing machine-based service bureaus is equivalent to buying computer and network time from vendors. This is a common practice and should be evaluated for each new increment of capacity. It is a form of financing when capital is short and a way to satisfy temporary or otherwise limited needs for specialized platforms. Outsourcing a major portion of the machine-based service bureau may also be helpful for a limited period of time during a migration to a new platform.

Permanent outsourcing may be cost-effective when there are economies of scale and multiple corporations can share infrastructure; a common example is in the field of communications, where few companies run their own private long-distance networks. However, this usually does not apply to software licenses, which are generally corporation specific.

Outsourcing should only be used when the same economies of scale cannot be attained internally. If outsourcing the entire function appears to save money, internal consolidation of data centers should also be considered as an alternative.

People-Based Service Bureaus

Some of these service bureaus can be outsourced as well. For example, installation and repair services are commonly outsourced, and training courses can be purchased for many common end-user computing packages.

Vendors offer commercial hot lines that support most of the common end-user computing products, but these are best used in combination with internal support functions. Inside staff should be the first line of support, calling on external resources for a specific class of questions. This approach ensures the required Quality of Service and handles internally developed packages and configurations. In general, the following guidelines apply:

- Hire enough staff to satisfy the lulls in demand; outsource to satisfy peak loads.
- Outsource only commodity and end-of-life services; keep new growth opportunities inside.

Technologists

No matter how big the IS organization, it can never afford to hire a specialist in every possible discipline. Contractors are therefore a valuable source of specialized expertise in less frequently used areas.

A preference to buying over making is another variant on outsourcing. Turnkey packages are attractive because they free scarce internal talent from the onerous burden of maintaining systems, allowing applications technologists to focus on new requirements. Packages should be used whenever the requirements for customization are limited. In most cases, clients appreciate receiving a proposal that offers a choice between custom code and a package — often this amounts to a choice between 100 percent of what they want for 100 percent of the cost, versus 80 percent of what they want for 20 percent of the cost.

As in people-based service bureaus, the same guidelines apply: Hire enough staff to satisfy the lulls in demand; outsource to satisfy peak loads. Outsource only commodity and end-of-life skills; keep new growth opportunities inside.

In every case, employees should be used to manage outsourced technologists in order to ensure quality, systems integration, architectural compliance, and responsiveness to the business.

Architects and Consultancies

These two functions are highly strategic and require an insider's deep understanding of the corporation. They not only require an intimate knowledge of the business, but success in these functions requires close relations with clients and the rest of the IS function. In spite of the willingness of many management consulting firms to sell these two types of planning, these high-leverage functions should never be outsourced.

Architect. Even in the smallest of organizations, the architect function is extremely important. Architects facilitate a consensus on standards so the IS function can be responsive to clients' strategic needs — tailoring solutions to their unique missions rather than blindly following a static top-down plan. They are also needed if the firm is going to successfully evolve toward integrated systems.

Where staff is lacking, the architect function should not be outsourced. It should be part of the responsibility of the chief technologist or perhaps the head of the department.

Consultancy. The consultancy function must not be ignored, however scarce personnel may be. It is essential to ensure a strategic return on IS investments and healthy client relations. (Return on investment is, of course, every bit as important to a small organization as it is to a large one.) Consultants are the primary liaison to clients, diagnosing the client's strategic needs without any bias for particular solutions and setting up contracts with the rest of the IS function. Consultancy requires an insider's understanding of the business and carefully cultivated relationships with key clients — the result of continuity over time. Outside consultants can train and assist internal consultants, but contractors should not be used to do their jobs for them.

Even in the smallest organizations, responsibility for strategic consultancy should be placed somewhere within the IS department. It may be as small as one person or (in groups of only a few people) a part-time responsibility of the top IS executive. Because this function depends on relationships with clients and an understanding of the corporation's strategy and politics, the consultancy function should never be left to outsiders.

HOW TO MANAGE OUTSOURCING VENDORS

When any degree of outsourcing is employed, it must be clear who in the organization is responsible for acquiring these outside resources. For example, in the case of external technical specialists, the appropriate technologist is expected to know where to find the right people and how to manage them. The internal manager of outsourcing contracts (in any area) is responsible for:

- shopping for the best deal, negotiating the contract, and managing contractor performance
- resolving problems in the relationship and maintaining healthy collaboration between the two parties
- generating entrepreneurial ideas within the established charter and domain and deciding whether to make or buy
- establishing clear contracts with internal customers and suppliers and retaining responsibility for fulfilling those contracts (whether outsourcing vendors are involved or not)

For all practical purposes, outside contractors should be considered part of the group that hired them. The fact that their paycheck is written by a different corporation does not change the nature of their work. All outsourcing vendors will automatically live within the bounds of the existing organizational structure, and clients need not worry about who is chosen to staff their projects.

CONCLUSION

In general, outsourcing the entire IS function is a serious mistake. Doing so risks higher costs, less flexibility, and a loss of strategic alignment. Instead, each group within an IS department should cultivate contacts with outside contractors and package vendors in its area of expertise and manage them as part of its staff. Each internal entrepreneur should proactively decide whether to make or buy in the course of every project.

Section II
Outsourcing to Win

Chapter 5
The Essentials for Successful IT Outsourcing

Ralph L. Kliem
Irwin S. Ludin

INFORMATION TECHNOLOGY (IT) OUTSOURCING is the use of a third party to provide services rather than using those in-house. It has become a growth industry and will continue to grow beyond the year 2000. Today, it has become commonplace for firms to outsource at least some aspect of their IT services. Some of the more popular services are:

- application development
- data center
- desktop/personal computers
- network (e.g., LANs, WANs)
- support services/help desk
- training
- year 2000

The above list is by no means exhaustive and can, in fact, include many services that are not IT in nature. However, this article will guide organizations through the pitfalls that often plague IT outsourcing activities, like:

- cumbersome transition into and coming out of an outsourcing relationship
- incomplete or vague contracts
- lack of an infrastructure for supporting an outsourcing relationship
- negotiating a contract with an unsuitable vendor
- poor communications with vendors

0-8493-0875-?/00/$0.00+$.50
© 2000 by CRC Press LLC

SUCCESS TIP #1: DETERMINE THE BUSINESS CASE FOR OR AGAINST OUTSOURCING

Many firms do not thoroughly analyze the need for IT outsourcing. Instead, they seek outsourcing because it provides immediate gain, only to later realize that it delivered long-term loss. As a result, some firms lock themselves into massive, long-term contracts only to find that such an arrangement is a liability rather than an asset (e.g., delivery of no longer necessary services at above market prices). A good business case, looking at different pricing alternatives (e.g., fixed or cost plus), and varying payback periods (e.g., three, five, or ten years) can help determine whether outsourcing will achieve savings (e.g., five to 20 percent), desirable levels of quality, and other objectives. Outsourcing should not occur, however, if the service is mission critical, can be done more effectively in-house, cannot provide a savings of five percent or more, or fear exists over losing controls (see Exhibit 5-1). When forming the evaluation team, the organization should be sure to:

- determine the required knowledge and skills (e.g., accounting, technical, or business management)
- designate a project manager
- determine the objectives of the team
- define each member's roles and responsibilities

When conducting the initial review, the organization should be sure to:

- define the objectives and scope of the review
- conduct an inventory of all assets (e.g., software, hardware, or data)
- determine which services are mission-critical; which are important but not critical; and which are nonessential
- determine existing capabilities for providing current services
- determine core competencies
- determine the internal service requirements
- define the requirements of internal customers

When conducting the preliminary review external review, the organization should be sure to:

- define the objectives and scope of the review
- develop criteria for selecting which vendors to look at
- determine the research approach (e.g., interview or literature review)
- determine the core competencies of the firms

When performing the cost/benefit analysis, the organization should be sure to:

- account for the time value of money
- determine a payback period

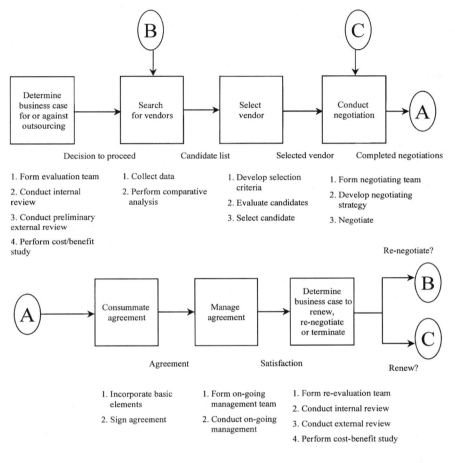

Exhibit 5-1. IT outsourcing process.

- determine the type of outsourcing agreement (e.g., co-sourcing, out-tasking)
- calculate different pricing options (cost plus, fixed price, time, and materials)
- list assumptions and constraints
- develop alternatives
- make a recommendation

SUCCESS TIP #2: SEARCH FOR VENDORS

It is very important to develop criteria for selecting vendors. The criteria should include overall reputation, market share and growth, responsiveness, expertise, flexibility in the types of outsourcing agreements, price, experience, size, and history.

It is important to ensure that the evaluation team has accepted the criteria and the selected vendors. This acceptance reduces resistance to the criteria and encourages buy-in from the team for the vendors that are selected.

When collecting information, the organization should be sure to:

- determine the criteria for looking at a group of vendors
- select the vendors
- determine the sources of information and their reliability
- determine exactly which information is needed (e.g., financial or market value)
- follow a consistent approach to avoid "corrupting" information

When compiling information, the organization should be sure to:

- organize the information in a readable, comprehensible manner (e.g., matrix, three-ring binder)
- not omit any important information

SUCCESS TIP #3: SELECT THE VENDOR

Selecting the vendor should be an objective process. Unfortunately, objectivity becomes sacrificed because "exemptions" are made to the criteria when applied to a specific vendor. Bias is introduced into the process and, not surprisingly, the results are also biased. Worse, it becomes difficult to obtain buy-in from team members and senior management. Whatever the criteria being used, however, the primary criterion is whether the vendor can provide services that will help achieve the goals identified during the determination of the business case. When developing the selection criteria, the organization should be sure to:

- create a specific, meaningful criterion
- use criteria that minimize bias and retain objectivity
- receive consensus from the members of the evaluation team

When evaluating candidates, organizations should be sure to:

- apply the criteria consistently to all vendors
- follow a methodical, logical process

When selecting the candidate, organizations should be sure to:

- receive input from members of the evaluation team
- reevaluate the selection to ensure objectivity and consistency
- communicate the results to all interested parties, including, for example, senior management and evaluation team members

SUCCESS TIP #4: CONDUCT NEGOTIATION

Effective negotiation requires extensive preparation before the event. It requires knowing as much as possible about the vendor, such as its history with other clients; the vendor's market size and growth; its financial condition; its management stability; and its reputation. It also requires that the selecting firm knowing something about itself, including its strengths and weaknesses, short- and long-term goals, and technological capabilities. Such information about the firm and the vendor enables development of a negotiation strategy that has win–win results.

During negotiation, it is important that all team members support the strategy. It is also important that one person be the primary negotiator. If the vendor senses the opposite, then the negotiation may not have the desired results.

While negotiating, it is also important to recognize trends in IT outsourcing, including:

- keeping the duration for contracts within two to three years
- reserving the right to review and perhaps even approve subcontractors
- focusing on a specific, narrow set of services
- describing circumstances for renegotiation and termination
- requiring technology transfer
- describing minimum service levels
- providing for penalties, damages, and incentives
- listing reporting requirements
- providing governance procedures

When forming the negotiating team, the organization should be sure to:

- determine the required knowledge and skills (e.g., legal, technical, business management)
- designate a project manager
- determine whom to select from the evaluation team

When developing a negotiation strategy, the organization should be sure to:

- determine the overall goals to achieve
- develop an in-depth knowledge and understanding of the vendor's style, goals, and history
- come prepared with facts and data to support the case
- conduct a worst/best case scenario analysis

When negotiating, the organization should be sure to:

- have a primary negotiator
- seek a win–win solution
- have the consensus of all members of the negotiation team

SUCCESS TIP #5: CONSUMMATE THE AGREEMENT

The contract is signed when the negotiation is concluded. There should be support by the entire team and senior management before it is signed. This commitment is important to ensure subsequent compliance with the contract, and to communicate to internal staff the willpower to make the outsourcing relationship work.

Prior to signing the contract, it is important to ensure that it covers some basic contractual elements. Failure to address the basic elements listed below could contractually obligate the firm in a manner that fails to protect its best interests (e.g., desirable quality of services at a competitive price).

When drafting the agreement, the organization should make sure it has incorporated at least the following basic elements:

- conditions for renegotiation and termination
- governance
- intellectual property rights
- length of the contract
- penalties, damages, and incentives
-
- pricing
- reporting
- services to provide and their levels
- subcontractor management
- technology transfer

Before signing the agreement, the organization should:

- ensure that all clauses, phrases, and terms are clearly defined
- ensure that there are no outstanding issues
- obtain senior management's support
- obtain consensus of the negotiating team

SUCCESS TIP #6: MANAGE THE AGREEMENT

Signing the agreement is not the end; it is the start of a new beginning. The relationship with the vendor must be managed to ensure the delivery of the desired quality of services for the money being spent.

For effective management, one person should be assigned responsibility for each contract. This person ensures the existence of ongoing communications, effective controls, and performance monitoring. The skills for managing a contract are less legal and technical and more account management in nature. The person should not only know contract management and have an understanding of the technology, but also possess good communications and relationship-building skills.

In addition to having the right person is having an infrastructure in place to manage the agreement. This infrastructure should include change management, scheduling activities, communication and information sharing, performance monitoring, and problem management.

When the organization forms the ongoing management team, it should be sure to:

- determine the required knowledge and skills (e.g., account management, contract management, business management, or scheduling)
- designate a business manager for the contract
- define each member's roles and responsibilities

When conducting ongoing management of the contract, the organization should be sure to:

- provide for continual communications with the vendors
- provide the means for ongoing oversight of the services being provided
- select software or develop a system for tracking and evaluating service delivery
- determine the data and metrics for tracking and evaluating service delivery
- perform a risk assessment to determine which controls should be and are in place
- set up an infrastructure for evaluating changes that are potentially outside the scope of the contract
- set up an infrastructure for problem management

SUCCESS TIP #7: DETERMINE THE BUSINESS CASE TO RENEW, RENEGOTIATE, OR TERMINATE

Once the IT outsourcing agreement is up for reconsideration, there are three options: renew, renegotiate, or terminate. *Renewal* accepts the terms of the existing contract. It often occurs if the customer feels the delivery of services is satisfactory or better. *Renegotiation* often occurs over dissatisfaction with the contents of the contract (e.g., it is too long in duration, or it is too costly). Increasingly, many firms are renegotiating because the technology is changing the needs for a service (e.g., movement from a mainframe-centric environment to a client/server one) or the pricing for services is not market driven. *Termination* occurs because the service is no longer necessary, is unsatisfactory, or costs too much. Terminations occur much less often than renegotiations.

Whether renewing, renegotiating, or terminating, it is important for the organization to conduct as comprehensive a study as when making the initial business case for or against outsourcing. It should use objective criteria, and make evaluations using data collected during the course of the initial contract. The data may come from metrics and documentation of past service delivery. If renegotiating or terminating, the organization should make sure the team and senior management support the decision, and understand the rights described in the contract to take such action.

When forming a reevaluation team, the organization should be sure to:

- define each member's roles and responsibilities
- designate a project manager
- determine the objectives of the team (e.g., renegotiate or terminate the contract)
- determine the required knowledge and skills (e.g., accounting, technical, legal, or business management)

When conducting the internal review, the organization should be sure to:

- define the scope and objectives of the review
- determine if capabilities exist for moving currently outsourced services in-house
- determine the requirements of internal customers
- determine which services are and are not currently being outsourced
- determine which services are mission critical, which are important but not critical, and which are nonessential
- document the quality of the past delivery of services
- evaluate the current delivery of services, using the metrics that were collected

When conducting the external review, the organization should be sure to:

- define the scope and objectives of the review
- determine the research approach (e.g., market analysis or benchmarking)
- develop criteria to determine what vendors look at

When performing the cost/benefit analysis, the organization should be sure to:

- account for the time value of money
- calculate the different pricing options, such as cost plus, fixed price, or time and materials
- determine the payback period
- determine the desired type of outsourcing agreement (e.g., co-sourcing or outtasking)
- develop alternatives
- list assumptions and constraints
- make a recommendation

THE DESIRED RESULTS

While IT outsourcing can be beneficial, it can also devastate a company. For that reason alone, management must see to it that all the necessary actions have been taken to ensure that the former occurs. In too many cases, firms are realizing that the outsourcing of their IT services could have been done better, or never should have occurred in the first place. As a result, everyone is frustrated and angry, and there are costs that no one ever thought would accrue. Fortunately, if the above actions are executed, such results need not happen.

Chapter 6
How to Manage Outsourcing for Best Results

Douglas B. Hoyt

OUTSOURCING IS OFTEN COMPARED TO A MARRIAGE. Each is a relationship in which both sides can benefit substantially. Yet both relationships have inevitable friction and conflicts. The key to success in both affiliations is for the parties to keep in mind the interests and desires of the other, and to try to please each other, and to resolve conflicts in a civilized way. The one difference is that marriages are intended to continue "until death do us part," whereas all outsourcing contracts have defined termination dates, which of course can be extended.

This chapter discusses the plans and actions computer operations managers, and others, must take to make an outsourcing relationship work smoothly and with maximum benefits for the client, as well as for the service vendor. There are always difficulties in these relationships — conflicts, obstacles, misunderstandings, and changed circumstances. These types of difficulties must be anticipated and approaches created for coping with them successfully. With careful planning and management, outsourcing can be a source of savings and other competitive advantages; some sloppily planned and managed outsourcing have been disasters.

TREND TO OUTSOURCING

Eastman Kodak was an early pioneer in the outsourcing movement. In 1989, Kodak contracted with Integrated Systems Solutions Corporation (ISSC), IBM's services branch, to do the computer work that Kodak had been performing at four of its facilities. Then in 1994, Xerox signed a 10-year outsourcing contract for $4.1 billion with Electronic Data Systems Corp. (EDS) to do a major portion of its computer work. AMTRAK expects to save $100 million over a 10-year outsourcing from its outsourcing arrangement.

Those are three examples of the well-publicized movement to outsourcing as a business strategy. It has been estimated that 80 percent of information systems work has been done by contractors by the year 2000.

WHAT TO AND NOT TO OUTSOURCE

Outsourcing has proven effective in accomplishing several goals: to reduce costs, to generate cash, to focus management's attention on the organization's prime purposes, to take advantage of an outsider's expertise, and to help expand globally. Functions inappropriate for outsourcing are systems work necessary to monitor the outsourcing vendor, a system that is part of a competitive advantage, and outsourcing that could expose key proprietary and confidential information.

TIPS FOR WORKING WITH THE CONTRACTOR

There are certain steps that can be taken at the beginning to establish a basis for working together constructively and cooperatively. Clear responsibilities for liaison are essential, regular meetings are helpful, and avoiding misunderstandings is important, yet having a mechanism for dispute resolution is essential.

Spirit of Partnership

Outsourcing arrangements work best when there is a basic feeling of trust and cooperation between the client and vendor. Truly, both should be working to accomplish common goals wherein each benefits in its own way. Both sides should gain substantially from the relationship. However, if conflicts dominate the relationship, lawyers probably get involved to protect what they see as their individual side's rights, and the original goal of mutual gain and benefit is not achieved.

Liaison Staff

One person should be appointed as chief liaison representative for the client in dealing with the outsourcing vendor on a continuous basis. Liaison individuals should have the authority to act for their employers and should be the normal route of communications between client and vendor, particularly for complaints. Therefore, the liaison person must be knowledgeable about the technology involved, be a diplomat, yet be able to be firm in monitoring and demanding proper performance from the vendor. The liaison officer must also be of unquestioned loyalty to the clients' interests (many systems technicians may see their best future career opportunities with an outsourcing services firm), yet see that the vendor's legitimate interests are respected.

The outsourcing contractor should be asked to set up a liaison counterpart, and both client and vendor should clearly define their liaison representatives' responsibilities and *modi operandi*.

The liaison function may vary in size and scope depending on the circumstances. McDonnell Douglas has a group of 15 to 25 employees managing its relationship with Integrated Systems Solutions Corporation (ISSC), IBM's services branch, with which it has a $3 billion outsourcing contract. Hughes Electronics has a staff of 50 to oversee the work of its outsourcer, Computer Systems Corporation (CSC), in its $1.5 billion outsourcing contract covering seven years, and is pleased with the way the relationship is working out.

Meetings

The spirit of working together can be strengthened by frequent meetings between representatives of the client and vendor on topics of interest to either party or to both. Having such meetings on an ad hoc basis, or perhaps regularly, under the guidance of the liaison representatives can get problems under control before they get out of hand, and foster an understanding of people on both sides about the interests and activities of the other parties, thereby encouraging a friendly and cooperative relationship and a feeling of participation, which are important factors leading to the success of the relationship.

Avoiding Misunderstandings

The best way to avoid misunderstandings is to have a contract clearly describing the work to be done and the standards of performance expected, and covering all the contingencies that are considered as possible to occur. But even with a well drawn up contract, there will be events that have not been anticipated, or one party may construe a part of the contract to mean something different from the other party's interpretation.

Resolving Conflicts

There are three general approaches to conflict resolution other than legal action, which it is recommended be avoided at all costs. They are:

1. a conflict resolution committee
2. referring the matter to higher executive levels
3. arbitration or mediation

The conflict resolution committee should probably be co-chaired by the two liaison representatives, with specialists added based on the nature of the issue, such as whether it is an accounting or technical matter.

If the committee cannot bring the matter to a compromise or other solution, it can be referred up the executive ladder — to the vice president level, then to the CEOs — to resolve. This process sometimes can settle the matter quickly. However, it often takes valuable executives' time away from their main functions, time they would take in researching and negotiating the issue.

Taking the conflict to arbitration or mediation is far superior to court action. Using the established processes of the American Arbitration Association can resolve issues faster, cheaper, and easier than suing, engenders less hostility, and can even be done without attorneys.

MANAGING THE TRANSITION TO OUTSOURCING

Making Detailed Plans

The key to a successful transition is a carefully and thoroughly drawn up plan listing all the events that must take place and their timing, including equipment transfers, data and software transfers, people transfers, and who (client and vendor people) is going to do what. Hopefully, much of the transition process has been spelled out in the contract; but even so, there are further details and dates to be made more specific, such as people's names instead of job names, and actual dates instead of time periods.

The transition is a time for the people on both sides to become acquainted with each other. Full discussion and conversations are encouraged during this period to try to establish working relationships that will help in the continuing operation of the contract. The liaison representatives of the client and the vendor should take the lead in coordinating the design of the transition plans, as they will take a major role in their implementation.

Running Systems in Parallel

Running the old system concurrently and in parallel with the new outsourced approach is the best way to confirm the validity of the new way of processing a system. Sometimes, it may be unduly expensive to run the whole system in parallel, and it may be possible to accomplish the purpose of parallel processing by doing it in part, say putting through 1000 of a total of 10,000 orders, which may be sufficient to verify the correctness of the outsourced process. Of course, some outsourced work is for systems that are new and have never been done before, in which case no parallel operation is possible.

Monitoring and Evaluating Contractor's Work

To achieve the client's desired results requires, first of all, to clearly define what known facts will be considered satisfactory, then to get feedback on how the actual performance compares to established standards, and finally to motivate the vendor to conform to or exceed the defined expected results.

Establishing Standards and Managing Expectations

All outsourcing contracts should not only define what work will be done by the outsourcing vendor, but what results are expected and how they will be measured. In order processing, for example, the contract might define the turnaround time from input to output, the maximum percent of errors that would be acceptable, and the cost to the client if the vendor has some control of that. For an outsourced help desk function, the standard might specify the maximum response time, the percent that needs referral to a second technician, and feedback from the users as to their satisfaction with the results.

While these performance standards should be in the contract, as the work gets underway, there may arise additional factors to be considered and adjustments and clarifications that need to be made to keep the standards practical and current. The refinements should be negotiated between the liaison representatives and others concerned, with the agreed new terms put in writing to confirm the agreement and to inform all concerned about them. Because the contracts often run for several years, the changing needs of the client, such as new products and new markets, and changing vendor conditions, such as new hardware or software or location, frequently create the need for revisions to the expectation results.

Performance Reports

It is essential to arrange for some report to be made regularly on each feature of the performance standards so that the outsourcing vendor's results requirements will be measured. Regular and prompt reports should be made by the vendor of items for which a performance standard has been established, measurable or not. Some of the reports will be by-products of other data processing functions, most will come from the vendor, but some may originate from the client, such as reports from users about their help desk performance. The liaison representative is a logical person to be responsible for coordinating, compiling, and disseminating the performance results.

Some aspects of contract requirements cannot readily be checked by reports. For example, keeping proprietary information confidential is a matter that can be verified only by keeping full communication with the right people, discreetly looking for possible breaches and diplomatically looking into anything noticed that raises suspicions.

Motivating Vendor to Conform

If the vendor's payments are tied to the performance results, that provision can be a principal motivating factor for the contractor to accomplish the outcome the client wants. Of course, having the vendor sharing the rewards and risks is a worthy plan where the circumstances make such an arrangement practical. It can make the vendor feel more like a partner than a contractor, and that spirit is desirable. Or, the contract may specify financial penalties when the vendor does not meet specified performance standards, generally a desirable type of provision.

The time to make terms for sharing the rewards and risks is when the contract is being negotiated; however, such an arrangement can be negotiated as an amendment to the original contract if both sides can see that it is to their benefit.

Whether or not the contract provides for the vendor's payments to be tied in to its performance criteria, it is essential for the performance report results to be communicated regularly and systematically to the client's management. The contractor should be thanked for meeting or exceeding set standards, and must be reminded of situations where the results criteria have not been met. If the performance is less than satisfactory a few times and the vendor is not brought to account, the contractor will not be motivated to hit the target. Thus, it is important to let the vendor know that the client is aware of the deficiencies and expects them to take corrective measures. Careful records of the deficiency copies of the reminder notices are important to keep, so that if the situation becomes a larger issue, the historical facts are documented for reference in discussions and negotiations about corrective action.

The client has one advantage in its pressures to the contractor to meet performance requirements. Outside service firms, for business reasons, are anxious to please their clients so that contract renewal can be achieved. Therefore, a request for improved performance should normally be met with respectful responses or negotiations to resolve the matter. If a contractor is seriously and repeatedly deficient in its compliance, the ultimate threat is to terminate the contract, which is the last resort and an undesirable conclusion for both parties; terminations under hostile circumstances can hurt the client as well as the vendor, since they inevitably cause disruption and the difficulties of moving the work back in-house or to another vendor under unpleasant circumstances.

HOW TO HANDLE EMPLOYEES WHEN DOWNSIZING

One of the most difficult parts of outsourcing and other types of downsizing is to manage the human relations aspects so that morale and loyalty are preserved and that the best employees are retained. Unfortunately, transferring employees out or letting them go inevitably strains the feelings of the other employees, and this part shows some of the tactics that can minimize the negative results of downsizing and even, sometimes, leave the new organization stronger than it was before.

Downsizing Methods

Downsizing is a major part of, indeed one purpose of, nearly all outsourcing programs. Cost reduction is an objective of most outsourcing, and that reduction is primarily in terms of fewer employees.

But there are a variety of ways that downsizing can be accomplished without outsourcing. One currently popular approach is reengineering, which consists of methodically examining the operating processes of an organization by analyzing the types and numbers of employees needed for each function as well as developing better approaches for performing these processes. Another downsizing method is to make "across the board" cuts, say 10 percent of each department; this approach, which is used to hastily meet a budget crisis, is generally not recommended as it usually makes cuts in the wrong places.

In the data processing arena, many companies have been able to reduce staff by converting mainframe systems to client/servers, by adopting CASE methods for programming, and other methods for accomplishing the work goals with fewer employees.

A typical example of downsizing was the recent plan by AT&T to reduce its staff by 40,000, a 13 percent reduction. NYNEX has laid off 16,000 employees.

Inevitable Anxiety and Resentment

Anxiety is an inevitable result of uncertainty. When a situation arises that will involve letting employees go, or requested to be considered for employment by an outsourcing services firm, results in anxiety for those affected. These employees' source of livelihood is put in limbo until the situation is resolved, even though the sources of their income may be improved under the new arrangement. Unfortunately, the uncertainty and resentment caused by downsizing usually also results in the lowering of morale of the employees who remain.

There are several general principles reviewed below for taking steps to minimize the disruption from downsizing, to maximize the morale and loyalty of the remaining employees, and to help to retain the employees the client wants.

Explain Process at Earliest Opportunity

The timing of the announcement of a downsizing plan to the employees concerned is a difficult decision, and usually not a perfect one. The plan should be explained before the rumors become prevalent. It can obviously be disconcerting for an employee to learn first of a downsizing plan from the newspapers.

While the plan must be discussed in advance with key employees who need to be consulted in preparing the structure of the downsizing effort, the planning phase should be as short as possible because, once the plan is known by top people confidentially, leaks and rumors almost inevitably follow.

Boeing's announcement in 1993 that it would reduce its workforce by nearly 20 percent over one-and-a-half years was received without any special alarm by its employees. The reason for the calm acceptance was that Boeing had made a point of revealing over the previous period that sales in the aerospace industry had been at a low level and that drastic corrective action was in order.

Explain Openly the Business Reasons for the Change

When the downsizing plan is announced, the important matters to emphasize and clarify are the business reasons for making the change and the fairness features of the plan for the employees.

There has been enough downsizing in recent years that it has become an accepted fact of life to most people. It has become recognized that in the evolving intensity of global competition, companies must often make major cost reduction efforts to beat or stay even with competitors. The real reasons for the decision to lessen staff can be to reduce a downward profit trend, to meet known cost levels of competitors, to generate cash for an important new venture, or some other of the many possible business considerations. These business reasons should be explained so that all concerned are made aware of the valid and logical necessity of the downsizing plan. It should be made clear how the downsizing program will make the organization stronger so that departing employees will understand the logic and reasonableness of the effort and remaining employees will feel more secure.

The fairness of the plan structure as explained should include the general terms of a financial package and career assistance for those that will leave, and the benefits of working for a computer service firm for those employees who may be made available for employment with the outsourcing vendor. The plan may give choices to some employees, making it somewhat voluntary, such as having them decide whether to accept a severance package or transfer to some alternative positions.

All of this open discussion of the business reasons and fairness will not eliminate some bitterness and lowering of morale. But done well, it should keep those disadvantages to a minimum.

Get Help from Human Resources and Legal Staff

When Philadelphia Newspapers, Inc., planned a downsizing effort in 1993, based on moving from its mainframe to client/servers, the unions threatened to walk out. The downsizing program had to be deferred until the labor dispute was resolved. That delay indicates the value of securing counsel and advice from legal and human relations specialists.

The human resources staff should participate closely in the planning of the downsizing steps. It is their job to be skilled in the handling of employee relations matters, especially those involving intense emotional feelings. Therefore, human resources' advice and guidance should be sought in laying out the plan. However, the execution is a line responsibility; that is, it is the line manager's proper role to make the announcements to the groups affected and, ultimately, to explain to each individual how the plan affects him or her.

The legal staff should also be consulted in designing the downsizing plan and the separation packages. Their advice is needed to make sure of compliance with the Employee Retirement Income Security Act (ERISA), the Consolidated Omnibus Budget Reconciliation Act (COBRA), union agreements, and other legal requirements.

Assess Individual Employees' Loyalty

Decisions regarding which employees are to remain and which are to be let go should be based mostly on their skills in relation to the client's needs. But the employee's loyalty to the employer is also an important factor in that decision even though there is no objective way to measure that loyalty. At best, loyalty can be judged by intuition, but there can be signs such as cooperative behavior, expressions of bitterness, and general demeanor indicating acceptance of management's decisions and plans.

When downsizing is a part of an outsourcing arrangement and some of the client's employees are to be employed by the services vendor, employees who are more loyal to their computer specialty than to their current employer may prefer to join the computer service firm rather than stay in an organization in which computer operations are not the primary function.

But loyalty can be a double-edged sword. Some employees who may not be the best qualified may feign loyalty, sensing the severe competition for survival in a downsizing situation. Their attempts to please may be appreciated, but should be tempered with a balanced evaluation of the employee's worth.

Encourage Valued Employees to Stay

Once it is known, from announcements or rumor, that a downsizing program is underway, some of the better employees may feel it is a good time to seek greener pastures. The employees whom the employer needs or wants to retain because of their skills and loyalty assessment, should be encouraged to stay. This may involve giving assurances as to future plans, possibly a pay increase because of added responsibilities, bonuses, or other financial incentives. These assurances are important particularly because of the general negative atmosphere that is generated by the downsizing, including lowered morale and anxiety due to the uncertainties involved.

Preach Loyalty Rationale Continuously

To those employees who will be retained, management should continuously be explaining the goals of the organization, why the prospects are good for reaching those goals, and how the individual employees fit into the plans and are wanted to help achieve those goals. These efforts are necessary to bolster the morale and offset the feelings of bitterness and resentment that are inevitable among some of the employees who are retained after seeing many of their associates leave, even though they may be given generous departure packages.

After downsizing, it is natural for remaining employees to feel insecure, anxious, depressed, and even resentful. Open communications can help. It is well to continue discussing the place of the downsizing in the organization's overall goals, and to seek employee views and help in planning how the work can best be done under the post-downsizing environment. Let employees vent their feelings without being recriminated for doing so. Such communication can foster a renewed feeling of trust and sense of value.

Offer Reasonable Severance Terms

It is essential for the public relations well-being of the organization to offer fair and generous settlements to employees who are asked or encouraged to leave. Such settlements may include provisions such as a cash amount based on the years of service, earlier pension starting dates, and career guidance and support.

The cash settlement is intended primarily to support the person until he or she is able to locate another position (though some have urged stock options instead of cash so that the ex-employee may share in increased profits from the downsizing). The earlier pension can be given by adding, for example, five years to the employee's actual age to enable him or her to achieve a retirement pension earlier than would be available otherwise. The outplacement assistance is usually provided by a consultant who guides the ex-employee in the techniques for seeking a new position and may also provide some of the résumé preparation and phone and office services helpful to the job seeker.

All these separation assistance tools help the organization's management to feel and say properly that it is doing what it reasonably can to help those who are put in a difficult position by the downsizing program, often due to no fault of their own.

Try to Give Choices Between Favorable Options. To the extent possible, it is wise to build into the severance arrangement choices for the employees so that the employees feel that there is a voluntary element in the plan and that they are not being forced unilaterally into their new status. For example, at a downsizing program at Sea-Land Service, many employees were offered a generous severance package, but given the choice of remaining with the company, which would try to, but not guarantee to, find them a lower-level position with the company if the package was rejected. With this choice, no employees left Sea-Land without the severance package.

SECURITY

The data in the hands of an outsourcing service may be the lifeblood of the client organization. It is, therefore, essential for the client's management to make sure that there are adequate backup copies of the operating data that the vendor possesses. This can often be accomplished by securing from the vendor current copies of the data so that operations could be continued should a disaster — like a flood, earthquake, or fire — destroy the client's data at the location of the outsourcing service. If the client relies on backup data that the vendor has arranged, such as with a firm like the Iron Mountain Depository or Comdisco, then the client must periodically audit those extra copies to verify that they are current, complete, and properly secured. However, even if the vendor does maintain an extra data security copy off-site, by keeping its own backup copy, the client is in a better position to terminate the vendor and resume its own work or use a new contractor. The backup data discussed here must include copies of the current software needed to run the other data.

The other major security concern is the exposure of proprietary information through the outsourcing vendor. Of course, the restrictions on the use of key business and technical data should be spelled out in the outsourcing contract. Whether they are or not, it behooves the client to check on the proper handling of information in the hands of the vendor, by observation, inquiry, and other means. If the contract does not spell out security requirements sufficiently, they should be discussed with and agreed to between the client and vendor, with the terms put in writing, in effect, as a supplement to the contract.

HOW TO TERMINATE A CONTRACT

The contract terms have much to do with how the contract is terminated, and there are may different reasons for ending a contract that affect how it best be done. A major factor in making a smooth transition to whatever the new arrangement will be is to prepare a careful plan and schedule of the items and events involved. Finally, both client and vendor may wish to renew the contract; but then there are always adjustments and improvements to make over the previous terms and features.

Terminating a contract before its scheduled end because of problems or changed circumstances cannot be done easily or quickly. It takes time to reestablish IS operations in-house or transfer the work to another contract service vendor. Therefore, if and when problems occur or conditions change, it is generally best to negotiate appropriate revised arrangements with the vendor rather than choose an early separation.

Reasons for Terminating

There are many reasons for terminating outsourcing contracts. One reason may be that the contract period is finished (though if the arrangement has worked well, a renewal would be the logical outcome). It may be that the client or the vendor has become dissatisfied for one reason or another and wants out. A good reason is that another vendor, possibly with some advanced technology, has offered terms that could save more money and provide specialized benefits. Or possibly, the client's needs have changed in terms of product or territory, or an acquisition or merger was made that has caused the vendor's services to be unsuitable.

Planning and Scheduling Termination

The transition to setting up the outsourcing arrangement required listing the myriad of details that had to be taken care of; a careful plan listing the equipment, software, and personnel changes to be made; and scheduling the events in a logical fashion. The termination process requires a similar listing of the hardware, software, and people changes and a time schedule for the events to take place. The scheduling process may be aided by GANTT or PERT charts, which help to identify the actions needed, their sequence, and the steps to follow up to keep the schedule on track.

The written or charted schedule also helps in coordinating the steps with the service contractor who, of course, must agree with the plan and cooperate to make it successful. There should be some guidelines about the termination steps in the contract, but they are never enough to be a working schedule at the time of the transition. Hopefully, the contract will set an elapsed period for the termination process that is ample enough to make it a smooth transition. If not specified in the contract, the pricing of the services in the termination period must be negotiated as one of the early steps.

RENEWING A CONTRACT

Long before the contract termination date, the computer services manager and others should be evaluating whether some other vendor might do the work better, whether the client has come to believe that it can do the outsourced work more advantageously in-house, or whether the contract should be renewed. If the decision is to renew, then the client should analyze in what ways the arrangement could be improved and whether a more advantageous price could be obtained, and begin to negotiate a revised contract — hopefully to the benefit of both the service firm and the client. The new contract should also reflect the many circumstances that undoubtedly have changed since the original contract was written, such as new technology used by the vendor and new products, customer groups, or geographical territories for the client.

SOURCES OF GUIDANCE AND SUPPORT

The operation and managing of an outsourcing or other downsizing program are matters in which it is helpful to talk with others who have been or are managing similar plans for their organizations. Informal meetings with peers in other such organizations about common problems can be a source of ideas and a feeling of support. There is considerable literature on these subjects; one thorough and pertinent source is *Computer Outsourcing* by Thomas R. Mylott III (Prentice-Hall, 1995).

Many organizations do buy, for a fee, the advice of experts who have experience in managing outsourcing and downsizing programs. These sources include the Outsourcing Institute and a variety of consulting firms.

The Outsourcing Institute

The Outsourcing Institute, Inc. [45 Rockefeller Plaza, Suite 2000, New York, NY 10111 (800) 421-6767] is a for-profit membership group to which both outsourcing users and vendors belong. Membership is free.

Consultants

Consultants, especially consulting arms of large public accounting firms, have been engaged to advise and counsel on whether and what to contract out, vendors to select, and how to negotiate and manage outsourced work. Firms like Andersen and PricewaterhouseCoopers provide such advisory assistance, though their fees range from $100 per hour to much higher.

The leading consulting associations can also refer inquiries to members, who can provide outsourcing vendor advisory services. These include:

- Institute of Management Consultants (IMC)
  521 Fifth Avenue, 35th floor
  New York, NY 10175
  (212) 697-8262
- The Association of Management Consulting Firms (ACME)
  521 Fifth Avenue, 35th floor
  New York, NY 10175
  (212) 697-9693
- Independent Computer Consultants Association (ICCA)
  11131 South Towne Square, Suite F
  St. Louis, MO 63123
  (800) 774-4222

Consultants' capabilities can also be researched through the Internet via Management Consultant Network International, Inc. (MCNI), reached via <http://www.mcninet.com/> or at (413) 755-0825.

CASE EXAMPLE: SEA-LAND SERVICE

As reported in the November 1993 issue of *Personnel Journal*, Sea-Land Service, a major cargo-shipping company based in New Jersey, in 1989 determined that its modest profits were due to excess staffing that had developed over the years. To overcome its inefficiency, the company decided, after careful planning, to redefine all jobs by analyzing what functions and how many people were really necessary for operating the business. By comparing the skills and abilities of its employees with its analytically determined staff guidelines, from CEO on down, the company was able to reduce its employee number by 800, or 15 percent. The restructuring of its organization eliminated five levels in its organizational hierarchy. These downsizing changes enabled the company to reduce operating expenses by $300 million and increase revenues 30 percent to $3.3 billion and increase profits by 35 percent to $151 million. All this improvement took place during a period of intense competition in this global industry.

The plan was designed to be as fair as possible by giving employees reasonable choices, with those choices being voluntary. Employees whose new positions would be two or more levels lower, or who lived over 50 miles from work, were offered severance packages and outplacement services. Those who turned down the severance arrangement would be helped in relocating within the company, though doing so made them forfeit the severance benefits. In the end, no one was laid off without benefits. The president of The Marshall Group, Bob Marshall, assisted Sea-Land in planning its staff analysis and restructuring program. The Marshall Group is a consulting organization based in Scottsdale, Arizona.

RECOMMENDED COURSE OF ACTION

The following points are highlights of the actions a computer operations manager should take to oversee and manage the work of outsourcing service vendors:

- Establish a relationship of cooperative partnership with the outsourcing vendor.
- When obstacles and conflicts occur, resolve them rather than fight about them.
- Even though there is trust and respect between client and vendor, monitor performance and demand results that were contracted.
- Select and rely on a strong liaison representation to coordinate relations with the contracting services vendor.
- Make careful and detailed plans for the steps to transfer the work to the outsourcing vendor and, at termination, to transfer the work to another vendor or in-house.
- Make parallel runs, if possible, with each change.
- Explain the downsizing reasons to employees — clearly, openly, and promptly — and reinforce those explanations regularly.
- Keep current copies of computer data and software in-house.

Chapter 7
Improving IT Performance as an Outsourcing Alternative

Richard D. Hays

OUTSOURCING HAS GROWN TO BECOME A PRIMARY FORCE shaping business, especially in the information technology (IT) arena. Owing to high costs, service that is often viewed as unresponsive and frustrating, and a willingness to see IT as an easily substitutable commodity, many organizations have targeted the IT function as a prime outsourcing candidate. Many IT executives have realized too late that their efforts to optimize internal technology have been eclipsed by the pressing need to deal with external communications and service effectiveness issues.

Many outsourcers have reduced costs and improved service levels. Others have found that their strategic focus has been sharpened by eliminating an IT function that was not central to their core technology. Still others have achieved improved access to information technology and expertise as a result of their outsourcing move.

For some organizations, however, the shift to outsourcing their IT function has been much less positive. Horror stories have resulted from the lack of flexibility and control that accompanies this shift.[1] Old problems and complaints that should have disappeared with the introduction of a new IT supplier remained. New limitations on control and flexibility have hampered strategic actions, and some have awakened to rude shocks as unanticipated parts of their agreement forced sudden and unpleasant lessons about the contracting process. For these companies, the promise of IT outsourcing is severely tarnished.

0-8493-0875-5/00/$0.00+$.50
© 2000 by CRC Press LLC

Symptoms of Poor IT Performance

Many disappointed volunteers in the outsourcing movement share a common original motivation and entry process. They were propelled into outsourcing primarily as a flight from a poorly performing internal IT unit (the more satisfied outsourcing companies are more likely to have had an original motivation rooted in broader strategic concerns). Frustration with cost and service quality in the existing IT unit and with repeated unsuccessful attempts to fix the problem have often precipitated a headlong rush to an outsourcing option. With no existing positive model of a well-functioning IT unit available, these organizations have been much more likely to jump into outsourcing for inappropriate reasons or negotiated much less favorable contracts and conditions. In addition, a quick move directly into outsourcing often means that fundamental factors that helped create the initial unsatisfactory IT performance remain unidentified and unaddressed — a neglect that sows the seeds of future discontent, even in an outsourcing mode. The following six symptoms of serious internal performance problems can help determine the level of concern about existing internal service performance within an IT organization:

1. *Conflict.* A high state of conflict and disagreement between IT and customer units is a continuing and dominant feature of the ongoing relationship.
2. *Complaints.* Customer units complain loudly and insistently about poor IT service or high IT costs.
3. *Duplicating service.* Customer units attempt to build their own internal duplicates of IT-provided services to gain better control.
4. *Executive frustration.* Senior corporate executives are frustrated with seemingly uncontrolled IT costs and the continuing need to referee conflicts between IT and its customer units.
5. *Organizational energy.* Considerable executive and managerial time, energy, and effort are being expended in dealing with interdepartmental conflict issues or in positioning for future conflicts.
6. *Customer impact.* The internal conflicts over IT costs or service quality are beginning to have an impact on the interface with external customers.

IT PERFORMANCE TURNAROUND

The risk and uncertainty surrounding outsourcing can be significantly reduced by achieving a performance turnaround in the existing IT unit before the formal consideration of outsourcing. Effecting such a turnaround requires commitment of substantial resources and effort, but yields three important organizational payoffs:

- Confrontation of key performance-limiting issues
- Creation of a solid comparative basis for outsourcing

- Achievement of greater cost and service benefits than outsiders can offer

Confronting Key Performance-Limiting Issues

If an existing IT unit is performing poorly, it is doing so for specific reasons. These reasons frequently have to do with fundamental structural factors that seriously impede the unit's ability to yield solid, cost-effective service. For example, a major source of difficulty for many internal IT units is unclear or conflicting service expectations. Lack of specific articulation and agreement between supplier and user of IT services breeds violation of unstated (but strongly held) expectations. In addition, senior management may want low cost, while line customer units want premium service. In such cases, the IT function is caught in the middle and can satisfy neither.

If these conflicts have not been addressed and resolved, moving to outsourcing only exacerbates problems. When an IT activity is poorly managed, the managers will probably not be any better at managing an external service provider. The question to ask is why executive management would want to bestow the benefits of improving an inefficient operation to an external market. Two responses have been suggested for this scenario. The first is to hire better IT managers, and the second is to improve the performance of the IT function before making the decision to outsource.[2] When fundamental problems such as poor performance or inefficiency are left unresolved, they are much more difficult to improve within the outsourcing arrangement.

Creating a Solid, Comparative Basis for Outsourcing

When moving directly from a poorly performing internal IT unit to outsourcing, a company has a very ill-formed basis for structuring and negotiating a contract. Significant evidence is emerging that shows that IT performance gains have much more to do with the adoption of effective management practices than with economies of scale.[3] Can the organization afford to give away an unknown (but probably large) premium to an outsider, based simply on the ability to bring in effective management?

Without the existence of a well-functioning internal IT unit that is operating within the unique variables and constraints of a particular company, the company has little basis for structuring the contract. The outsourcing contractor is much more experienced and knowledgeable about the factors that will determine final cost and performance — a rather one-sided basis for negotiations.

Achieving Greater Cost and Service Benefits

A well-known research study carefully examined six firms with IT units that were judged by their own company to be performing unsatisfactorily.[4]

Each firm placed its IT function out to bid in an outsourcing mode but, after considering both external bids and a bid from their own internal IT unit, elected to grant a contract to their internal unit (a practice known as insourcing). The performance of each unit was then monitored as changes were made — changes that were more extensive than were possible in the old mode of a totally captive unit.

The results were impressive. Costs were reduced from 20 percent to 54 percent and, in many cases, service improved as well. It was concluded that internal IS departments, given the freedom and capability to change, often possess strong cost advantages over any outsider and offer greater insight into the unique organizational service needs as well.

The emerging success stories in insourcing are causing new questioning as to why an external agent, using essentially the same people and equipment as the internal unit, should be able to deliver more cost-effective service and produce a profit as well. In fact, once internal IT units start to see the overall problem from this perspective, the challenge to use their own resources to exceed what an outsider could offer can become a positive and motivational vision. They already have the basic resources that would become available to an outside supplier — why not work on the revised perspective, practices, and processes that will provide the same cost and service benefits?

Each of these benefits can be substantial, but the combination of all three provides a commanding reason to seriously consider the turnaround option. Many companies have avoided the turnaround option because of the difficulty in designing and executing such a complex organizational change. However, the change technology and experience base are available to help structure an IT performance turnaround that will most likely succeed (even in cases with low reform success in the past).

DETERMINING THE APPROPRIATENESS OF A TURNAROUND

Individual organizational characteristics determine whether a turnaround attempt should be made prior to outsourcing. While no simple answer exists, affirmative responses to the following questions should bias the IS manager's thinking toward investing in a turnaround effort:

1. *Is IT central to the core business and strategy?* IT is often viewed as a substitutable and replaceable commodity, particularly if historical performance has been poor. However, a more in-depth analysis may reveal that IT is more central to effectiveness of strategic actions than is apparent on the surface. If the overall strategy of the business depends on IT functioning and performance to any substantial degree, outsourcing could mean loss of control and flexibility in a key area — actions that could seriously blunt the overall strategic impact.

2. *Could IT become a source of competitive advantage?* For many companies, IT is more than just crucial to strategic action — it is a fundamental source of external competitive advantage. American Airlines, Otis Elevator, USAA insurance, FedEx, and Frito-Lay all gain primary competitive advantage from their IT competence. Envisioning how IT could move to a role of providing a basic competitive advantage may be extremely difficult if present IT issues center on adequacy of basic functioning.

3. *Are IT needs complex, relatively unique, or dynamic?* An outsourcing contract can be most effective with fairly straightforward service needs and a moderately steady-state situation. The loss of flexibility as conditions change (i.e., either organizational needs or technology changes) can become a substantial limitation with a rigid contract.

4. *Is frustration with the present IT function a primary outsourcing motivator?* Successful outsourcing arrangements tend to be grounded in strategic analysis rather than based on a flight from a frustrating existing internal unit. Identification of, and assault on the fundamental issues creating the present performance problems is necessary, even in an outsourcing mode.

SETTING UP THE TURNAROUND

Once it has been determined that a turnaround is an appropriate endeavor, the following actions should be taken to help ensure a successful effort. These include:[5]

- *Situational assessment.* IS managers should assess the initial situation to determine the need for change, the general extent of changes needed, and the capability of the parties involved to manage and embrace the change. Asking pointed questions about the general need, the IT unit, and the customer units can help focus thinking about the need to change and make this need more salient to all.

- *Enrollment of stakeholders.* It is important to ensure the continued understanding and support of senior managers, customer managers, and IT leadership in the organizational change process. Top managers and customer unit leaders must have specific information on the need for change, the benefits of a successful effort, required resources, impact on others, and scheduling. IT leaders needs to grapple with the significant issues involved with a major change process.

- *Final commitment.* All of the setup work should be committed to a specific and written document that serves as a public agreement on such issues as the need for the change, the goals of the turnaround, and the general process to be used. Top management, customer unit leaders, and IT leadership all need to have a shared understanding and agreement about the important organizational change ahead. The team that will actually manage the change process will need to organize itself to ensure effective project management.

BUILDING THE INFORMATION BASE

Any successful organizational change effort must be grounded in firm information and analysis. An IT turnaround effort requires a clear vision of the existing problem situation and its causation, detailed insights into the real service needs to customer units, and a deep understanding of their own internal processes and procedures. An effective change plan must be founded on this solid information base.

The process of constructing the needed information base can serve as the launch pad to a new IT culture centered on internal customers — units with service needs that must be identified and filled if IT is to be successful. Extracting the views of these internal customers and other stakeholders regarding the following questions is essential to the construction of an effective IT change plan.

- How do they view present IT service?
- What is their perception of the present IT function?
- What are the service needs?
- What specific topics are causing the most difficulty within the units?
- What is the desired balance between cost and service responsiveness?
- How strongly do the units feel a need for basic change?

Surveys and interviews can provide important insights into the causal forces that shape today's problem situation. Focused exploration of customer unit service expectations can reveal the nature and form of their service beliefs (and provide an opportunity to identify those that may be unreasonable or excessively costly).

DESIGNING THE TURNAROUND PLAN

Once the information base regarding the existing problem, customer service expectations, and existing processes is understood in depth, a plan to direct the IT turnaround effort can be constructed. The plan must set specific and measurable goals, define the needed changes, and identify the required processes for change.

Defining IT Performance Standards

Many of the goals of the plan will be derived from newly defined IT performance standards. Considerable work needs to be expended on working directly with customer units to define these standards. They will reflect both the specific service expectations of the customer units and the practical and professional pragmatics of the IT unit. The standards need to be as specific and measurable as possible and explicitly agreed upon by all as the definition of excellent service. This definition of excellence will serve as the guide for the efforts of the IT unit, as well as the standard used by the customer units to judge service.

The process of negotiating and defining these standards may be one of the most difficult tasks of the entire turnaround, but it is also one of the most important. One survey of IT departments in a variety of industries searched for factors that contribute to high internal customer satisfaction.[6] The IT units that ranked high on service satisfaction had significantly better and more precise specifications regarding the service to be performed than did their less-well-rated counterparts. For these IT units, the considerable investment in defining expectations and clarifying standards paid off strongly in service satisfaction.

FROM PLANNING TO IMPLEMENTATION SUCCESS

Three supporting elements are key to converting a turnaround plan from an abstract concept to an implementation success. They are discussed in the sections that follow.

1. Aligning the IT Culture

Customer-centeredness must become the driving force of the IT culture. Most poorly performing IT units have an internal culture centered around the enhancement of their own technology or processes. The conversion of this well-established culture to an entirely new focus that targets the service needs of customer units is a prodigious task, unlikely to respond to gentle prodding. Gaining an explicit understanding of the functioning of the present internal IT culture and producing a specific articulation of the desired culture are necessary but difficult and foreign processes for most IT units. Designing the actual cultural changes and reinforcements may be even more foreign.

2. Developing Service-Oriented IT People

Building the skills and attitudes needed to produce service-oriented people in the IT unit is also a necessary support step for the change plan. Being skillfully solicitous of, and receptive to, customer feedback (particularly negative feedback) is a trainable skill. This skill escapes even many external service companies, but is no less crucial to an IT unit dealing with internal customers. IT agents must provide respectful and responsive service interactions with internal customer units and be able and willing to gain feedback on service rendered — an invaluable element in improving future service.

Ensuring Capability for Service Recovery

Many IT units deliver service adequately but destroy their relationship with customer units when they face service recovery situations. Because the best of service will sometimes fail, the skill that the IT unit has built to recover positively from these unanticipated shortfalls will heavily shape the customer's view of the service they have received. Recovery situations are particularly difficult because of the higher interpersonal skill level and service commitment needed to handle disgruntled and emotionally charged customers who have just received service that violates their expectations.

RECOMMENDED COURSE OF ACTION

At the completion of a successful IT performance turnaround, the company has a greatly expanded range of alternatives. When a cost-effective and service-sensitive IT unit is in place, the motivation for outsourcing erodes. The loss of flexibility and control associated with outsourcing is just too great a cost without the negative prod of poor and costly existing service. The process of creating a truly effective internal IT unit causes fundamental problems to be addressed and, at a minimum, establishes an excellent basis for negotiating an outsourcing contract.

If outsourcing is still a consideration, the outsourcing options themselves become richer as new performance experience is gained. A more sophisticated view moves from asking a simple "outsource or not" question and looks at the effectiveness of selective outsourcing of specific functions. Assessing IT performance and achieving a performance turnaround is thus a practical alternative to outsourcing.

Notes

1. Lacity, M.C., Willcocks, L.P., and Feeny, D.F., "IT Outsourcing: Maximize Flexibility and Control," *Harvard Business Review,* 73 (May–June 1995), pp. 84–94.
2. Earl, M.J., "The Risks of Outsourcing IT," *Sloan Management Review* (Spring 1996), p. 27.
3. Lacity, M.C. and Hirschheim, R., *Beyond the Information Systems Outsourcing Bandwagon: The Insourcing Response,* (New York: John Wiley, 1995), p. 168.
4. Lacity and Hirschheim, p. 36.
5. Hays, R.D., *Internal Service Excellence: A Manager's Guide to Building World Class Internal Service Unit Performance* (Sarasota FL: Summit Executive Press, 1996).
6. Pfau, B., Detzel, D., and Geller, A., "Satisfy Your Internal Customer," *Journal of Business Strategy,* (November–December 1991), p. 11.

Section III
Outsourcing and Process

Chapter 8
How to Select an Outsourcing Vendor

Douglas B. Hoyt

THE OUTSOURCING OF COMPUTER OPERATIONS WORK has proven to be an important means for many organizations to help them become or stay competitive today. With new IT technologies, global competition, growing availability of competent services vendors, and reengineering efforts to redefine and improve traditional business processes, outsourcing has become an increasingly prevalent way to fulfill business improvement opportunities.

THE CHALLENGE

It has been estimated that 73 percent of the leading companies contract out part of their IS functions, that $6 billion of client/server work was outsourced in 1996, and that 80 percent of information systems activities has been done by contractors by 2000. Because organizations are finding that outsourcing can cut costs, sharpen management's focus, get access to expertise, and foster global expansion, computer operations managers should help lead the way to finding improvement opportunities via IT outsourcing. When outsourcing has been decided on by their managements, the managers must help to implement those decisions so that they work to the organizations' best advantage, by securing the most appropriate vendors and laying the groundwork for a mutually beneficial relationship.

One or More Vendors?

Most organizations that outsource some computer work use several vendors. One reason is to select the best vendor for each function specialty. A second reason is to not "put all your eggs in one basket;" sometimes it is better to have more than one vendor for a single function, for comparison purposes and to protect against total disaster if one fails. Having several

0-8493-0875-5/00/$0.00+$.50

vendors can prove to be an advantage when it is decided to change vendors or return the work in-house, an eventuality that must be considered in every outsourcing action.

Having one vendor do everything that is outsourced simplifies the management of the work outsourced, and is fine so long as the vendor proves competent and reliable. But many outsourcing arrangements have their rocky periods, and their termination must be anticipated in all cases.

SOURCES OF OUTSOURCING VENDORS

Many of the larger and better-known outsourcing vendors are known to most computer operations managers from discussions with peers and reports in the press and magazines. Some vendors may have approached the managers' organizations in efforts to sell their services. Word of mouth and general knowledge sources can be valuable, especially when they reflect opinions of results the vendors have achieved from people or media in which the prospective client has trust.

However, even though a worthy source may be known from prior knowledge, it is usually wise to look at other alternatives to make sure that the vendor selected is the one best suited for the job to be done. Sources to consider in seeking the best service vendors are: The Outsourcing Institute, research services, consultants, and computer resellers.

The Outsourcing Institute

The Outsourcing Institute, Inc. (45 Rockefeller Plaza, Suite 2000, New York, NY 10111; (800) 421-6767) is a for-profit membership group to which both outsourcing users and vendors belong. One of its services to members is its *Buyer's Guide,* a list of outsourcing vendors detailing the services they provide and industries and geographical areas they cover. Membership is free.

Research Services

Dataquest Professional Service Trends and The Gartner Group publish reviews and reports on potential vendors. It has been said that such information should be sufficient for projects of $100,000 or less, and that consultants are suggested for advice on more sizable work to be contracted out.

Consultants

Consultants, especially consulting arms of large public accounting firms, have been engaged to advise and counsel on whether and what to contract out, vendors to select, and how to negotiate and manage outsourced work. Firms like Andersen and PricewaterhouseCoopers provide advisory assistance, though their fees range from $100 per hour to much higher.

The leading consulting associations can also refer inquirers to members who can provide outsourcing vendor advisory services. These include:

Institute of Management Consultants (IMC)
521 Fifth Avenue, 35th floor, New York, New York 10175
(212) 697-8262

The Association of Management Consulting Firms (ACME)
521 Fifth Avenue, 35th floor, New York, New York 10175
(212) 697-9693

Independent Computer Consultants Association (ICCA)
11131 South Towne Square, Suite F, St. Louis, Missouri 63123
(800) 774-4222

Consultants' capabilities can also be researched through the Internet via Management Consultant Network International, Inc. (MCNI) at http://www.mcninet.com/, or by telephone at (413) 755-0825.

Resellers

Many resellers of hardware and software also provide outsourcing services for a variety of computer operations, usually related to the products they sell. When a reseller does offer to perform outsourcing work, it will be more motivated to make its customer pleased, because its bread-and-butter profits depend upon the sale of computer products to the same customer. Therefore, resellers are an important outsourcing option to consider.

HOW TO EVALUATE VENDORS

The final decision in selecting an outsourcing vendor may well be an intuitive judgment, such as a belief that "these are people I feel I would like to work with, and I sense that they are reliable and honest." A feeling of mutual respect and trust based on such opinions can be important to a successful, continuing business relationship.

Nevertheless, the decision should be made only after a thorough analysis of the many characteristics that are essential to the success of contracted work. This analysis must include feedback from the vendors' other customers, and verification of the vendor's expertise and experience, financial stability, and reliability. Checks should be made into the financial stability, size, and potential conflicts of interest with the firm being considered. It is good to get at least two proposals and compare them, based on a carefully written request for proposal (RFP), or in a statement of the work that is to be required.

Checking References

The best reference is a referral from someone who is known personally and trusted, and who has experience with the vendor. Lacking an unsolicited recommendation, it is well to discuss the vendor with some of its present or past clients, meet with them, and talk over in some detail the work done, how it met expectations, the vendor's technical expertise resourcefulness, reliability, and related matters. It is important to make sure the clients met with are representative and random, not selected favorites of the vendor.

Appraising Expertise and Experience

One major reason for wanting to contract out some computer work is usually that vendors have greater expertise and experience than the client in the function involved. Therefore, it is essential to evaluate and verify the nature and degree of these factors in the vendors being considered. The sources of research into this area are multifold: vendors' literature, published articles, discussions with potential vendor representatives, consultants, and — most important — information from the vendors' past and current clients.

When appropriate, it may be wise to ask the potential vendors for résumés of the persons who would do the work or be in charge, and evaluate their qualifications in the specializations required. The presence of certifications can be significant, such as the ISO 9000 series certification, demonstrating quality control discipline, and CCP, Certified Computer Professional.

Financial Stability

The client must be assured that any outsourcing vendor selected will be around long enough to complete the contract, usually a matter of from one to ten years, and also be available to continue if it is desired to renew the contract. The vendor should be comfortably profitable, so as not to be influenced to cut corners to survive.

If a public company, review the potential vendor's financial statements. Secure credit reports from credit agencies like Dun & Bradstreet and Moody's. Look back some years, as enduring years of success are an indication of likely future success at surviving and performing. Review published reports in periodicals like *The Wall Street Journal* and *Business Week* for any significant events such as legal or labor problems in the vendor's history.

Size

Values related to a vendor's size should be evaluated. Smaller-sized firms may be more flexible, cheaper, more eager to please, but are harder to assure long-term survival. A one-man firm may be risky if the function is a critical one. Large firms indicate strength by having achieved that size and having greater resources, but may be more rigid and demanding in their relationships with clients. These are all matters to consider, along with the nature of the job to be done.

Conflicts of Interest

An outsourcing firm serving competing clients can be inappropriate where the revelation of proprietary information is at stake. For example, Electronic Data Services (EDS), a subsidiary of General Motors until recently and now a key outsourcing vendor to GM, would not be asked to be a vendor for Ford or Chrysler. However, the serving of competitors can be acceptable and be of benefit to all, especially when the cost of developing a specialized expertise can be spread among many clients, and the protection of proprietary information is assured; examples are Automated Data Processing (ADP), which provides payroll service for thousands of clients, and Hyatt, which provides reservation systems know-how to its competitors.

Fair Prices

The relative prices of competitive vendors are often a key factor. However, it sometimes is difficult to compare prices because vendors have different price structures. Also, there are many approaches to incorporating incentive and flexible pricing systems, and that nature of these systems is also one part of the price evaluation analysis. The price structure alternatives are reviewed in the section below about terms to build into a contract.

THE REQUEST FOR PROPOSAL (RFP)

Major outsourcing contracts are often based on a request for proposal (RFP) sent to potential vendors. If an RFP is not used, it is essential for the client to prepare a statement of the work to be contracted out, including requirements such as functions to be performed, turn-around time, location, and equipment. All those who have worked with outsourcing arrangements agree that a principal ingredient for success is to have in advance a well thought out, complete statement of the work to be done, and related requirements. The statement should specify results expected, in measurable terms where possible, e.g., cycle time, volumes, or costs. This statement ensures that the client has fully analyzed what is wanted and that the vendor has a complete and correct understanding of what is expected.

Whether an RFP or work description is used, the prospective vendor's competence should be evaluated by analyzing the qualities of the vendor's proposal, its promptness, clarity, and completeness, qualities that will be desired in the work to be done under the contract.

TERMS TO BUILD INTO A CONTRACT

Books have been written on contract terms and negotiation methodologies. The main features of contracts are reviewed here with comments about available options. The important thing about the contract is to look at it as a means for the client and vendor to discuss and come to a clear and common agreement about what is to be done, how the process will work, and the pricing. The contract is the foundation of the relationship, which must be mutually beneficial if it is to be successful. Nothing can damage a relationship more than differences in the understanding of what is expected.

Requirements Statement

This section covers the nature and details of the work to be done, cycle times, where it will be done, programs and equipment to be used, and related matters. This part is normally a repeat of the requirements statement given to the prospective vendor as part of the exploratory process, possibly revised or refined based on discussions with the vendor. One feature that is important to include is the specific measures the vendor will take to ensure prompt recovery in the event of a disaster, including backup for data and facilities. Other features to include are the methods the client plans to use to monitor the performance of the vendor during the contract, and the standards and criteria that will be applied in determining the acceptability of the results.

Term or Duration

For a contract to maintain an organization's computer hardware, a term of one or two years may be appropriate. In such contracts, it would make for minimum disruption to change from one vendor to another. But for a contract in which an outsourcing vendor is going to buy much or all of the client's computer hardware, hire maybe 100 of the client's employees, and perform some of the client's basic computer operations, many such contracts are made for terms of seven to ten years or more. These major contracts would involve significant problems for the client as well as for the vendor if they are terminated or changed in a few years.

Some recommend keeping the periods short to allow for flexibility and changes. The client's needs may change, with new products, new markets, new competitors. Provisions must be made in the contract to facilitate these types of new conditions. Since hardware or software may develop in a year or two that may enable the vendor to cut its costs significantly, provision must be made to permit the client to receive at least part of that benefit. So, if the term is lengthy, terms must anticipate the need for flexibility to adapt to changes properly and fairly for the client and the vendor. Finally, short contracts give the vendors more incentive to perform well in order to secure renewals.

Pricing and Incentives

If a major part of the client's purpose in outsourcing is to reduce or control costs, make sure that the contract terms will provide the means to measure and fulfill the accomplishment of that objective.

A simple price per unit of work basis is fine for short-term arrangements where there is a uniformity of the tasks to be performed. However, for longer term or more complex agreements, it is generally desirable to incorporate incentives based on performance, as well as provisions for renegotiating when conditions may change. Incentives can be made to reward or penalize the vendor for variations in measurable results, such as speed of a cycle time and percent of defects. With such terms, the vendor can share the risks and rewards of poor or exemplary performance.

An example of revenue sharing is a 10-year agreement with Perot Systems Corp. to provide client/server outsourcing for Europcar International. After the second year when a distributed system is established, the contract provides that Europcar will pay Perot a share of its revenue.

THE FLEXIBILITY TO MAKE AMENDMENTS

It is a good idea to incorporate in long-term contracts provisions for renegotiation of the price and other terms, to meet changes in the assumed conditions on which the original terms were based. Changes in technology, products introduced, entering global markets, disaster crises, and unanticipated conditions may alter the client's needs as to what is outsourced and how it is done. Therefore, these types of unforseen events must be provided for in the contract terms so that the client can make changes as new conditions require. Vendors my feel uncomfortable with contract terms that give this flexibility, but will usually consent to them because of their reasonableness and to be competitive.

Noncompete Terms

In situations where the vendor is in a business similar or possibly the same as the client, the client should insert a contract provision that the vendor will not do business with the client's clients for a specified period of time, such as two or five years, or possibly in certain territories. Outsourcing vendors in their work often have access to the clients' customer and potential customer lists, as well as to information about the clients' product features or services methods that give the client a competitive advantage. The noncompete agreement terms prevent the outsourcing firm from using such information to compete with its client for a specified period. It should also state that the vendor will not recruit any of the client's employees without prior written consent.

Nondisclosure Terms

When the vendor is in a position to learn from the client information about systems and methods, products, or services that give the client a competitive edge, the contract should contain terms that prevent the vendor from disclosing that proprietary and technical information to third parties. The provision can state examples of restricted information, such as lists of customers and potential customers, marketing plans, computer programs, documentation, and manuals. It may also specify that the vendor may not reverse engineer or decompile any of the client's software.

Ownership of Innovations

When the work to be outsourced includes the design and development of new systems, the contract must clearly specify who owns the new system and programs, and what restrictions apply to their sale or use. The new programs logically belong to the client because it paid for them. It is also logical for the vendor to own them since the vendor did the work. These arrangements must be negotiated, for the programs often have considerable value and may have an important influence on the client's competitive position if they were to be obtained by a competitor.

Use of Licensed or Purchased Software

Purchased and licensed software terms normally specify that the purchaser or licensee may not make the software available to other organizations without the vendor's permission. Therefore, if any such software is to be used by the outsourcing vendor, permission must be obtained from the software provider. If the permission is granted, the software vendor will insist that similar restrictions apply to the outsourcing vendor. Those restrictions must be built into the contract between the client and outsourcing service.

Subcontractors

If it is possible for the outsourcing vendor to use subcontractors, the contract must specify that any subcontractors are bound by nondisclosure, noncompete, and other provisions of the prime contract. If the client wishes to review and approve any subcontractors, the contract should so state.

Acceptance of Results

Where the work contracted out is fairly routine, such as processing the payroll or invoices, the results should be defined in the contract in terms of turn-around time, percent of errors, and similar yardsticks. But if the work is creative, such as designing a new system, the contract should specify who is responsible for making the decision of acceptability and should give at least some general criteria on which that decision will be made.

Asset and Staff Transfers

When hardware and software are to be purchased by the outsourcing contractor from the client, those items, as well as the financial terms, must be spelled out in detail in the contract. When employees are to be transferred to the vendor's payroll, those staff members must be specified or, if the personnel transfers are to depend on interviews and reviews by the vendor, those arrangements and understandings should be made clear in the contract's provisions.

Documentation

Where the vendor will be upgrading or establishing new systems and programs, the contract should spell out the responsibilities and requirements for the documentation. In the case of instructions for the client's user personnel, the vendor (probably with the assistance of specified client personnel) should keep an up-to-date set of complete and clear users' instructions. The programming documentation and the instructions for the computer operating personnel must also be maintained completely and clearly in such a manner that they will be useful to those who will take over the system if and when it is decided to return the operations to the client or to another vendor. Who maintains and who owns the source code must be explicitly spelled out.

Arbitration of Disagreements

Hughes Aircraft Corp. outsourced a major part of its computer operations to Computer Sciences Corp. for $1.5 billion. Hughes' contract provided for a committee representing several people from the client's and vendor's staff to resolve differences that arise. Hughes found that that arrangement was very helpful in keeping the process moving ahead smoothly. It is suggested that a similar provision be considered in outsourcing contracts.

It is also recommended that the American Arbitration Association be specified in the contract as the agency to resolve any serious conflicts, instead of taking them to court. Arbitration is cheaper, faster, equally fair, and a bit less unfriendly. It can even be done without attorneys, though they are usually present.

Termination

Every contract has an end, and that event must be carefully provided for in the contract. Naturally, when preparing a contract, everyone's prime attention goes to how to get the transition started, and it is instinctive to think that the termination arrangements can be worked out later, or when the need arises.

Because every contract does end, the various possibilities must be thought out and planned for. The end may come when the client wishes to transfer the work to another vendor, decides to bring back the operation in-house, or the nature of the job is so modified that other arrangements must be made. The termination may be initiated by the client or the vendor, and the timing of the advance notice must be specified. Hopefully not, but the termination may be caused by the client or the vendor being dissatisfied with how the contract is working. It could be that either the client or vendor goes out of business. All of the myriad possibilities must be taken into account and provisions written to make the change as undisrupting as possible however it happens.

As the start of an outsourcing transition does not usually occur instantaneously, neither does the termination; it may be reasonable or necessary for the vendor to assist in the final conversion, and the terms for doing so should be planned and reflected in the contract terms.

HOW TO NEGOTIATE — STRATEGIES AND TACTICS

General Concepts

The objective of any outsourcing arrangement is to establish a relationship and a process that is beneficial to both the client and to the vendor. Anything less is an unsatisfactory result. No outsourcing relationship is without its frictions and problems. However, if on balance either the vendor or client is seriously unhappy, then the other party cannot be pleased either.

Nevertheless, in the negotiation game, both the client and the vendor use strategies and tactics to gain favorable terms for themselves. The client should have prepared an RFP or other detailed statement of what it wants, and the vendor often will start off with a standard contract with boiler-plate terms that are favorable to it. Then, both parties sit around a table and discuss all the features they want, and give and take to come to an accommodation that each considers is to its individual benefit.

Many articles and books have been written on the art and tactics of negotiation. Only the basic principles are covered here. The basic needs are to be forthright and fair, to consider as many contingencies as possible that may arise, and to try to listen to and understand the concerns of the other party. The contract provision areas outlined above can be used as a checklist. Attorneys are good at thinking of other issues, like which state's rules apply, and most have skills at negotiating methodology. Bringing in purchasing, audit, and human relations, in addition to information systems specialists, can further help to make sure all relevant issues are considered.

Roles of Attorneys and Others

The computer operations manager, the CIO, or other IT executive should normally take the lead in determining what work to outsource, in reviewing possible vendors, in selecting the most likely one or more to negotiate with, and in negotiating the final contracts. The attorneys, either internal or outside, should be helpful from the beginning in seeing that the RFP, work statement, and contract are clear and unambiguous to all concerned, and cover all the legal issues that can be reasonably expected to arise.

In addition to the computer and legal officials, many organizations have found that other staff members are valuable in the planning and negotiation processes. These include: human relations, who advise about the handling of employees to be transferred or terminated, and the morale of those who remain; auditors to help assure adequate controls of the work to be outsourced; and purchasing, which has the experience in selecting and negotiation with vendors.

DIRECTV® — Case Example. As reported in the August 1996 *Managing Office Technology*, DIRECTV® is a top direct satellite company based in El Segundo, California, with a goal or achieving 10 million subscribers by 2000. With an 18-inch dish, DIRECTV delivers over 175 channels, both on a subscription and pay-per-view basis. Anxious to concentrate on its demanding marketing aspirations, DIRECTV elected to outsource its information systems and the preparing of invoices.

DIRECTV selected Output Technologies in Kansas City, Missouri, to prepare and mail over 34,00 invoices each day. The data about the purchases to be billed are collected for each customer by a smart card attached to the TV, and are relayed to DIRECTV and then to Output Technologies over regular phone lines. Output Technologies also inserts information and marketing material in with the invoices, selecting the inserts by considering their weight and the needs of different demographic areas.

Output Technologies checks for input errors and reports quality problems to DIRECTV. It also provides security by using protected transmission lines, and by having alternate facilities which could continue in the event of a disaster.

"This dynamic outsourcing relationship has given the broadcast satellite service a competitive advantage in the market by allowing DIRECTV to focus on its core competencies."

After deciding to outsource its bill processing and related functions, DIRECTV compared the capabilities of several potential vendors, and selected Output Technologies because research showed that this vendor had a strong computer facility and volume capacity, its client references were favorable, it demonstrated a record of accuracy in bill processing, its operating methods were sound, and it had the capability and flexibility for customized projects. This vendor selection has proved to be sound after some years of working together.

CONCLUSION

The following points are highlights of the action a computer operations manager should take to secure the right outsourcing vendors and negotiate favorable terms with them:

- After researching where and how outsourcing can be beneficial to the organization, and supporting such research initiated by others, the computer operations manager should take the initiative in seeking the best vendors to do the work and in negotiating favorable terms with them.
- Select more than one vendor when the best expertise and experience desired is not to be found in any one vendor.
- Research thoroughly the reputation, capabilities, soundness, and compatibility of vendors selected, because the liaison is like a marriage that requires working together harmoniously to make for a successful alliance.
- Provide flexibility needed to adapt to changing needs and conditions, by provisions to renegotiate arrangements as circumstances warrant.
- Take advantage of the skills and participation of attorneys for their negotiation and legal talents, of human resources for guiding employee changes and morale, and auditors and purchasing personnel for their advice and assistance as to controls and vendor relations.
- Provide for arbitration of problems so as to avoid the hassles of court proceedings.
- Make sure the work requirements are clearly documented and fully understood by vendor and client personnel so as to avoid misunderstandings, a most common source of outsourcing problems.
- Include provisions for the vendor and client to share improvement benefits, so that the vendor is motivated in that direction.

Chapter 9
A Step-by-Step Guide to Writing a Successful RFP

John R. Vacca

THE TENDERING PROCESS THAT LEADS TO AN OUTSOURCING ARRANGEMENT and involves a written request for proposal (RFP) is the one most widely used internationally by enterprises wishing to identify an outsourcing solution and a supplier of outsourcing services. This process begins with a Request for information (RFI) document issued by a potential enterprise to find out information from the market about the types of services that might be suitable for that enterprise. From the information received, the enterprise identifies the potential recipients of the RFP.

The RFP contains, among other things, a statement of the enterprise's requirements. The RFP is, in legal terms, an invitation to treat; and the response (often called a proposal) made by the outsourcer is (usually) an offer. Care must be taken by the enterprise to ensure, either by words in the RFP or in the acceptance of the proposal, that the acceptance or the response is subject to the negotiation of a formal agreement.

The content of the RFP is the key to ensure that the subsequent outsourcing contract contains the rights and remedies the enterprise requires. The RFP must be fully researched and comprehensive in its statement of the enterprise's requirements. The RFP must cover the enterprise's business needs, both at the executive level (i.e., addressing the customer's reporting requirements) as well as at an operational level (addressing, for example, the more detailed functionality required).

The RFP is the cornerstone of a contract. However, too often legal and negotiating input is not sought before it is issued. Sometimes, enterprises, through inexperience, neglect to involve their legal and negotiating advisors in the proposed outsourcing project — particularly with the completion of the documentation recording the outsourcing requirements — until the proposed contract negotiating date is imminent. This scenario leaves little time to negotiate the terms of an agreement and to include terms that were not included because legal professionals were not previously involved.

If a lawyer is not involved at an early stage, the opportunity will be lost to generate representations and to mold aspects of the RFP that will make the enterprise's requirements clear and indisputable. If that occurs, the enterprise's legal advisor or negotiator must try to recover lost ground by picking up and incorporating omissions in the contract. The involvement of the enterprise's legal advisor and negotiator at the construction stage of the RFP can avoid many subsequent problems. They are able to guide an enterprise, not only as to the content of the RFP for legal purposes, but as to the time within which negotiation of the documentation should be undertaken — the timeframe invariably being underestimated by the enterprise, often to its detriment.

It is essential to capture the RFP and the outsourcer's proposal as part of the contract. The incorporation of these documents captures the requirements and representations of the parties so that they do not have to be restated in the contract document. Where the requirements and representations are not adequately spelled out in the earlier documents, time must be spent in ensuring correction and incorporation in the final documents, or alternatively, in a fresh and agreed-to statement of requirements.

The contract must allow for variations to, or subsequent versions of, the RFP and proposal, and for those subsequent documents to be subject to the same contractual structure provided by the original agreement. The draftsperson must ensure that a priority is established between different documents in the event of conflict, usually providing that later documents override earlier documents. The body of the new agreement overrides the schedules and sometimes for a priority between various provisions within the body of the new agreement.

Even if an enterprise insists on pre-contract documentation being made part of the written contract, the outsourcer still has a number of mechanisms available to dilute or nullify that documentation. When it comes to committing to contract, the outsourcer may resort to a number of tactics designed to reduce the levels of commitment made to the enterprise in the sale cycle.

The enterprise's statement of requirements (usually contained in the RFP) needs to be both all-encompassing and unambiguous. After all, an enterprise expects its outsourcing contract to be drafted by their advisors in similar terms. In general, the quality of statements of requirement issued by an enterprise, or by management consultants on behalf of the enterprise, leaves much to be desired.

An enterprise must thoroughly understand its functional, operational, and selection requirements, and must be able to articulate them in unambiguous written terms. If, throughout the process undertaken to identify an outsourcer, the enterprise keeps in mind the nature of the contract that it wishes to execute with the outsourcer and implements adequate quality management processes, then its pre-contract documentation will not become a plethora of loopholes for the outsourcer to exploit.

Another area in which an enterprise creates loopholes for outsourcing suppliers to exploit, is in the priority afforded to requirements. Statements that rate the importance of requirements as "highly desirable," "desirable," or "nice to have" are common. It is obvious that these are not statements of requirement, but preference. To avoid doubt, the importance of the requirement is best left unqualified, with the outsourcer being required to state specifically the extent to which the requirement "can," "cannot," or "can only partly" be satisfied. It is then up to the enterprise to determine the acceptability of the outsourcer's response.

A precise articulation of requirements is achieved by (1) a comprehensive analysis of the requirements; (2) an objective assessment of the interpretation that the outsourcer will make when the written requirements are read; and (3) an anticipation of how a (usually) computer-illiterate judge or arbitrator may interpret the expression if a significant dispute arises.

In composing a statement of requirements, many enterprises think only of the functionality required from the outsourcing services. Operational and selection requirements are often ignored. When the outsourced system produces five-minute terminal response times, the enterprise may find that there is nothing in the pre-contract documentation or the contract itself that addresses the requirement for tolerable response times. The upgrade that the outsourcer agrees to undertake (at the expense of the enterprise), and an ebb in enterprise morale, which could have been easily avoided, will ensue. Unfortunately, few standard and even some negotiated IT contracts contain response time warranties. Even when response time warranties are written into the contract, they are frequently drafted inadequately and consequently provide the outsourcer with more loopholes to exploit.

Now, look at how to prepare an RFP. The questions to ask before writing are:

- Which functions should be outsourced?
- Who should provide the services?
- What are the measurements for success?

The following step-by-step guide will help produce a highly effective and successful outsourcing RFP.

STEPS TO EFFECTIVE OUTSOURCING

For those enterprises with unique needs or special requirements that cannot be handled by standard services, a request for proposal (RFP) may be necessary. The following are steps that an enterprise should follow in order to write a highly effective and successful outsourcing RFP.

1. Define objectives.
2. Identify which functions should be outsourced.
3. Develop a written RFP: results and benefits.
4. Define the nature and scope of the contract/work.
5. Select the outsourcers that should be on the RFP list.
6. Evaluate the proposals.
7. Negotiate the final price: fees, payments, and duration.
8. Project completion: additional outsourcing issues and services.

Step 1: Define Objectives

The enterprise will have specific business objectives for deciding to outsource services. These will have been identified and confirmed in the work that was undertaken during the enterprise analysis phases prior to selecting a preferred outsourcing services supplier (outsourcer).

The major objective now is to negotiate a supply agreement with the preferred outsourcer for the delivery of the required services at an agreed cost and level of performance. There are seven components to an agreement achieving this objective. These are:

1. *Service specification:* sets out, in specific and measurable terms, the services required, how they are to be delivered, and the duration they are required.
2. *Service levels:* sets out the performance standards (service levels) that relate to each of the services to be provided.
3. *Roles and responsibilities:* document the obligations of the outsourcer and the enterprise and the boundaries of responsibility.
4. *Transition period and acceptance:* sets out how any existing services will be handed over to the outsourcer, the services accepted by the enterprise, and the transition of staff.
5. *Prices, payment, and duration:* agrees on the price and payment for delivery of the services, including the basis of charging for any additional or optional services.
6. *Agreement administration:* sets out how the agreement will be managed and administered. This will include provision for resolving disputes and the remedies in the event of nonperformance.
7. *Outsourcing issues:* issues that are specific to outsourcing and will need to be considered during contract negotiations.

In addition, although there are similar motivations, each enterprise is a little different, each with a different set of priorities. The RFP must be clear on goals. Here are some examples:

- reduce or control operating costs
- gain access to world-class capabilities
- free internal resources for other purposes
- access resources unavailable internally
- obtain levels of service specific to requirements

Step 2: Identify Which Functions Should Be Outsourced

While an enterprise may be considering outsourcing the management of its services, it does not have to outsource every function. Each operation should be analyzed and evaluated overall and in terms of quality and cost-effectiveness. This requires a thorough assessment of each and every facilities operation and service. Only outsource those functions that can be operated better, faster, or cheaper.

In other words, the enterprise (purchaser) will have set out in the RFP the services required. These services may have been specified in some detail or set out in enterprise terms requiring the outsourcer to propose services to meet the enterprise needs. The outsourcer will have submitted and agreed with the enterprise, a detailed RFP setting out how it will provide the services to meet the enterprise's requirements specifications. A comprehensive specification of these services will generally form the basis of the agreement and should set out the following in some detail:

- services the outsourcer is required to deliver to the enterprise, including the tasks of the enterprise's work activities (e.g., help desk support or communications administration)
- deliverables that result from the services provided
- how the outsource services will be provided to the enterprise
- how third-party outsourcers will be managed
- how problems will be managed and resolved

The outsourcer may also be contracted to provide additional services, including (1) training for the enterprise's staff involved with the outsource work activities; and (2) advisory services for system enhancements, as required, to meet any changes in the enterprise's business needs.

Step 3: Develop a Written RFP — Results and Benefits

Once the decision has been made to outsource, it is important to articulate in writing exactly what is expected to be accomplished. Some enterprises have found it very beneficial to engage an outside outsourcing consultant at this point.

A good strategy in creating a comprehensive RFP is to meet with a few outsourcerss to discuss the assignment. In talking about objectives, the functions to be outsourced, and then hearing the outsourcer's questions, one can get a good idea of what should be included in the RFP and how to phrase requests. This phase is referred to as an RFI (request for information) and includes a larger number of prospective service providers than in the RFP phase.

At this point, one should start to get a feel for the outsourcers and begin to determine which outsourcers should be selected to bid on the job. Be sure to deal with senior-level decision-makers, those with whom one feels comfortable and those one feels can have a good working relationship that could extend over a number of years.

The tangible results of the preceding activity include: (1) written functional specifications and request for proposal outlining the enterprise and reporting requirements and the hardware/software required to satisfy those requirements; and (2) a written comparative analysis and proposal summary analysis of all proposals submitted. The intangible results of this activity include:

1. an unbiased opinion and evaluation of enterprise requirements with no regard to any particular hardware or software product
2. application of technical expertise and experience to this project, gathered by the evaluation, selection, and installation of thousands of applications in hundreds of enterprises
3. a review by project-oriented professionals who are not hindered by the day-to-day operation and internal enterprise structure.

Step 4: Define the Nature and Scope of the Contract/Work

It is important to look at not just what the enterprise is doing today, but to identify the optimum service that will ensure uninterrupted business in the future. After identifying the functions to be outsourced, be as specific as possible as to exactly what must be accomplished within each function, including written standards and specifications and quantitative measurements for success. For example (1) the server goes down; it must be brought up within two hours, unless there is a castrosphic incident like a denial-of-service attack, or the like; (2) if a network cable wears out or is damaged, it must be replaced in three days; (3) if the air-conditioning system filter within a telecommunications closet is obstructed with debris or is damaged, it must be replaced within eight hours; or (4) if the thermostat within a telecommunications closet is not regulating the temperature properly or is damaged, it must be replaced within the hour. Determine what will be considered ongoing service and what is emergency service. It is also important to define what should be included as standard service and what services could be offered for bids at a later date. Remember: anything that is not included in the scope of the contract becomes an incremental cost in execution.

Therefore, have the outsourcing consultant review enterprise functions and accounting procedures — both manual and computerized. The review should include discussions with IT management and key personnel to determine where computerized systems might be installed or upgraded to increase efficiency, reduce manual processing requirements, reduce costs, and provide better management information and reports.

Based on the outsourcing consultant's findings, the consultant should prepare functional specifications that, when combined with the general specifications, will serve as an RFP that will be sent to computer hardware and software vendors that will be able to satisfy this RFP.

These functional specifications will be presented to the enterprise for review and comments. The outsourcing consultant should then select — together with the enterprise — a number of qualified outsourcers who are known to be qualified to handle a project such as this. The RFP is then mailed to these outsourcers and the outsourcing consultant should then hold an outsourcer conference with all outsourcers to whom the RFP was sent in order to answer outsourcer questions, have the outsourcers meet enterprise personnel, and have the outsourcers see who else is bidding.

The outsourcing consultant should assist the enterprise in the final selection of an outsourcer by reviewing — together with the enterprise — the proposals submitted by the outsourcers and preparing a comparative analysis and proposal summary analysis of the proposals, based on a series of factors that the outsourcing consultant believes are important indicators of the outsourcer's capability to deliver a system. Once an outsourcer is selected, the outsourcing consultant should assist in the preparation of a contract by helping negotiate equipment delivery and program payment schedules with the outsourcer and by providing the enterprise's attorney with draft contract clauses that the outsourcing consultant has found to be acceptable to outsourcers, while providing the greatest available protection to the enterprise.

Step 5: Roles and Responsibilities — Select the Outsourcers Who Should be on the RFP List

From all possible outsourcers, try to narrow down the list to the three to five that will provide the best solutions. Check their references, consider their track records, and visit their sites — all in advance of offering them a chance to submit a proposal. Only consider outsourcers that have successfully managed facilities similar to yours.

Contemplate whether a single outsourcer can perform all the functions the enterprise currently accomplishes utilizing multiple departments. If not, what combination of outsourcers will be needed to provide the quality and level of service required? Also think about how a team of outsourcers will interact and how that team will be managed.

Furthermore, in addition to selecting who should be on the RFP list, the roles and responsibilities of both the outsourcer and the enterprise in the delivery of the outsource services must be documented in the agreement. Roles and responsibilities for the enterprise should include:

- reasonable access to the enterprise's site as required by the outsourcer
- the appointment of a suitably qualified and experienced in-house person to act as an account or relationship manager between the outsourcer and the enterprise
- allowance for the outsourcer to conduct due diligence before taking up the agreement to ensure that the enterprise's expectations are reasonable
- reasonable access to the information, institutional and enterprise knowledge, and documentation of the enterprise's business
- timely response to any requests from the outsourcer for information, advice, or any action required by the enterprise
- negotiating new contracts and the renegotiation of existing contracts for specified service level agreements with secondary service providers
- identification of the staff whom the enterprise would like to transition to the outsourcer

Roles and responsibilities for the outsourcer should include:

- appointment of a suitably qualified and experienced account manager to manage the delivery of services and the relationship with the enterprise
- delivery of the agreed services
- compliance with the enterprise's policies and procedures as they relate to the delivery of services and occupational safety and health
- confirmation that the skills and competencies of the enterprise's staff, identified by the enterprise as transitional, are appropriate for the delivery of the required services
- securing the services of the staff confirmed as transitional
- provision of additional and suitably skilled staff to perform the services
- management of any agreements with third-party suppliers of information technology services
- quality assurance of the delivered services
- compliance with security and confidentiality obligations
- reporting on the delivered services
- provision of warranties for delivered services
- services transfer assistance in the event of termination

Step 6: Evaluate the Proposals — Transition Period and Acceptance

Having received the proposals, one must go through a period of transition and acceptance. That is, one must analyze and evaluate the solutions, including the strategic advantages, alignment of personnel, and an assessment of the risks involved. Other considerations include:

- Do they (outsourcers) have a good solution? Can they manage the process better than the enterprise can?
- Have they precisely offered solutions to meet the enterprise's objectives?
- Have they responded to all the points in the RFP? How crisply and specifically did they respond? Do the answers sound boiler-plate or did they consider the enterprise's unique situation and provide customized solutions?
- How will they handle the transition? What are the costs involved?
- Do the cultures of the enterprise and the outsourcer(s) match? Are these people with whom the enterprise wants to work for a long period of time? Will they work with the enterprise to achieve mutual goals?
- Is the pricing fair?

Here, transition management is a key aspect of the outsourcing process. Transition management should be priced and form a part of the agreement between the outsourcer and the enterprise, and appear as a schedule to the agreement as new services.

Step 7: Negotiate the Final Price — Fees, Payments, and Duration

Once the outsourcer has been determined, there may be points in the proposal that need further negotiating. Price can be one of these points. While pricing is important, it should never be the only criterion for selection. It is critical to weigh the solution and the mitigation of risk against the cost. If, however, one needs to drive down the price or the favored outsourcer is substantially more expensive than all other bids, it is important to remain flexible and try to operate in a full-disclosure atmosphere when discussing the costing process. Remember, the enterprise and the outsourcer may be in business together for many years to come. It may even be possible to unbundle the solution, and relinquish some less-important services of a more favorable cost.

Fees and Payment. The outsourcer's fees should be on a per diem basis. The outsourcer should provide an estimated range of fees prior to beginning the engagement. Most outsourcers require a retainer to begin the project, and will work out a payment schedule with the enterprise.

Prices and payment terms should be included in any agreement. The pricing may be set based on a number of different formulae; and an agreement will include one or more of these formulae, as appropriate, for each component service. These should include:

- pricing model for each work activity to be outsourced
- total fixed fee for all services provided
- specification of which services are part of the agreement and which services will be an additional charge, if required, to the enterprise at a later date
- pricing models for any optional services or resources that the enterprise may require and that do not form part of the standard outsourcing service
- one-time costs for the transition period
- formula for charging for additional services delivered or where service levels are exceeded
- formula for rebates that would apply in the event services are not delivered or service levels are not met
- basis for a review of charges in the event of any extraordinary reduction or increase of outsourcing work as a result of changes in the enterprise's business
- basis for any review of charges over the term of the agreement and any index (consumer price index [CPI]) for capping or linking any increases
- any charges that will apply on termination, including any transfer of assets

The agreement should set out in some detail how the pricing is arrived at and state the assumptions or constraints that underpin the model. This will support the calculation of any future variances and will avoid disputes arising from differences in interpretation of the pricing model. Also, the procedure for invoicing should be clearly defined, as should the terms of payment.

Time and Duration. The agreement should also specify the term during which the outsource services will be provided. This may include the basis for any right of renewal of the agreement and any milestones for reviewing the agreement during its term. It may also cover any termination charges for early termination of the agreement by either party.

In other words, the outsourcer's workload will determine when they can start the project. Once the outsourcer begins, the RFP should be completed within 30 to 60 days. An outsourcer conference should be held ten days after proposals are mailed. Outsourcers are expected to respond to the RFP 30 days after the RFP is submitted to the them. The enterprise should evaluate the proposals and select outsourcer finalists 15 to 30 days after proposals are received. This timetable assumes adequate cooperation by the enterprise's personnel and ready availability of the necessary information.

Project Completion. The enterprise should consider the engagement complete when the proposals have been analyzed and recommendations for the final outsourcers have been made. Having determined the provider or team of providers that most exactly meet enterprise needs, one is ready to embark on an outsourcing relationship that, properly managed, can provide the enterprise with the most productive, leading-edge facilities management possible.

Step 8: Project Completion — Additional Outsourcing Issues and Services

Finally, additional services may be required by the enterprise in visiting and evaluating outsourcing references, evaluation of detailed specifications, testing of the software, and implementation of the system. The scope of every outsourcing RFP will vary according to the requirements of the enterprise and its special business, technical, or service needs. The parties to the RFP will need to take these into account in each instance with the appropriate additions to the schedules and clauses to the RFP. Such additions are likely to include the following.

Insurance. The outsourcer should have adequate public liability insurance. This insurance should cover loss or liability through injury or damage.

Other Third-Party Suppliers. Arrangements should exist as to which party (enterprise or outsourcer) will hold and which party will administer the terms of any RFP currently in place between the enterprise and other third-party suppliers. Maintenance contracts must be transferred to the outsourcer unless the outsourcer has agreed to provide maintenance services for all equipment and software.

Software Licenses. Where software used to provide outsourced services is supplied by third parties, the appropriate licenses must be obtained. Any licenses currently held by the enterprise that relate to services being provided may need to be extended to cover the activities of the outsourcer.

Ownership of Information. The ownership of data and information needs to be agreed to by the enterprise and the outsourcer. Should a dispute arise and the agreement terminated, it must be clearly stated who owns the information and data.

Scope of Work. Identification of the key work activities to be performed by the outsourcer is essential and is typically set out in the RFP. The enterprise should specify in detail the nature of the services that will be outsourced and the requirements of the enterprise in relation to those outsourced services. The outsourcer will have responded to the RFP with a proposal, setting out how it will perform the work activities. Both the RFP and proposal can be incorporated into the contract to support the definition of the work that must be performed and the requirements that must be met by the outsourcer. In defining the scope of work, the following additional issues should be considered:

- What, if any, technology, personnel, or other resources must be provided by the enterprise? Will there be any transfer of personnel or assets from the enterprise to the outsourcer? If so, how is that to be achieved? The transfer of personnel is fraught with employment law issues that need to be carefully considered. If information technology facilities are to be provided, where will they be located?
- What will be required to maintain these facilities and who will do the maintenance? Is the outsourcer likely rely on another outsourcer to provide maintenance?
- Is the outsourcer responsible for information technology planning or will this be done by the enterprise?
- Is the outsourcer responsible for ongoing system design and system modifications to meet new or changed future requirements of the enterprise? This issue should be made clear during the RFI and RFP stages — but often is not.
- Is the outsourcer responsible for the development of software and, if so, is there a component in the charges for this activity?
- What are the procedures for maintenance and support of software? That is, who pays for upgrades and who supports software licensed to the enterprise?
- Who is responsible for disaster recovery and enterprise continuity arrangements?
- Who is responsible for asset replacement, capacity planning, and software upgrades?

The parties should recognize that in most cases the enterprise's business requirements will change during the term of the outsourcing arrangement. It is also likely that the technology requirements will change as existing equipment and software become outdated or relatively more expensive to support. Over the term of the agreement, new technology might also become available that reduces the cost of service delivery. There should be provisions that enable either party to request and benefit from additional services, changes to the scope of existing services, or the deployment of new technology during the term of the agreement.

Contract Duration and Commencement. The commencement date of the contract should be decided as early as possible to minimize transition difficulties when service provision is handed from the enterprise to the outsourcer. Given the complex problems that can arise during the hand-over of information technology services, it may be prudent to include a defined transition period as part of the term of the contract.

The length of term will depend entirely on the nature of the outsourced services and the business requirements of the enterprise. From an outsourcer's perspective, the price of the services is likely to be influenced by the capital costs involved in providing the resources required to maintain service delivery. An initial term of three years is typically seen as a minimum. The terms of renewal should be based on performance and current conditions at the time.

System Specification. The system specifications should be defined for function, performance, and availability as part of the RFI and RFP phases. The service specifications, such as response times and system reliability, should likewise be defined in the RFI and RFP phases.

Service Level Agreements (SLAs). Service level agreements are put in place to define the minimum level of service that must be provided. They are, therefore, the basis for measuring the outsourcer's performance. SLAs will typically be included in the contract schedules and cover a number of areas of service, including system availability and response times, and quality standards.

Measuring and monitoring service levels can be achieved through user satisfaction surveys and analysis of performance data such as system response and job turnaround times. It is not always easy to identify performance measures that accurately reflect the standard of service required by the enterprise's users. Moreover, SLAs can be ineffective documents unless the enterprise has practical and realistic remedies in the event of non-performance. Such remedies might include the withholding or deduction of agreed-upon rebates from fees otherwise payable to the outsourcer, should the agreed-upon level of performance not be maintained. Both the enterprise and the outsourcer need to be aware that SLAs are not inflexible, and there should be a review period in the SLA to cover changing enterprise requirements and new technology.

Reporting and Review. Closely linked to the SLA are management reporting and review of performance. Procedures for reviewing the performance of the outsourcer should be defined in consultation with the enterprise and the outsourcer during regular meetings. Each party should nominate dedicated representatives who will be responsible for liaising with the other party's representative and communicating information and decisions. Such meetings should regularly involve senior management from both parties and include adequate focus on future developments and forward planning.

System Access and Security. Access to the enterprise systems by the outsourcer needs to be considered in the context of current privacy legislation, which is intended to protect personal information about identifiable individuals. Outsourcers may only require system access at certain levels to enable them to perform their service.

The level of security measures required to protect the enterprise's system and information from unauthorized access will continue to require rigorous planning, implementation, and management. Outsourcing services will bring additional issues of protection, confidentiality, and ethics that the parties will need to ensure are documented and agreed-to with regard to their responsibilities and obligations.

Facility Ownership and Control. If the outsourcer is to perform certain services using the enterprise's equipment, who will own these assets? The outsourcer may enter into an arrangement to purchase these assets or they may be handed back upon termination of the outsourcing arrangements. In either event, a detailed inventory of assets will need to be compiled.

What will be the relationship with suppliers of third-party services such as communications or network services? Outsourcers may need to rely on competitors to supply services to enable them to provide service to the enterprise. This may require facilitation by the enterprise.

Personnel Issues. Although the issue of personnel is often crucial, it is sometimes overlooked by those involved in outsourcing. People are fundamental to an enterprise and are required to maintain enterprise continuity during the transition period.

The arrangements for the retention, redeployment, or other options for existing staff must be negotiated. This issue is critical as the outsourcer will require the institutional knowledge of enterprise's staff. Enterprise continuity must be maintained during the transition, which requires that enterprise's staff be kept fully informed where appropriate.

Staff may need to be transferred from the payroll of the enterprise to the payroll of the outsourcer. A transition plan should be used to minimize the risk of service disruption and employment-related legal claims.

The employment contracts or collective agreements under which enterprises staff are employed may require negotiations to be held with the relevant staff or their representatives. The early involvement of professional human resource managers and employment law specialists to advise and assist with contractual and privacy issues is critical to any transition to outsourcing.

The enterprise might also specify that a certain number of staff should be hired by the outsourcer, and the outsourcer might require a certain number of people for the purpose of acquiring system and enterprise knowledge. In such cases, there should be an agreed-upon process for the outsourcer to select, assess, and engage the appropriately skilled staff from the enterprise. The enterprise should also be made aware if any of the outsourcer's staff are being shared with other clients.

Intellectual Property Indemnity, Warranties, and Disaster Recovery. Each party should generally indemnify the other against claims of intellectual property rights infringement arising from the use of facilities and resources that they supply to the other as part of the outsourcing arrangements.

Appropriate warranties should be provided, including:

- warranty of authorization and title
- performance warranty
- compliance with specifications
- service quality

Finally, agreement should be reached between the enterprise and the outsourcer concerning enterprise continuity, should any of the outsourcer's facilities fail.

CONCLUSION AND SUMMARY

A two-stage proposal process is recommended with plentiful scoping time built in. The first stage would be designed to glean through the crowd and select a short list of outsourcers to bid on the RFP. Find three, four, or five promising outsourcers, even if they have not yet cranked out a proposal with numbers. To do this, the enterprise should prepare a scoping document that the greater mass of interested developers can use as a starting point.

This initial document should be heavy on goals and vision. For example, if an enterprise is putting up a Web site, what does one want that site to do? What is the reason for putting up a Web site in the first place? This document needs to state more than just the project's vision; consider the following example.

CmsasCo seeks an outsourcer to help build a World Wide Web site to perform the following functions: build and reinforce the enterprise XYZ brand around the world; sell XYZ products; and provide economical customer support capabilities.

Describe the enterprise (CmsasCo) and its products; give a bit of information about the time one has in mind for the project; and describe the resources to be devoted to the project. Talk to the people who respond and set up short meetings with the ones who either come recommended or who one has a good feeling about. Then, if an Internet strategy consultant is not going to be used, get ready to prepare a proper RFP.

Restrict the bidders to three or, at most, four outsourcers. If it is a big project, one might want to consider a paid pitch — give the final bidders $3,000 each to offset the cost of preparing their proposals. This may sound like a waste of money, but put yourself in the bidders' shoes for a moment.

A well-prepared proposal for a large project is going to take considerable time and resources to produce. Quite a few proposals come to nothing. Often, the rumor mill can make it sound like the enterprise asking for proposals already has a favorite developer and just wants competing proposals for comparison purposes or to keep its favorite developer honest. A paid pitch means that the best development outsourcers can devote the time needed to prepare the best proposals.

It is recommended that the enterprise specify that proposals be arranged so that they can be easily compared. Ask for specific facts and figures in the format, in order to make a good comparison. Say something like:

Proposals shall contain the following sections:

- executive summary containing a brief description of project development approach and costs
- enterprise information, including financial details
- qualifications, including previous clients with contact information and relevant URLs
- description of the development process
- asset and draft delivery methods
- project stages
- milestones
- quality control
- testing
- proposed team and their qualifications
- proposed schedule
- costs and payment details
- terms and conditions

Keep in mind that what the enterprise is trying to do is select an outsourcer that can be trusted. During the development process, both the enterprise and the outsourcer will make mistakes; the enterprise will be late with deliveries, and so will the outsourcer. The enterprise needs to select an outsourcer that will forgive enterprise sins as the enterprise forgives those of the outsourcer. Although one should try, it is almost impossible to include everything in an RFP or in a proposal. The proposal needs to set the way for the enterprise and the outsourcer to work together. Outsourcers almost always say they will deliver everything needed for the project in a neat little pile at the very beginning of the project, and the enterprise will probably assume it can do so too. *This never happens!* The outsourcer will be the first one to be late with a deliverable. The RFP should state what the enterprise expects to happen when the enterprise is late and when the outsourcer is late.

Make sure the RFP sets out a schedule for the proposal and development process. For example, a schedule for outsourcing Web site development might be:

- March 10:request for qualifications goes out
- March 20:qualifications due
- March 22:short list of outsourcers selected
- March 30:RFPs sent to short list of outsourcers
- April 15:response to RFP due
- April 20:successful outsourcer notified
- April 22:purchase order for project issued
- April 24:initial project scoping meeting
- May 30:project development begins
- July 30:site goes live

There will be several other milestones set once the project gets underway, but outsourcers need to know these dates upfront.

If time has been spent talking to the short list of outsourcers, the enterprise can probably write the RFP in such a way that its project goals and vision are clearly stated. If the outsourcers have been given a good idea of the budget range, the enterprise probably already has a reasonable idea of what is going to be involved in the project. The RFP should focus on the details of how the enterprise will relate to the development outsourcer during the build process.

It is vital to provide short-listed outsourcers with a contact person who they can talk with when they have questions about the project. It is not in the enterprise's best interest to have the outsourcers working on proposals in equal ignorance — the best thing is for them all to feel free to contact the enterprise and find out what the enterprise really wants. One is going to have to spend a lot of time with these people later, so why not spend some time finding out what they are like? Set some time aside for explaining the project during the time the outsourcers are working on their proposals.

Be sure to mention who is going to pay for corrections. If the copy provided has errors in it, who is going to pay to fix them?

The enterprise may want to consider mentioning that the RFP is a private, copyrighted document that can not be shown to others. Many development outsourcers use freelancers and part-time help; be sure to ask for this to be detailed and explained. It is not necessarily bad if they use freelancers, but one wants to be sure that the RFP does not get all over town and into the hands of one's competitors. Consider asking the short list to sign a nondisclosure agreement.

Finally, if the enterprise can detail exactly what it wants — great; but do not forget to set out a comfortable working relationship. One wants to hire a specialist development outsourcer because they probably know more about all this than the enterprise. Listen to them. If they say one's goals are unrealistic and the budget is absurd, they may be right.

Nevertheless, this chapter has taken the initiative to provide some constructive guidance to help participants involved in the procurement of outsourcing services understand the key issues involved in writing a highly successful outsourcing RFP. This chapter is useful to many enterprises in assisting them to reach early and constructive agreements on the requirements of an outsourcing RFP agreement.

Chapter 10
Outsourcing IT Services

David Massey

PROJECT OUTSOURCING SIMPLY MEANS ACQUIRING SERVICES from an external organization instead of using internal resources. By using outsourced resources, IT managers can use contingent staff to accomplish strategic goals without incurring the fixed overhead. By focusing on leading-edge and highly specialized skill sets, outsourcing providers can often provide services better, or at a lower price than the client organization.

Typical reasons for outsourcing go beyond simple contingent staffing. Outsourcing is about partnerships with providers and clients. For the partnership to work, the provider must know the business of the client as well as the technologies being outsourced. Often, there is a need for specialized knowledge or skills, both technical and industry-specific, or early skills in leading-edge technologies that are not yet widely deployed. Outsourcing vendors are wholesalers of highly specialized talent. Outsourcing providers are able to maintain economies of scale with regard to specialization. By deploying these highly skilled specialists to multiple clients, outsourcing providers can justify the enormous expenditures necessary to develop those specialists.

Perhaps the most important considerations in the decision to outsource are more strategic than technical. IT managers often outsource cyclical, specialized, or unique projects to enable their permanent staff to focus on the company's core business. Services that do not add value directly to the organization are appropriate candidates to be outsourced. Unless skills cannot be provided or developed internally, outsourcing should not be used for services that relate to the core business of the company. Functions that are well suited for outsourcing include system construction and implementation, application testing and training, system and user documentation, system maintenance and enhancement, and system integration.

Advantages and Disadvantages of Project Outsourcing

The first step in outsourcing involves the decision to do so. Not all projects are well suited to outsourcing. In evaluating potential outsourced projects, the IT manager must make a business case that outlines the drivers for outsourcing as well as the expected business benefits. This analysis must weigh the impact on all the project's stakeholders, classifying potential risks and documenting assumptions.

A side benefit of this analysis is that it forces the IT manager to produce a detailed project proposal that outlines the scope of a project and defines what the project is committed to deliver. It also includes the estimated budget, time frame, resources, controls, and standards within which the project must be completed. It is the foundation for moving forward and preparing detailed plans. Once the project is clearly understood, it can be evaluated against the advantages and disadvantages inherent in outsourcing.

Outsourcing can allow an IT manager to control and predict costs effectively. By delegating work outside the company's core business to outsourcing partners, the client can focus on its core business with greater stability, predictability, and reduced total cost of ownership (TCO). Outsourcing partners allow the internal IT department to be more flexible and responsive, to locate and utilize highly focused expertise, and build a department based on a business-driven service model.

These benefits, however, are not without some cost. Relying too heavily on outsourcing can be more costly in the longer term. Unanticipated revisions can demand additional funding. The outsourcing vendor has a disproportionate control over quality, and the client is at risk if changes occur in the vendor organization. Companies relying on outsourcing partners often find there is limited skills transfer between their staff and the outsourcing provider, and the morale of internal staff may be impacted by the dynamics of their relationship with outsourced staff.

Delivery and Pricing

The staff utilized in an outsourced project can operate in many different modes. Each of these modes has advantages that make them suitable to certain projects, or for dealing with certain providers.

Routine Assignments

If the work to be done is relatively routine (e.g., system maintenance, coding, and testing under in-house supervision), any firm or individual provider can be considered. Small or independent contractors often offer lower rates, although large firms may be cost competitive if they wish to place employees immediately.

Project-Oriented Work

The success of a project depends on a cohesive, effective project team. A larger provider with a reputation for project management can choose from among many employees to assemble a team with the necessary skills for the client organization. A clearly structured project management methodology helps ensure that the project management aspects of development receive the required attention.

Specialized-Skill Assignments

A specialist is often needed when an assignment requires in-depth knowledge of a particular area. If a contracting firm that specializes in the required skill cannot be found, large firms, especially regional or national consulting organizations, with a large employee base should be used.

As in any field, a specialist costs more than a generalist. The client should thoroughly examine the credentials of anyone suggested for a specialist's assignment.

The Cost of Outsourcing

The cost of outsourcing can be significant. IT managers can leverage their outsourcing budget by structuring the relationship in a manner appropriate to the work being done. Most outsourcing projects take one of three forms. Costs are usually allocated at the end of each project phase; however, it is not unusual for a client to request estimates or billing for each project deliverable. An entire contract need not use a single price structure. Occasionally, any or all of these structures are used in different parts of the same project.

Fixed-Price. This is the simplest arrangement. The client and provider agree on a fixed price, and the project is completed. Clients are usually uncomfortable with this arrangement unless the provider supplies detailed justification for the project cost.

Time and Materials. This is the most common arrangement. The client pays an hourly rate for the provider's services and provides the means and resources to perform them.

Not to Exceed. The "not to exceed" project is actually a time and materials (T & M) project with a fixed-price ceiling. The provider is paid the T&M hourly rate for the limit of the contract, after which the outsourcing provider must absorb the cost of any overrun. Such arrangements are usually advantageous to the client, and few providers are willing to enter into them unless they are absolutely certain that the scope of effort is well within the limits of the project.

125

EVALUATING OUTSOURCING PROVIDERS

The method for evaluating outsourcing proposals should be established early. Too often, the evaluation is based simply on bottom-line price comparisons. Ideally, IT managers will also focus on completion time, relevant experience, and methodological approach. Large, complex projects usually illicit proposals that are equally large and complex, as well as tedious. However, the only way to evaluate a proposal properly is to read it thoroughly. IT managers must pay attention not only to what is presented, but the manner in which it is presented. The care and professionalism demonstrated may indicate the provider's overall commitment and attitude. Because the proposal is a marketing tool, the contracting firm will not overlook the opportunity to present positive information about itself. Information on the provider's history, mode of operation, past successes, and unique methodologies are often included and should be considered in the decision-making process.

Regardless of the scope or complexity of the project or how they are staged, projects can be viewed on a nontechnical level as consisting of three main phases: discovery, invention, and implementation. Each of these phases, which in reality must coexist throughout a project, are described below.

Discovery Phase

Proposals often evolve over a series of early, informal meetings with all interested providers. This gives the client an opportunity to see how the provider responds, and gives the providers a chance to review the project in detail and to withdraw if they choose. These informal meetings occasionally foster ideas that can alter the scope and complexity of the project.

The main goal at this stage is to produce a requirements definition, which is crucial to the overall success of the outsourcing initiative because it is at this point that the fundamental characteristics of the project are determined. The deliverable from this phase, often referred to as the discovery phase, is a document that sets the scene for the entire project. This document generally includes sections on the master project plan, goals and objectives, performance targets and acceptance criteria, and the legal terms of the relationship. The amount of detail in each section depends on the nature of the project and the amount of information collected.

Not all projects survive past the discovery phase. The thrust of discovery is to convert areas of uncertainty into areas of certainty through technical investigation, interviewing, and occasionally, prototyping. In some cases, this effort reveals that the project is unnecessary, or has little or no chance of success. Usually, however, the project moves from discovery to the next phase — invention.

Invention Phase

In the middle of a project, the emphasis shifts toward invention. Invention also represents moving from uncertainty toward certainty. At this phase, software is designed or a system is engineered. In complex projects, a series of inventions may be required. As the project moves away from discovery, overall risk tends to decrease, but so does the ability to meaningfully influence the direction and outcome of the project.

Implementation

Unlike previous phases, implementation does not involve a high degree of uncertainty. Here, the potential developed in the previous phases is realized. It is important to realize, however, that the previous phases must be wound down as implementation moves ahead. It is counterproductive to leave discovery and invention open while attempting implementation. IT managers who do not realize this often find that the first 90 percent of a project takes the first 90 percent of the time, and the last 10 percent takes the other 90 percent of the time.

METHODOLOGICAL APPROACHES TO PROJECT DEFINITION

System development methodologies can be generally divided into four main categories. Prototyping is often proposed as a fifth methodology, but prototypes can be developed at any stage within the four main methodologies below. Despite their obvious differences, these methodologies generally share certain characteristics. They are typically used to analyze information flows and data structures for large, structured applications where the scope of the application is fairly well defined in advance. The primary objective is to provide a detailed specification of data flows and structures that can be directly translated into systems designs. These methodologies require extensive investments in time and resources to achieve the level of detail required.

1. Traditional Analysis Methodology

Traditional methodology is based on the system flowchart. Data is represented in hierarchical input process output (HIPO) charts. The traditional methodology is less effective as the size of the team and the complexity of the information system grow.

2. Structured Analysis and Design Methodology

Structured analysis and design emerged in the mid-1970s as an outgrowth of structured programming. It was embodied, for example, in methodologies by Yourdon and DeMarco, and is often referred to as the data flow modeling methodology. Many methodologies for analyzing requirements of data processing applications have been developed. They include

IBM Business Systems Planning, Yourdon's Structured Analysis Techniques, SofTech Structured Analysis and Design Techniques, and others. Most businesses using structured analysis and design or CASE methodologies have developed some hybrid based on Yourdon, and incorporating the best of the other models. As with its programming counterpart, structured programming, structured analysis and design adds dimensions that allow it to be rigorous, repeatable, and measurable.

By 1984, another dimension, computer-aided software engineering (CASE), was added to structured analysis and design. CASE uses computer software to assist in modeling from a functional perspective. In CASE analysis, the analyst begins by modeling what the system will be asked to do, rather than modeling the system. By focusing on the functional flow of data, without regard to the systems through which they flow, these methodologies allow the development of systems that meet the information and process needs of an organization, rather than adapting either of those to the system. Most structured analysis methodology focuses on the data flow diagram (DFD). A data flow diagram graphically represents a system as data flows, processes, data stores, and external interfaces.

Although CASE can trace its roots as far back as the 1960s, it was the advent of the personal computer, and systems based on it, that brought CASE to the forefront. Simply, CASE automates the creation of data flow diagrams based on user specifications. CASE can be divided into Upper CASE and Lower CASE. Upper CASE tools focus on the planning, analysis, and early design of systems. Lower CASE emphasizes the design, implementation, and evolution of systems.

The most significant contribution of CASE is the ability to automate the generation of data flow diagrams, entity–relationship diagrams, HIPO charts, Warnier–Orr diagrams, and object-oriented diagrams. Without some Upper CASE tool, analysts would have to rely on programs like Visio or Microsoft PowerPoint to render these diagrams. Unlike CASE tools, these programs provide no assistance in defining the model, and require the analyst to regenerate diagrams by hand when changes are made.

3. Information Modeling Methodology

Like structured methodology, information modeling methodology approaches the design of information systems from an information perspective rather than a functional perspective. The major focus of logical modeling is to derive a business event partitioned model that reflects the most customer-oriented, stable, and maintainable view of the business policy. This business event partitioned model will flow naturally into the complete organizational view systems and on into systems design. The analyst using this methodology asks what information the system must provide to its users. Key proponents of this methodology include Texas Instruments and Knowledgeware Corporation.

The key difference between information modeling and CASE is that information modeling focuses on information, whereas CASE focuses on functions. The bias inherent in each of these methodologies can lead them to different results, depending on whether designs are driven by functions or data.

4. Object-Oriented Methodology

Just as structured analysis and design methodologies emerged as a complement to the structured languages of the 1970s, object-oriented methodology emerged in the 1980s with the popularity of object-oriented languages. Object-oriented languages differ from the structured, deterministic, and sequential paradigm of languages like COBOL in that they focus on objects, rather than functions or data.

Because object-oriented languages are unique, the methods of analysis they call for are also unique. Object-oriented analysis, like the languages, must focus on objects, attributes, responsibilities, and messages. In fact, the most difficult aspect of adopting an object-oriented methodology is when analysts experienced in the function- or data-centric methodologies must unlearn these techniques and adjust to object-centric thinking. Even more difficult, many organizations maintain heterogeneous systems that incorporate object-oriented systems with systems that focus on data or function. Clearly, the applicability of any of these four methodologies will depend on the type of system.

Object-oriented methodology uses abstraction as a method of isolating properties that are not relevant to a particular function from those that are. These functions are then distributed among components, or encapsulated. Each software component isolates a single function, therefore hiding that function to users of the object. One of the most important attributes of these components is referred to as polymorphism; that is, the fact that a component can take on different forms based on the conditions in which it is operating. This allows greater reuse of objects, whether by sharing, copying, or cloning, and adjusting them.

PROJECT DELIVERY

At some point, the finished system needs to be turned over to the users and brought into production (after user training on the new system, of course, has taken place). Project delivery generally follows one of two methodologies. The first is the "big bang" approach. The second is phased implementation.

The "big bang" approach entails pulling the plug on the old system and bringing up the new system and requiring that everyone use it. In this approach, there is no safety net. If one uses this approach, careful testing and deployment are critical.

The second, more common, approach is phased implementation. Various portions of the new system are brought up one at a time, either by subject or by class of users. In most cases, running the new system in parallel with the legacy system requires double entry into both systems while the bugs are being worked out. Such an approach is clearly more costly than the "big bang" approach; but if something goes wrong, there is always the legacy system to fall back on.

"Big Bang" Delivery

"Big bang" delivery begins with the analysis phase. During analysis, the project team must capture all of the user specifications for the project and completely detail all business processes that will be involved. This is the most important step in systems design. Analysis may include subphases, often referred to as information gathering and requirements analysis. The deliverable from this phase is the requirements document. A carefully prepared requirements document is one of the major keys to system success. The requirements document should include the following: analysis function hierarchy, legacy system documentation, business rules, and requirements mapped to the function hierarchy.

Following analysis is the design phase. The design phase is where the blueprints are drawn for building the system. Design is complete when the design documents can be handed over to another team to build. The specifics of the build process depend on the technology in question.

Following the build phase comes testing. Testing is one of the most important, but usually most neglected phases in the system design process. The key to proper testing is to use multiple tests. No single test, no matter how carefully conducted, will find all of the errors in a system. It is better to perform several different tests less carefully; these usually catch more errors at less cost to the organization. The second goal of the test phase is to perform user acceptance testing. Once all errors have been corrected, the user must accept the system to move on to implementation.

Staged Delivery

Staged delivery provides for delivering a project in successive stages. Staged delivery differs from "big bang" delivery only in the iterative nature of the design, build, test, and implementation cycle. This cycle can be repeated any number of times until the full project is delivered. During iterations, the legacy system can be phased out as the new system is phased in.

Staged delivery can make critical functionality available to users early in the project life cycle. Delivering in stages also reduces the technical risk of unsuccessful integration because it forces integration to occur more often. Reporting requirements are also reduced because there is no more accurate status report than a working component.

Staged delivery allows closer monitoring of costs, since overruns can be identified and addressed early in the project life cycle. Staged delivery, however, adds to the overall cost of a system, most notably because of the costs associated with mounting multiple release efforts within a single project. Still, the added benefits of increased estimation accuracy, flexibility, and visibility, as well as the overall reduction in risk, usually more than justify the increased overhead.

OUTSOURCING AND THE VIRTUAL CORPORATION

Somewhere along the continuum of a company that does not outsource and one that consists entirely of contingent staff lies the "virtual corporation." In a virtual corporation, tasks such as human resource management, finance, sales, and marketing might all be devolved to external agencies. Virtual corporations are often so tightly organized that the casual observer may have difficulty determining where the client company ends and outsourcing partner starts. Eventually, they operate as a single organization with shared culture, goals, and processes.

Certain business conditions make the virtual corporation a particularly useful way of reducing risk. For companies involved in highly complex industries and markets, it can be difficult to excel in all functional areas. Complexity shifts the advantage away from broad-based organizations toward specialists — it is a process that favors outsourcing. Not only do senior managers need to keep up with trends across a wide range of disciplines, but also the resources and skills required for success in some areas of the enterprise might actually work to inhibit success in other areas.

Another factor that favors outsourcing and the virtual corporation is an environment of rapid change. Managers often find it difficult to allocate resources in an unpredictable climate. Even more problematic is knowledge management in such an environment. Managers may cultivate new skill sets and competencies only to find they are quickly obsolete. In these circumstances, the benefits of outsourcing are very clear.

Companies often start by looking at outsourcing and the virtual corporation cost-cutting programs. While they do play that role, the real benefits of outsourcing derive not from such a defensive application, but rather when they are used proactively to gain strategic competitive advantage with existing resources.

CONCLUSION

Outsourcing is a tool that can give companies a competitive edge by allowing them to focus on core business while tapping highly skilled and specialized resources cost effectively. To make the best use of outsourcing, IT managers must establish relationships with outsourcing partners who understand their client's business and technology environment.

Outsourcing providers often use complex and arcane methodologies to manage resources and deliver services. IT managers must be fluent in these methodologies to ensure that their own organization goals are not made secondary to those of the outsourcing provider, and that they do not become the servant of the provider's methodology, rather than the master.

There is no question that outsourcing is a necessary practice if corporations are to remain competitive in today's complex economy and marketplace. The strategic decision is not when or whether to outsource, but to what extent. By keeping internal control over core business functions, and closely managing outsourcing of appropriate projects, IT managers can achieve maximum efficiency within their departmental budgets.

Chapter 11
Outsourcing as a Means of Improving Process Maturity: An Approach for More Rapidly Moving up the Capability Maturity Model

Brian Keane

BECAUSE IT CAN TAKE YEARS TO PROGRESS TO HIGHER LEVELS within the Capability Maturity Model (CMM), many organizations are outsourcing. Outsourcing is an approach for improving productivity and lowering costs by contracting the support or development of one or more software applications to a software services firm. Productivity and quality objectives can be aligned with the CMM and structured into an outsourcing contract.

Software services providers can be significantly effective in assisting the move up the CMM. This effectiveness is gained through the tight management controls, formal processes, and constant measurements that are the hallmarks of organizations high in CMM. IS managers can use outsourcing as a means for obtaining and implementing "best-in-class" processes in their organizations.

Most IS organizations are level 1 organizations — far from the level of flexibility required for today's competitive business environment. Even with the CMM providing guidelines for process improvements, lower-level

0-8493-0875-5/00/$0.00+$.50
© 2000 by CRC Press LLC

organizations find it difficult to implement new processes and advance from their current level. Process reengineering of any kind is undoubtedly challenging, and in an IS organization it can be even more difficult. In fact, it can take years to progress from one level of maturity to the next, and the move from level 1 to level 2 requires the most commitment, effort, and expertise.

Outsourcing is a viable method for introducing and more quickly institutionalizing new processes within an IS organization. This section of the chapter provides background on outsourcing and discusses how outsourcing can be used to accelerate the implementation of process improvements. The discussion focuses on application outsourcing — contracting a software services firm to manage and be accountable for one or more software applications — as an example of the processes and methods that are available to IS organizations. In this presentation, highlights from the methodology of Keane for application management are included to illustrate the environment and processes required to move up the CMM.

A note on terminology. Outsourcing is a term used to describe the contractual transfer of an internal corporate function to an external service provider. Typical IS functions that may be outsourced include data center operations, help desk operations, new application development projects, and maintenance and support for applications. The term outsourcing is reserved for situations where the service provider supplies its processes and takes direct responsibility for the daily operations of specific portions of the IS requirements of a corporation according to a predefined level of service. This mixture of processes, expertise, and accountability is the foundation for the major benefits that can be gained from outsourcing. In this article, supplemental staffing is not considered a form of outsourcing.

OUTSOURCING AND THE CMM

When measured on the CMM scale of maturity, the best outsourcers rank quite high. While a consulting company may be successful in an occasional outsourcing engagement through excellent staffing, it cannot provide reliable and predictable levels of service, quality, and profitability across multiple projects without a well-managed set of outsourcing processes documented in a methodology. Highly experienced outsourcers develop a set of world-class processes that they customize and apply to each of their projects. The experience of the outsourcer over many projects allows it to select and combine the best and most effective practices from many organizations. These procedures are documented within the methodology of the outsourcer and are used to train its staff. Since outsourcers tightly manage their projects, process usage is enforced. By using the same processes from project to project, the outsourcer is able to shift its consultants as needed between projects.

IS organizations at the lower end of the CMM need years of effort and massive cultural change to achieve the level of process maturity present in a best-in-class outsourcer. Fortunately, IS organizations can take advantage of the knowledge and experience of the outsourcer to move them up the scale of maturity faster than is possible through other means. Outsourcing engagements offer IS organizations a number of powerful benefits.

Access to Best-in-Class Processes

A top outsourcer will have a separate team that manages its outsourcing processes. This team is responsible for maintaining and continuously improving the processes of the organization using the experiences from all of its ongoing projects. As a result, the processes of the outsourcer evolve far faster than those of most IS organizations. Because the livelihood of the outsourcer is based on its ability to provide its services at maximum efficiency, the outsourcer has considerable incentive to improve its process effectiveness.

Ability to Watch the Procedures in Action

Implementing an outsourcing project within the IS organization provides staff members with the ability to watch the new processes and tools in action. This enables side-by-side comparisons of existing IS processes against those used by the outsourcer. Any doubts or misgivings about the value of more efficient processes will be dispelled by this exercise.

Hands-on Training

Any large-scale outsourcer will have well-prepared training materials, skilled trainers, and training facilities to prepare its own staff for outsourcing assignments. These resources can be applied to training internal staff. IS staff members can supplement their learning by working alongside the outsourcer staff on an actual project.

A Means to Overcome Cultural Resistance

Often, the required cultural change is the most difficult obstacle to overcome. The current practices of the IS organization are heavily ingrained in its staff members, and they often strongly resist changes to the status quo. An interesting paradox is that this resistance vanishes if a staff member takes a new job in a new company. The staff member expects to learn and assimilate new procedures as part of the job move. It is far easier to add staff members successfully to an existing process environment than it is to change the process environment of existing staff members. Outsourcers take advantage of this phenomenon when staffing their outsourcing projects. By putting the process environment in place at the start of the outsourcing project and transitioning staff into the environment, the outsourcer avoids the resistance that occurs when IS organizations attempt to change. The same principle can be applied within the IS organization by allowing the outsourcer to set up the project environment and then transferring IS staff to new assignments within the project.

KEY COMPONENTS OF A SUCCESSFUL OUTSOURCER

Selecting an outsourcer to assist the IS organization in moving up the CMM is different from selecting an outsourcer strictly for assuming responsibility for a given function. The outsourcing project must be performed on site, and it requires an outsourcer with the experience and desire to share its methods. These requirements preclude offshore outsourcing organizations. Some outsourcers will consider their practices proprietary and will be unwilling to transfer knowledge to the IS organization. The IS organization must find an outsourcer that is willing and able to provide its procedures and the required training. Because claiming expertise is easier than providing expertise, the IS organization must evaluate the claims of each outsourcer carefully for accuracy before selecting a vendor.

The list that follows provides information about the key components of the service offering of a successful outsourcer. IS organizations should consider these components in detail when evaluating outsourcers.

Project Management Experience

Large-scale project management experience is one of the most important characteristics of a successful outsourcer. If the outsourcer does not have a solid track record of achievement, all of the other components in this list are suspect. For example, the methodology of the outsourcer represents the codification of this knowledge. If the outsourcer has limited experience, how strong can the methodology be? While experience in managing ongoing outsourcing projects is crucial, experience in managing the implementation and transition into a new project is especially important when using outsourcing to move up the CMM.

Methodology

The methodology of the outsourcer documents its processes and methods. The methodology describes which processes are used, how those processes are implemented, how they are used during project operation, and how they are managed. It is the primary training and reference document for the project. IS organizations should review the methodology in great detail. The methodology describes how the IS organization will operate if the project is successful. The evaluators must ensure that the methodology meets their long-term requirements and is sufficiently complete to serve as a meaningful training tool. The methodology must support the processes required to move up the CMM. It must also include the supporting metrics, quality reviews, and process improvement activities to ensure that the processes are used effectively.

Central Support Team

A central support team is needed to maintain the methodology and capture best practices from multiple projects. Such teams are a primary vehicle for building continuous improvements into the methodology. The team receives project metrics from each ongoing project and assists in conducting management reviews of project quality. The existence of a central support team is indicative of the commitment of the outsourcer to its practice and to the ideals expressed in the CMM.

Experienced Staff

While training courses are valuable, actual project experience is even more important. A successful outsourcer will have staff members who have worked on multiple outsourcing engagements. These staff members know how to implement the processes in the methodology in a variety of circumstances.

Training Materials

Examining the quality of the training materials of the outsourcer is another good method for determining its value in a process improvement effort. Lack of good-quality training materials indicates poor training on the part of the outsourcer and casts doubts on the experience of its staff. Good training materials will be highly tuned from use on multiple assignments and will provide a strong foundation for training IS staff members.

A MODEL FOR AN APPLICATION MANAGEMENT METHODOLOGY

Highlights of the Keane application management methodology (AMM) are offered below as an example of a methodology that supports the environment and processes required to move up the CMM. The AMM is customized to fit the needs of individual organizations; however, the fundamentals remain the same.

Project Management Processes. These processes manage ongoing project operations, personnel issues, and project performance to level of service agreement commitments. There are three major groups of processes in this category: project management, level of service management, and training.

Customer Assistance Processes. The customer assistance function ensures that user support is based on centralized and common practices. This approach enables fast response to requests, management controls on workload, and a collection point for project performance metrics.

Project Operation Processes. These processes include those needed to execute the tasks necessary to implement scheduled application maintenance and enhancement projects. They include processes for the estimation, prioritization, specification, and programming of project tasks.

Asset Management Processes. Asset management processes ensure the integrity of client application assets and effective project management through release management and configuration management. Application assets include source code, load modules, documentation, test cases, and other application components.

Production Control Processes. These processes ensure the quality of project deliverables and the integrity of the client's production environment. They include processes for system testing, acceptance testing, production turnover, and project close.

Operational Improvement Processes. These processes identify methods to improve project operations and implement continuous quality improvements. They embody the principles of continuous process improvement as defined by the CMM. Metrics from all project tasks and from process operations are continuously monitored to identify opportunities for improvement.

Management Review Processes. These processes sit above all phases of an outsourcing project. They define the methods used by project management, client management, and Keane management to audit and review the quality of project performance regularly.

IMPLEMENTING AN OUTSOURCING PROJECT

When an IS organization decides to pursue an application outsourcing project, there are many activities that must occur to prepare the environment for outsourcing. Similarly, when a project is completed, there are activities to wind down operations and return the project to the IS organization. As a result, outsourcing projects are usually organized into four distinct phases.

Phase I: Planning and Definition

This is the initial phase of the application outsourcing engagement. This phase evaluates the existing environment to develop a complete inventory of project assets and determine the types of improvements necessary to set up the project. A level of service agreement is created to document the project performance commitments, and a transition plan is created to begin the assumption of project responsibilities.

Phase II: Transition In

This phase addresses the turnover of the project to the application management team. In some cases, Keane introduces its employees to the application environment, whereas, in other cases, Keane acquires client employees to form the application management team. During this phase, depending on the team makeup, members either focus on acquiring the business and technical knowledge necessary to support the application(s) or they focus on learning and implementing the Keane process model. Team members also begin high-priority improvement activities. At the end of this phase, the application management team has full responsibility for the project, and the processes of the project are fully implemented and operational.

Phase III: Project Operations

This phase covers most of the outsourcing engagement. The application management team is totally responsible for the support of all aspects of the outsourced applications following the standards agreed upon in the level of service agreement. In addition to supporting the daily support activities for the application(s), the project team also focuses its attention on increasing its efficiency at supporting the project. The team will implement any necessary procedural and technical improvements in the early stages of this phase to reap the benefits over the life of the project.

Phase IV: Transition Out

This is the final phase of the outsourcing project where the outsourcing team returns control of the application(s) to the IS organization. As part of the transition, the IS staffers are trained in the new processes and tools that were established during the project. At the end of the transition out, the IS organization is supporting the application(s) in the new, higher-level operational environment.

CONCLUSION

Businesses are finding that strong processes are critical to their efforts to improve organizational flexibility. This chapter was developed to provide insight into how process improvements can help IS organizations face the challenges of a growing application portfolio, new technology shifts, and an increasingly fast-paced business environment.

The CMM is an excellent vehicle for assessing the quality of existing processes and determining the steps needed to improve those processes. Organizations can use the model to identify deficiencies, adopt practices, and meet specific goals through evolutionary steps. The CMM does not require any specific software technology, organizational structure, life-cycle model, or set of documents. In addition, unlike other mechanisms for establishing processes, the CMM can be used to create an organization where processes are not only defined, but practiced, shared, and continuously improved.

Moving up the CMM is not without its challenges, especially for lower-level organizations. Once processes are redesigned, it is much more critical, and difficult, to get the practices adopted throughout the organization. Under continued pressures and project deadlines, IS professionals do not have the time to familiarize themselves with newly defined procedures. As a result, the adoption of new practices is slow and, in some cases, impossible. Because it can take years to overcome such barriers and progress from one level of the maturity model to the next, organizations are forming outsourcing agreements with vendors that are willing to transfer their processes.

Outsourcing is a valuable tool for IS organizations seeking to accelerate their move up the CMM. The following section details some of the services a major software services firm provides to assist clients with their process improvement objectives.

IS Productivity Assessments (ISPA)

Before attempting to improve their process maturity, IS organizations need to understand their current situation. Through a detailed assessment of the IS organization, IS managers can ascertain where improvements are needed, determine which improvements would provide the greatest value and establish a baseline from which to measure future improvements.

Keane offers a comprehensive evaluation of an IS organization through its ISPA service. This service is based on the principle that productivity is ultimately a synthesis of people, processes, and technology. An ISPA goes beyond typical process maturity evaluations by including people and technology factors in its evaluation. Evaluations of issues such as application software quality and staff training enable Keane to develop an improvement strategy that will maximize the benefits of the recommended process improvements. This strategy is documented, along with the current status of the IS organization, in a complete report that also includes a project plan for implementing the recommended improvements.

Outsource Full Responsibility to Keane

This is the traditional outsourcing model. The IS organization increases its process maturity by outsourcing areas of low maturity. This arrangement allows the IS organization to concentrate its resources on its strengths. Keane takes responsibility for all aspects of the project, including staffing and process improvements. Keane operates the project following CMM principles, as contained in its AMM, and the corporation receives the benefits that ensue from more mature processes.

Outsource and Transition

This method is similar to the outsourcing service described above, except that the application(s) is transitioned back to the IS organization after the new project environment has been put into place. This method is useful for overcoming cultural barriers to change. Keane takes responsibility for the project using its own staff. The project team members implement the Keane process model and operate the project until all processes are fully tuned. At that stage, the IS organization can continue to outsource or it can reassume responsibility for the project. During the transition-out period, project team members fully train the IS staff members in all aspects of the project and the new processes. Cultural resistance is reduced by effectively moving IS staff members into a new assignment rather than attempting to change familiar processes on their current assignment. The IS organization can use its newly trained and experienced staff members to seed other projects in its portfolio.

Outsource a Pilot to Keane

A pilot project is used as a proof of concept. Keane assumes responsibility for the project and fully implements its outsourcing model. The IS organization observes the process and can compare its operations against those used by Keane. It enables the IS organization to see precisely how the new processes will operate in its environment. When the organization is ready, it may decide to outsource additional projects, or it may seek assistance from Keane to implement the model for internal IS projects. This method provides the IS organization with the methodology, staff, and training necessary to improve its processes successfully. The pilot project provides a demonstration of the benefits that can be gained when the new processes are fully implemented across the organization.

© Keane, Inc. 1998.

Section IV
Outsourcing Selective Functions

Chapter 12
Outsourcing Network Management and Information Systems

Nathan J. Muller

WITH COMPUTING AND NETWORKING ENVIRONMENTS getting ever more powerful, complex, and expansive, an increasing percentage of the corporate budget is being used for their support. Much of this money is spent on such brick-and-mortar aspects of computer operations as hardware and software and lines and circuits. In addition, many companies can no longer afford the salaries of qualified technical people to run computer systems and networks or skilled programmers to develop the sophisticated applications needed to run the core business.

Instead of hiring, training, and retaining internal staff to perform cabling, hardware maintenance, systems integration, and network management functions, companies can become far more competitive by focusing internal resources on strategic or business-specific applications that can add measureable value to the enterprise in the form of new products and services. Overhead functions that support these efforts can be offloaded to outside organizations for a monthly fee.

With the current competitive environment and the trend toward downsizing, many companies are experiencing hiring freezes and staff reductions, coupled with increased pressure from senior management to get more work done in less time. All of this is occurring at the same time the enterprise is becoming more and more dependent on an information systems network that must be operational 24 hours a day, seven days a week.

Consequently, many companies are turning to service firms that specialize in managing networks, integrating diverse computer systems, or developing business applications. Outsourcing involves the transfer of network assets or staff to a vendor, who then assumes profit and loss responsibility for some or all of the client's network and data processing operations.

APPROACHES TO OUTSOURCING

There are two basic approaches to outsourcing — each of which can benefit organizations facing tough financial times. First, the outsourcing firm can buy a company's existing information systems and network assets and lease them back to the company for a fixed monthly fee. In such an arrangement, the outsourcer can also take over the network management payroll. This relieves the client of a cash outlay, which can be applied in turn to its financial recovery.

The outsourcer maintains the data communications equipment, upgrading to state-of-the-art systems within the budgetary parameters and performance guidelines in the agreement. In some cases, equipment leasing is part of the arrangement. Aside from its tax advantages, leasing can protect against premature equipment obsolescence and rid the company of the hassles of dealing with used equipment once it has been fully depreciated.

With the second type of arrangement, the company sells off its equipment and migrates the applications to the outsourcer's systems. Often, these are managed by the company's key personnel, who have been reassigned to the outsourcer's payroll and receive a comparable benefits package. Because the outsourcing firm may provide a wide array of services to a broad base of clients worldwide, employees can even find new career opportunities with this type of outsourcing arrangement.

OUTSOURCING TRENDS

The trend toward outsourcing is not new in the information systems arena. Service bureau activity, in which in-house data centers are turned into remote job-entry operations to support such applications as payroll, claims processing, credit card invoicing, and mailing lists, has traditionally been associated with data center outsourcing. Under this arrangement, mainframes are owned and operated off site by the computer service company.

As applied to networks, however, the outsourcing trend is quite recent. An organization's LAN may be thought of as a computer system bus, providing an extension of the data center's resources to individual users' desktops. Through WAN facilities, data center resources may be extended further to remote locations. Given the increasing complexity of current data networks, it is not surprising that companies are seeking ways to offload management responsibility to those with more knowledge, experience, and hands-on expertise than they alone can afford.

In this context, outsourcing firms typically analyze the user's business objectives, assess current and future computing and networking needs, and determine performance parameters to support specific data transfer requirements. The resulting system design may incorporate equipment from alternative vendors as well as the exchange facilities of any carrier. Acting as the client's agent, the outsourcing firm coordinates the activities of equipment vendors and carriers to ensure efficient and timely installation and service.

In a typical outsourcing arrangement involving WAN facilities management, an integrated control center — located at the outsourcing firm's premises or that of its client — serves as a single point of service support at which technicians are available 24 hours a day, 365 days a year, to monitor network performance, contact the appropriate carrier, or dispatch field service as needed, perform network reconfigurations, and perform any necessary administrative chores.

WHAT TO OUTSOURCE

Networks are growing rapidly in size, complexity, and cost; technical experts are expensive and difficult to find and keep; new technologies and new vendors appear at an accelerating rate; and users clamor for more and better service while their bosses demand lower costs and increased work performance. Consequently, the question may no longer be whether to outsource but what to outsource.

The prevailing view among users is that outsourcing commodity-like operational functions, sometimes called tactical functions, is a low-risk proposition. It is possible to save both money and headaches by letting someone else pull wires, set up circuits, and move equipment. Outsourcing mission-critical or strategic functions, however, involves more of a risk to the company. If the outsourcing firm performs these functions poorly, for whatever reason, the client company's competitive position could become irreparably damaged.

One way for a company to take a partial step toward outsourcing is to outsource network management for the second and third shifts and weekends, while keeping control over the more critical prime time. As confidence in the vendor grows, more can be outsourced.

TYPICAL OUTSOURCING SERVICES

- the specific activities performed by the outsourcing firm may include:
- routine equipment moves, adds, and changes
- integration
- project management

- trouble ticket administration
- management of vendor-carrier relations
- maintenance, repair, and replacement
- disaster recovery
- long-term planning support
- training
- equipment leasing

Each of these is discussed in detail in the following sections.

Moves, Adds, and Changes

Moves, adds, and changes constitute a daily process that can consume enormous corporate resources if handled by in-house staff. This process typically includes such activities as:

- processing move, add, and change orders
- assigning due dates
- providing information required by technicians
- monitoring move, add, and change service requests, scheduling, and completions
- updating the directory database
- handling such database modifications as feature, port, and password assignments
- creating equipment orders upon direction
- maintaining order and receiving logs
- preparing monthly move, add, and change summary reports

In assigning these activities to an outside firm, the company can realize cost savings in staff and overhead, without sacrificing efficiency and timely order processing.

Integration

Current information systems and communications networks consist of a number of different intelligent elements: host systems, LANs and servers, cable hubs, and WAN facilities, to name a few. The selection, installation, integration, and maintenance of these elements requires a broad range of expertise that is not usually found within a single organization. Many companies are therefore turning to outsourcing firms for integration services.

The integration function involves unifying disparate computer systems and transport facilities into a coherent, manageable utility, a major part of which is reconciling different physical connections and protocols. The outsourcing firm also ties in additional features and services offered through a public switched network. The objective is to provide compatibility and interoperability among different products and services so that they are transparent to the users.

Project Management

Project management entails the coordination of many discrete activities, starting with the development of a customized project plan based on the client's organizational needs. For each ongoing task, critical requirements are identified, lines of responsibility are drawn, and problem escalation procedures are defined.

Line and equipment ordering is also included in project management. Acting as the client's agent, the outsourcing firm negotiates with multiple suppliers and carriers to economically upgrade or expand the network without sacrificing predefined performance requirements. Before new systems are installed at client locations, the outsourcing firm performs site survey coordination and preparation, ensuring that all power requirements, air conditioning, ventilation, and fire protection systems are properly installed and in working order.

When an entire node must be added to the network or a new host must be brought into the data center, the outsourcing firm performs acceptance testing of all equipment before bringing it online, thus minimizing potential disruption to daily business operations. When new lines are ordered from various carriers, the outsourcing firm conducts the necessary performance testing before cutting them over to user traffic.

Trouble Ticket Administration

In assuming responsibility for daily network operations, a key service performed by the outsourcing firm is trouble ticket processing, which is typically automated. The sequence of events is as follows:

- An alarm indication is received at the network control center operated by the outsourcing firm.
- The outsourcing firm uses various diagnostic tools to isolate and identify the cause of the problem.
- Restoral mechanisms are initiated (manually or automatically) to bypass the affected equipment, network node , or transmission line until the faulty component can be brought back into service.
- A trouble ticket is opened:
  — If the problem is with hardware, a technician is dispatched to swap out the appropriate board.
  — If the problem is with software, analysis may be performed remotely.

If the problem is with a particular line, the appropriate carrier is notified. The client's help desk is kept informed of the problem's status so that the help desk operator can assist local users. Before the trouble ticket is closed out, the repair is verified with an end-to-end test by the outsourcing firm. Upon successful end-to-end testing, the primary customer premises equipment or facility is turned back over to user traffic and the trouble ticket is closed.

Management of Vendor-Carrier Relations

Another benefit of the outsourcing arrangement comes in the form of improved vendor–carrier relations. Instead of having to manage multiple relationships, the client needs to manage only one: the outsourcing firm. Dealing with only one firm has several advantages in that it:

- improves the response time to trouble calls and alarms
- eliminates delays caused by fingerpointing between vendor and carrier
- expedites order processing
- reduces the amount of time spent in invoice reconciliation
- frees staff time for planning
- reduces the cost of network ownership

Maintenance, Repair, and Replacement

Some outsourcing arrangements include maintenance, repair, and replacement services. Relying on the outsourcing firm for maintenance services minimizes a company's dependence on in-house personnel for specific knowledge about system design, troubleshooting procedures, and the proper use of test equipment. Not only does this arrangement eliminate the need for ongoing technical training, the company is also buffered from the effects of technical staff turnover, which is usually a persistent problem. Repair and replacement services can increase the availability of systems and networks while eliminating the cost of maintaining inventory.

Disaster Recovery

Disaster recovery includes numerous services that may be customized to ensure the maximum availability and performance of computer systems and data networks:

- disaster impact assessment
- network recovery objectives
- evaluation of equipment redundancy and dial backup
- network inventory and design, including circuit allocation
- vital records recovery
- procedure for initiating the recovery process
- location of a hot site, if necessary
- installation responsibilities
- test run guidelines

- escalation procedures
- recommendations to prevent network loss

Long-Term Planning Support

A qualified outsourcing firm can provide numerous services that can assist the client with strategic planning. Specifically, the outsourcing firm can assist the client in determining the impact of:

- emerging services and products
- industry and tariff trends
- international developments in technology and services

With experience drawn from a broad customer base, as well as its daily interactions with hardware vendors and carriers, the outsourcing firm has much to contribute to clients in the way of assisting in strategic planning.

Training

Outsourcing firms can fulfill the varied training requirements of users, including:

- basic communications concepts
- product-specific training
- resource management
- help desk operator training

The last type of training is particularly important because 80 percent of reported problems are applications oriented and can be solved without the outsourcing firm's involvement. This can speed up problem resolution and reduce the cost of outsourcing. For this to be effective, however, the help desk operator must know how to differentiate among applications problems, system problems, and network problems. Basic knowledge may be gained by training and improved with experience.

Equipment Leasing

Many times, an outsourcing arrangement will include equipment leasing. There are a number of financial reasons for including leasing in the outsourcing agreement, depending on the financial situation. Because costs are spread over a period of years, leasing can improve a company's cash position by freeing up capital for other uses. It also makes it easier to cost-justify technology acquisitions that would have been otherwise too expensive to purchase.

Leasing makes it possible to procure equipment that has not been planned or budgeted for. Leasing, rather than buying equipment, can also reduce balance sheet debt, because the lease or rental obligation is not reported as a liability. At the least, leasing represents an additional source of capital and preserves credit lines.

With new technology becoming available every 12 to 18 months, leasing can prevent the user from becoming saddled with obsolete equipment. This means that the potential for losses associated with replacing equipment that has not been fully depreciated can be minimized. With rapid advances in technology and consequent shortened product life cycles, it is becoming more difficult to sell used equipment. Leasing eliminates such problems.

OUTSOURCING LAN MANAGEMENT

As the size, complexity, and expense of local area network management get to be too big to handle, companies consider outsourcing the job. Certain routine LAN functions (e.g., moves, adds, and changes) are regularly outsourced. Such functions as planning, design, implementation, operation, management, and remedial maintenance are increasingly outsourced, and LAN operation and management are the services most needed by many current companies.

Providers of this type of service can be categorized into two groups with a third rapidly emerging. First, computer makers such as IBM, Digital Equipment Corp., Unisys Corp., and Hewlett-Packard Co. have introduced comprehensive LAN operation and management services packages. Second, management and systems integration firms (e.g., Electronic Data Systems Corp., Andersen Consulting, and Network Management, Inc.) have become less rigid in terms of the services they provide.

The strengths of the computer firms include a sound service and support infrastructure, knowledge of technology, and a diverse installed base. Their weaknesses include an orientation toward their own products and skills that are limited to certain technologies or platforms.

Systems integration and facilities management firms approach LAN outsourcing from the time sharing, data center, and mainframe environments. Their strengths include experience in data applications, familiarity with multivendor environments, and a professional service delivery infrastructure. Their weakness is that they often lack international networking capabilities, though this is changing.

The emerging category of outsourcing firms includes telecommunications companies, including interexchange carrier, regional Bell operating companies (RBOCs), and value-added network providers. Although AT&T has the service infrastructure to become a major player in LAN outsourcing, it must combine the support infrastructure of its telecommunications and computer divisions to ensure success in this area. Although US Sprint Communications Co. and MCI Communications Corp. have developed LAN connectivity and integration services, they have limited operation and management capabilities relative to AT&T.

Among the strengths of these firms is that they typically have a large service and support infrastructure, significant experience in physical cabling and communications, network integration expertise, and remote management capabilities. In addition, they have considerable investment capital available as well as strategic partnerships and alliances worldwide.

The regional Bell operating companies have strong regional service presence but limited data communications and applications experience. They are also limited by law to providing only a narrow range of services, limited domestically to operating within designated serving areas, and are subject to close state and federal regulation.

The strength of the value-added network providers is their ability to manage an internetwork of LANs as part of their packet network and frame relay services. Their chief weakness is that they do not have extensive service infrastructures and staff.

The custom nature of LAN outsourcing makes discussion of price difficult. Vendors change users per event, hour, or year for certain service elements; however, LAN outsourcing service packaging and pricing is still determined by the custom bid.

REASONS FOR OUTSOURCING

The reasons a company may want to outsource are varied. They include:

- difficulty in using technical personnel efficiently
- insulating management from day-to-day system problems and decisions
- concern about buying expensive technology that could become obsolete shortly after purchase
- greater flexibility to deal with fast-changing worldwide markets

Beyond these considerations, outsourcing arrangements may encompass several strategic objectives; First, to free capital tied up in buildings and equipment; second, to save money in absolute terms on an annual basis in the form of operating expenses; third, to move to more advanced information systems and network architectures; and fourth, to bring in — through the outsourcing firm — the necessary personnel and technical knowledge to consolidate operations that had not been available in-house.

Despite the many reasons to outsource, there are still many concerns associated with putting such critical resources in the hands of outsiders. Many of these concerns can be overcome with experience and knowledge of typical outsourcing arrangements.

Many corporate executives are concerned about giving up control when considering the move to outsource. However, control can increase when corporate management is better able to concentrate on issues that have potentially greater returns. Instead of consuming valuable resources in the nuts-and-bolts aspects of setting up an automated teller machine (ATM) network, for example, bank executives can focus on developing the services customers will demand from such a network and devise test marketing strategies for potential new financial services.

A common complaint among corporate executives is that outsource firms do not know their companies' business. In any outsourcing arrangement, however, users continue to run their own applications as before; the service provider just keeps the data center or network running smoothly. In addition, outsourcing firms typically hire at least some members of the client staff who would have been let go upon the decision to outsource and who are familiar with the business.

Companies that are considering outsourcing should examine their current information system and network activities in competitive terms. Activities that are performed about the same way by everyone within a particular industry can be more safely farmed out than those that are unique or based on company-specific skills. Most important, the company must take precautions to remain in a position to recommend and champion strategic systems and new technologies, which may involve high initial payout and possible cross-functional applications.

As the company opts for external solutions, standards that were internally developed do not suddenly lose their relevance. Oversight of standards that address hardware, communications, and software should remain an internal responsibility to ensure compatibility of information systems and networks across the entire corporation.

In-House Commitment to Outsourcing

Outsourcing can increase service quality and decrease costs, but management control cannot just be handed over to a third party. The fact that work has been contracted out does not mean that company staff can or should stop thinking about it. Typically, there is still a significant amount of supervisory overhead that consumes resources.

Someone within the company must ensure that contractual obligations are met, that the outsourcing firm is acting in the company's best interests, and that problems are not being covered up. Just as important, considerable effort is usually required to establish and maintain a trusting relationship. To oversee such a relationship requires staff who are highly skilled in interpersonal communications and negotiation and who are knowledgeable about business and finance.

THE DECISION TO OUTSOURCE

Strategic, business-oriented issues play a significant role in the decision to outsource. It is essential that potential users take stock of their operations before making this decision. Arriving at the correct solution requires an examination of the company's unique characteristics, including its human resources and technological infrastructure.

For example, it is advisable to compare the costs of in-house operations with the services that will be performed by the outside firm. This entails performing an audit of internal computing and networking operations to determine all current and planned costs for hardware, software, services, and overhead. These costs should cover a minimum of three years and a maximum of seven years and should include specifics on major expenses that may be incurred within that timeframe. This establishes a baseline figure from which to evaluate more effectively the bids of potential outsourcing firms and monitor performance after the contract is signed.

A detailed description of the operating environment should be prepared, starting with computer and network resources. This description should include:

- hardware configuration
- direct-access storage device requirements
- backup media and devices
- systems software
- applications software
- communications facilities and services
- locations of spare bandwidth and redundant subsystems
- restoral methods
- applications at remote locations
- critical processing periods
- peak traffic loads

The next step is to identify potential outsourcing firms. These vendors can then be invited to visit corporate locations to view the various internal operations, thereby obtaining an opportunity to understand the company's requirements so that these can properly be addressed in a formal proposal.

A company that turns to outsourcing to alleviate problems in managing information systems or networks should realize that transferring management to a third party may not turn out to be the hoped-for panacea. Although outsourcing represents an opportunity for companies to lower costs and enhance core business activities, before such an arrangement is considered, it should be determined how well internal staff, vendors, consultants, and contract programmers are managed. If there are difficulties in this area already, chances are that the situation will not improve under an outsourcing arrangement. In this case, perhaps some changes in staff responsibilities or organizational structure are warranted.

Vendor Evaluation Criteria

Most vendors are flexible and will negotiate contract issues. Each outsourcing arrangement is different and requires essentially a custom contract. It is important to identify all the issues that should be written into the contract. This can be a long list, depending on the particular situation. The following criteria, however, should be included in any rating scheme applied to outsourcing firms:

- financial strength and stability over a long period of time
- demonstrated ability to manage domestic and multinational computer systems and data networks
- number of employees, their skills, and their years of experience
- ability to tailor computer and network management tools
- history of implementing the most advanced technology
- an outstanding business reputation
- fair employee transfer policies and benefits packages

The weights of these criteria should be set by the company in keeping with its unique short- and long-term requirements.

Software suppliers may impose inhibitive transfer fees on licensed software if an outsourcing vendor takes over internal operations. This is often a hidden and potentially costly surprise. The common assumption among software users is that they can just move software around as they please. For the most part, software firms do not allow third parties to provide use to customers without a new license or significant transfer fees. They see this as necessary to safeguard their intellectual property rights. Outsourcing firms hit by these fees must pass them on to their clients if they expect to continue in the outsourcing business. If these fees are sizable, it could sway the decision on whether to outsource.

Requirements of the Outsourcing Firm

The outsourcing firm should be required to submit a detailed plan — with timeframes — describing the transition of management responsibilities. Although timeframes can and often do change, setting them gives the company a better idea of how well the outsourcing firm understands the company's unique requirements.

Performance guarantees that mirror current internal performance commitments should be agreed upon — along with appropriate financial penalties for substandard performance. The requirements should not exceed what is currently provided, unless that performance is insufficient, in which case the company should review its motives for outsourcing in the first place.

Satisfactory contractual performance guarantees for network operations can be developed if sufficient information on current performance exists. It is more difficult to develop such guarantees in the applications development arena, and this is why some companies avoid outsourcing this function.

A detailed plan for migrating management responsibilities back to the company at a future date should also be required. Despite the widely held belief that outsourcing is a one-way street, proper planning and management of the outsourcing firm can keep open the option of bringing the management function back into the corporate mainstream. Despite this option, the company may decide that, after the five or ten years of the contract are up, the outsourcing arrangement should be made permanent.

Structuring the Relationship

Companies that outsource face a number of critical decisions about how to structure the relationship. Entering into a long-term partnership with the outsourcing firm can be risky without proper safeguards. As previously noted, poor performance on the part of the service provider could jeopardize the client company's competitive position.

It must be determined at the outset which party will respond to computer system and network failures, and the degree to which each party is responsible for restoral. This includes spelling out what measures the outside firm must take to ensure the security and integrity of the data, financial penalties for inadequate performance, and what amount of insurance must be maintained to provide adequate protection against losses.

The outsourcing relationship must make explicit provisions for maintaining the integrity of critical business operations and the confidentiality of proprietary information. The firm must ensure that the outside firm will not compromise any aspect of the relationship.

The typical outsourcing contract covers a lengthy period of time — perhaps five to ten years. Outsourcing firms justify this by citing their need to spread the initial costs of consolidating the client's data processing or network operations over a long period of time. This also allows them to offer clients reasonable rates.

The relationship must provide for the possibility that the client's needs will grow substantially. The outsourcing firm's ability to meet changing needs (e.g., from the addition of a new division or the acquisition of a small company) should be evaluated and covered under the existing contract.

Companies entering outsourcing relationships must also establish what rights they have to bring some or all of the management responsibilities back in-house without terminating the contract or paying an exorbitant penalty. However, this should not be done lightly, because it can take a long time to hire appropriate staff and bring them up to an acceptable level of performance.

To avoid getting locked into the outsourcing arrangement, organizations should stay away from sharing data centers, networks, and applications software and from relying on customized software, applications, and networks. It can be difficult for a company to extricate itself from outsourcing arrangements when its operations are tightly woven into those of other companies operating under similar arrangements. The contract should be structured so that it can be put up for bidding by other parties.

Contracts should provide an escape clause that allows the user to migrate operations to an alternative service provider should the original firm fail to meet performance objectives or other contract stipulations. Because it is difficult to rebuild in-house systems or network staff from scratch, it is imperative that users do not outsource anything that cannot be immediately taken over by another firm. In fact, having another firm on standby should be an essential element of the company's disaster recovery plan.

CONCLUSION

The pressures for third-party outsourcing are considerable and on the increase. Requirements to service large amounts of debt have made every corporate department the target of close budgetary scrutiny, the corporate network and data center included. In addition, competition from around the world is forcing businesses to scale back the ranks of middle management and streamline operations. Outsourcing allows businesses to meet these objectives.

Although outsourcing promises bottom-line benefits, deciding whether such an arrangement makes sense is a difficult process that requires considerable analysis of a range of factors. In addition to calculating the baseline cost of managing the in-house information system and data network and determining their strategic value, the decision to outsource often hinges on the company's business direction, the state of its current data center and network architecture, the internal political situation, and the company's readiness to deal with the culture shock that inevitably occurs when two firms must work closely together on a daily basis.

Chapter 13
Outsourced Systems Development
Raoul J. Freeman

THE OUTSOURCING OF LARGE-SCALE SYSTEMS DEVELOPMENT ACTIVITIES is becoming more prevalent, yet the success of these activities is not. In many cases, the repeated failure of large-scale outsourcing projects is caused by lack of management attention to a common set of factors. Given the magnitude of investment involved in large-scale efforts, IS managers must learn to manage these factors before a system is approved for funding and in a way that ensures on-time and within-budget delivery of effective systems. This chapter draws from the experience of several large-scale systems development efforts in the public sector to present recommendations that help ensure the success of large-scale outsourced development projects.

CHALLENGES IN LARGE-SCALE PROJECTS

Well-known failures in the area of large-scale systems development include the State of California Department of Motor Vehicles (DMV) registration system, the Denver Airport baggage-handling system, and the Bank of America trust system. Failure, however, is not reserved to the well known. A study of 24 large U.S. companies reports that 68 percent of major projects using client/server technology overshot their schedules, 55 percent overspent their budgets, and 88 percent involved significant redesign. Large projects (i.e., those in excess of 5,000 function points) are canceled about a quarter of the time, and projects in the 10,000 to 20,000 function point range are canceled half the time. About 67 percent of projects that are completed overshoot their original schedules and budgets by nearly 100 percent.[1]

IS managers responsible for projects that are significantly larger than others they have managed face challenges not only regarding day-to-day management and integration, but also in terms of their ability to conceptualize whether the scale factor will affect system operation. Missed intermediate milestones in large projects involving new technology require special attention, because the development is occurring in relatively uncharted territory. It is at these milestones that managers need to make decisions to continue the project, cut back on functionality, or spend additional money. If such decisions are postponed, the sponsors of the system may find themselves at a point of no return.

FACTORS TO MANAGE IN LARGE-SCALE PROJECTS

Analysis of outsourced systems development projects ranging in value from $1 million to $100 million and involving, among others, the State of California, County of Los Angeles, and Los Angeles Unified School District revealed several factors that significantly contributed to failure or delay in multiple instances. In each project, managers failed to give appropriate consideration to one or more of the following areas:

- acceptance testing standards
- contract specifications, especially:
  — measurable business effects or outcomes
  — requirements specifications
  — arbitration and cost-reimbursement clauses
  — mechanisms for settling management disputes
- project management and metrics
- resource reserves for system implementation
- software examination
- length of the development cycle
- independent quality assurance
- technology transfer
- system ownership

Because absence of proper attention to these factors contributes to failed systems development efforts, management of these factors is a vital, although not necessarily sufficient, ingredient for ensuring project success.

DEVELOPING APPROPRIATE ACCEPTANCE TESTING STANDARDS

Standards for acceptance testing should be adopted for all systems development efforts. IS managers should ensure that any deviation from such standards is approved by an independent technical body and that wherever possible a parallel acceptance test is conducted.

Parallel testing need not be conducted in real-time, which can reduce costs, but any live or parallel test must be sufficiently long to ensure that conditions occurring at significant calendar times throughout the year are experienced. There must be no cold turkey starts of a system without adequate testing of critical system capabilities, and there must always be a fall-back plan in case of failure.

IS managers should ensure that proper documentation of the acceptance test is maintained and that ad hoc judgment is not allowed to substitute for contractually obligated performance. When the new and the old systems can accept the same transactions, comparison is facilitated. When they cannot, a set of specialized transactions needs to be devised to fit the new system.

Under such circumstances, it is possible to encounter a reconciliation-of-reports problem between the new and old systems. IS managers should not let the issue rest with a promise from developers that these minor errors will be fixed down the road. Independent sign-off that the acceptance test plan meets standards and that the test actually done corresponds to the planned test helps ensure that the area of acceptance testing does not become the cause of a failed development effort.

ENSURING CLEAR AND COMPREHENSIVE CONTRACT SPECIFICATIONS

IS managers must ensure that technical contract specifications are clear and based on design objectives. Before a request for proposal (RFP) is issued, the IS manager should hire independent technical and legal professionals to review and approve the specifications.

Such a review should focus not only on what is included but also on possible areas of omission (e.g., lack of a binding-arbitration clause). The contract should clearly delineate resources to be supplied by the vendor and the user in terms of number of person hours, qualification of personnel, calendar time when people are to be available, hardware, documentation, and training. The manager must also ensure that all contracts contain specifications to cover various contingencies.

Independent review of contract specifications clearly has costs in terms of money and time. Is the insurance worth buying? Although managers have to make that judgment for themselves, it is a well-known fact that ambiguous contract specifications lead to lawsuits.

In Los Angeles County, independent review by outside legal counsel following review by in-house counsel has produced valuable results. In addition, independent technical review outside of the sponsoring agency is being instituted through a new office of the chief information officer. Previously, independent departments or users issued their own RFPs without central oversight.

Specifying Measurable Business Effects or Outcomes

IS managers should ensure that measurable outcomes or expectations from the implementation of a system are included in contracts at the outset, preferably as stipulations but at a minimum as goals. Examples of such outcomes include a reduction in the amount of manual labor required and increases in the efficiency of service (e.g., the amount of paperwork needing to be redone will be reduced from two to one percent). Failure to meet such specifications would be cause for cancellation of the project and for arbitration damages.

IS managers should ensure that the amount of manual intervention and support required by any new system once operational is also detailed. Lack of this specificity can lead to delivery of all kinds of fancy systems that do not achieve business outcomes.

Consider the example of a new order-entry system. High-level business outcomes for the system could include the following:

- reductions in staff that save * million dollars a year
- reduction of one minute in the average length of time a customer spends on the phone while the clerk fills in the screen

These expected outcomes might be difficult to include in a contract, however, because a vendor might balk at being responsible for total user information performance and the actions of user personnel. Still, an effort to include such outcomes should be made.

Specifying Business and System Requirements in Clear and Cost-Effective Terms

IS managers must ensure that contract specifications clearly reflect the user's business requirements. It should not be assumed that a given system will magically meet specific user requirements even though it may contain laudatory general capabilities. The full requirements of the user must be anticipated for several years, and systems acquired must be flexible enough to accommodate such requirements.

System requirements should be based on the system's handling most, but not necessarily all, transactions. Automated handling of 100 percent of transactions may necessitate the development of excessive code and generate additional development expense.

Ensuring that a stated requirement accurately reflects the needs of the user can be accomplished through independent evaluation of business and systems requirements. Some RFPs have been found to contain 20 to 30 pages of minute requirements, many of which the user did not need, and to omit others that the user did need. If an outside agency is hired to evaluate requirements, it should be made liable for the validity of its findings.

Including Binding-Arbitration and Cost-Reimbursement Clauses

IS managers must make every effort to ensure the inclusion of a contractual requirement for binding arbitration to handle disputes and a penalty structure agreed upon by both sides. Penalties, such as treble damages for revenue losses resulting from lack of system performance, should be immediately payable without further legal recourse. Los Angeles County, for example, lost a substantial amount of money from inaccurate Medicare and Medicaid billing resulting from information produced by an out-sourced system that turned out to be faulty.

Contracts should stipulate that a vendor guarantee financial resources to cover the cost of a fallback position that permits the continuation of the client's essential user services. Alternatively, contract provisions should ensure that the user is reimbursed for losses incurred as a result of curtailment of essential services. The size of a performance bond, if any, should be commensurate with the size of the project and the dollar magnitude of the operation it concerns.

Is it realistic to try to include binding-arbitration, cost-reimbursement, or measurable-effects clauses into contracts? Although it has been difficult to include such clauses into public contracts in the past, progress is being made in this area. Smaller vendors, however, are still hesitant or incapable of providing these type of guarantees.

Developing Dispute-Settlement, Change-Control, and Early-Warning Mechanisms

Because any project involving a user and a developer will have disputes and changes, IS managers must ensure that appropriate mechanisms are in place to meet such contingencies as they arise. Basic management practices and alertness warrant that such mechanisms be enforced as well; a sound structure that is not enforced serves no purpose.

Any systems development contract should therefore include a variety of levels for settling disputes, starting with gentle persuasion and ending with CEO summits. The failure of lower-level management to settle a matter or escalate it to a higher level of review should be a cause for disciplinary action. Failure to meet milestones or provide deliverables should be pursued within the managerial chains of both contractor and user.

IS managers should ensure that the outsourcing contract contains an adequate mechanism for change control that is fair to both the user and contractor. Early-warning conditions must be specified, and IS staff must be kept cognizant of development or implementation progress. Potential problems should be brought to the attention of appropriate managers.

DEVELOPING EFFECTIVE PROJECT MANAGEMENT

Project management is a major factor in the success or failure of systems development efforts. It involves tracking progress and then making changes to keep projects in control and heading along the path to completion in an efficient manner. Projects should be managed by an experienced project manager who has been involved in the development of systems of the same dollar magnitude. When an individual with this experience is not available internally, IS managers should consider hiring someone to fill this function.

Effective project management requires establishing a standard — including well-defined project review cycles — that considers deliverables, effectiveness of what is delivered, metrics (e.g., function points), and tightly defined reporting formats. Progress tracking can only be accomplished when there is a well-defined and unambiguous measure to track. Function point analysis meets this criterion and is suitable as well for change control and measurement of scope creep (i.e., percent change in function points between phases of the software development life cycle). The methodology is also readily communicated to users.

IS managers should recognize that use of any metric can involve the fudging of numbers at lower levels. This is particularly commonplace with percentage of completion estimates. A savvy manager, however, should be able to detect or have a feel for how things are going. If they are going badly, the manager should know how easy or difficult the cure or fix is going to be.

Some managers, however, simply do not want to face up to the fact that a project is in trouble. Although these managers know, either overtly or subconsciously, when a project is in trouble, the seemingly dire consequences of shutdown or other drastic remedial action lead them to decide not to acknowledge reality and just hope for the best. Some of the factors that play a role in such cases follow:

- Top management, for its own political agenda, has made successful completion of the system a matter of paramount importance.
- IS managers find continued operation under the present system such a distasteful prospect that even a slim chance at producing a better system is deemed more desirable than an aborted effort or rescoping of functionality.
- Managers have developed an affection for the new system that hinders them from acknowledging the tell-tale signs of failure.
- The reward/punishment system favors going forward.

Disregarding the facts, for whatever reasons, can cause IS managers to continue a development effort that should be curtailed or altered. Once certain levels of commission are passed, it becomes increasingly difficult to stop a project. The manager gets more deeply enmeshed and hangs on to increasingly unrealistic hopes for success.

ALLOCATING SUFFICIENT BUDGET RESOURCES
FOR IMPLEMENTATION

The success of outsourced systems development also depends on the sufficient budgeting of resources for system implementation, including user training, dual operation, conversion, physical facility changes, and documentation. To accommodate peak personnel requirements during implementation and changeover, IS managers should consider the use of temporary employees and overtime and allocate funds for these purposes.

Training funds should be budgeted not only for the people doing the training but also for the people taking the training. These individuals require overtime or replacement help to do their jobs while they are being trained. IS managers should advise user managers in advance of the need for such allocations.

Because a thorough evaluation of implementation costs increases the price of a system, some IS managers do not conduct full cost evaluations. In addition, overruns in development or programming costs lead managers to co-mingle implementation funds with operating funds or even with other funds for development of the system.

The practice of robbing Peter to pay Paul or banking on the idea that there always will be a way to find the money for implementation is fraught with danger. It usually results in inadequate or shoddy implementation. The saddest of all development experiences is to see the hard work of systems development go to waste or at a minimum used inadequately because of improper implementation. The following sample scenario illustrates the results of this practice.

A lack of implementation funds for a newly development welfare-payments system causes users to be improperly trained. As a result, a number of transactions are mishandled. Needy members of the public do not receive their allotted benefits. The media picks up on this, and the system is accused of having all sorts of glitches. Governmental committees hold hearings, and consultants and advisory committees are called in to investigate what was in fact an effectively developed but poorly implemented system.

The preceding scenario could have been avoided had the IS manager set aside adequate funds for implementation and safeguarded the funds from other use. An independent assessment of the adequacy of implementation resources also helps to avoid problems later on.

EXAMINING SOFTWARE

In any turnkey system, provision must be made for examination of the source code. This examination provides an assessment of how easily user-required changes can be accommodated, as well as the ease with which the user can assume control of the system if necessary. Examination of the source code can be done by user personnel or by an agreed-upon third party and should address the documentation and structure of the code, methodology used in development, ease of change, modularity, and programming language.

SHORTENING THE LENGTH OF THE DEVELOPMENT CYCLE

The length of time between the inception of system specification and the end of system implementation must be kept to a minimum. IS managers should endeavor to cut major systems development projects into smaller more manageable projects that have shorter lead times and are more amenable to careful oversight.

The rapid pace of changing requirements and technology mandate that the development cycle never be allowed to exceed two years. Projects with estimated completion time exceeding two years should be redefined; IS managers should consider using ready-made software and integrating if possible. Although this approach might seem inefficient, the nature of today's development environment warrants its use.

REQUIRING INDEPENDENT QUALITY ASSURANCE

Large-scale outsourced systems development efforts benefit from independently monitored quality assurance. Hiring an independent entity represents an additional expense, but it provides an insurance policy for management that is justified by the high stakes of large projects. Los Angeles County is using this approach to ensure that when a user department outsources a large-scale project, an independent contractor monitors vendor quality and adherence to standards.

ENSURING TECHNOLOGY TRANSFER

IS managers need to ensure that appropriate technology transfer to the user agency or department occurs. This transfer involves the careful delineation of the information that must be transferred to the sponsoring agency and of the form in which the information will be transferred. Managers who leave these issues up to contractor personnel are courting disaster, particularly in the area of system maintenance.

MANIFESTING SYSTEM OWNERSHIP

Because having a high-level manager take a personal interest in a system (i.e., manifesting ownership) helps keep everybody involved in the development on their toes and ensure that things get done, personal attention by user and IS managers at all levels is certainly another key ingredient of a successful outsourced development effort.

How can an IS manager tell that system ownership has occurred among colleagues? The amount of time other managers spend on the project and the number of questions they ask regarding the system are some of the indicators of system ownership. But most important is an attitude that demonstrates involvement.

CONCLUSION

The need to specify requirements and objectives has been a prime consideration throughout this approach. Sometimes, however, such specificity is not available, as is the case when a project involves changing conditions or the development objectives become determined as the project progresses. Such conditions are not ideal for outsourcing, except perhaps on a time and materials basis, and reinforce the need for careful consideration of the outsourcing decision.

Once such a decision has been made, IS managers should actively manage the factors known to have a direct effect on the success or failure of development efforts. Before a system is approved for funding, a manager must secure detailed presentations from the contractor describing how these factors have been addressed. Furthermore, periodic checks should be made during the systems development life cycle to ensure that management of these factors has been kept on track.

Does consideration of all the factors ensure a project's success? Not necessarily, but it does improve the project's chances of success. IS managers who follow the recommendations provided in this chapter help ensure that if outsourced systems development efforts fail in the future, it should at least be for reasons other than the ones described here.

Notes

1. R. Garner, "Management Meltdown," *Open Computing* (January 1995), pp. 36-42.

Chapter 14
Applications Maintenance Outsourcing

Joseph Judenberg

THE ISSUE OF THE STRATEGIC VALUE OF INFORMATION SYSTEMS has given rise to the concept of selective outsourcing. This approach entails outsourcing selected data processing functions or applications. Activities with little strategic implication are more likely candidates for outsourcing than functions that are more strategic in nature. It is generally agreed that strategic activities should be kept in-house. One form of selective outsourcing that has significant benefits and opportunities in the current IS environment is application systems maintenance outsourcing.

IS managers who want to accelerate the move to new technology—whether it is client/server, object oriented, or multimedia—know that this migration requires qualified, dedicated resources. Because IS must continue to be responsible for the legacy systems that currently support the business, there is significant contention for management attention, knowledgeable resources, and project manager focus. Outsourcing of applications maintenance is a potential solution to this dilemma.

BENEFITS OF OUTSOURCING MAINTENANCE

Applications system maintenance is defined as the performance of those activities required to keep a software system operational and responsive after it has been accepted and placed into production. It includes two major sets of activities:

1. promptly fixing software problems that cause the system to be non-operative or to perform incorrectly
2. implementing changes, improvements, and enhancements to the system

When an outside firm is selected for outsourcing software maintenance for an applications system or group of systems, it assumes responsibility not only for implementing corrections and enhancements, but also for managing the process.

Although each situation is different, companies have achieved benefits from properly structured maintenance outsourcing arrangements. Opportunity areas and benefits of selective outsourcing include:

- freeing up existing maintenance staff to work on new development activities
- improving internal staff morale by removing the perceived drudgery of maintenance and providing opportunity to work with new technologies
- offering potential career paths for employees not moving to the new technologies
- reducing costs of providing maintenance
- supporting fluctuating maintenance demand with external variable costs rather than internal fixed costs
- improving service to applications system users with more responsive systems modifications and enhancements
- allowing management to focus on high-priority areas

Several of these benefits directly relate to IS management's need to support new business initiatives through technology.

Staffing Issues

The usual approach is to hire new staff to work on applications development requiring newer technologies. When it is difficult to find staff, consultants are usually engaged, but this approach poses some serious problems.

Existing staff members may feel neglected because they are relegated to maintenance work and not given the opportunity to advance their skill levels, while new employees or consultants are given the more exciting assignments using the latest technologies. Many of the IS department's current employees have knowledge about the business that could be valuable in development of the new applications. In addition, the cost of hiring consultants or new employees with the required skills is often high.

Applications maintenance outsourcing offers an effective solution to these problems. Retaining a firm to assume responsibility for maintenance of one or more legacy systems is a strategy that frees up existing staff members so they can be trained in new skills and can bring to bear their accumulated knowledge of the business. Retaining the in-house staff is usually less costly than hiring new employees and can be more cost-effective than hiring consultants. The cost of outsourcing maintenance should be significantly lower than the cost of hiring a firm to provide new development capabilities.

Use of maintenance outsourcing also provides a solution to another problem faced by organizations moving to new technologies. Studies have shown that a higher than expected percentage of the existing staff will not make the grade on newer technologies. Approximately 20 percent or more do not even want to learn new skills. Of those that do learn, about 20 percent are unsuccessful. The outsourcing arrangement can be structured so that the outsourcing supplier acquires some of the existing maintenance staff. This ensures knowledge and continuity in the systems maintenance work and accommodates those employees unwilling or unable to adapt to the new environment.

ASSESSING THE MAINTENANCE OUTSOURCING SUPPLIER

The most critical factor in a successful maintenance outsourcing arrangement is finding the right supplier. Although terms and conditions must be defined and a contract executed, flexibility and mutual understanding for the other party's interests are crucial and yield the spirit of cooperation that's needed to sustain an ongoing relationship that benefits both parties.

Key issues and questions to consider in assessing an outsourcer are as follows:

- Prior track record:
  - Does the firm have a history of performing similar tasks? It is advisable to evaluate the number of engagements and their success as described by the references provided by the outsourcing firm.
  - Have current clients achieved the benefits they were seeking? Are these benefits similar to what your organization expects?
- Proven staff and management:
  - Does the firm have a large staff experienced in maintenance and in the applicable methodologies and approaches?
  - Will the individuals to be assigned have relevant business or applications experience?
  - What is the quality and experience level of the management team to be assigned, and how long will they be committed to the contract?
- Level of commitment:
  - Is maintenance outsourcing a key business for the outsourcer firm?
  - Is there a corporate commitment in support of maintenance outsourcing, as evidenced by a corporate support staff, corporate tools and methodologies, adequate local support, and a general sense that this business is important to the firm?
- Personnel issues:
  - Does the outsourcer have an approach for absorbing the organization's employees if necessary? Does the approach protect these

employees' interests? Is it consistent with your organization's human resources policies?
- Phased approach to assuming responsibility:
  — Does the firm have a standard, proven approach for assuming total responsibility?
  — During the transition period, are tasks and responsibilities for them clearly delineated?
  — Are the costs for transition defined and attributed?
- Methodology for managing maintenance:
  — Does the supplier have a methodology that defines all the phases in the maintenance life cycle, all the tasks to be performed during these phases, and responsibilities for such tasks?
- Appropriate procedures:
  — Either as part of the methodology or as stand-alone tools, does the supplier have formal, documented procedures for managing service requests, testing, and quality assurance?
- Project management discipline and tools:
  — Is there a management control tool that tracks service requests and the tasks required to accomplish them?
  — Are regularly scheduled status reports defined and required?
  — Is level of service (discussed in more detail in the next section) tracked and reported on?
- Use of automated tools to improve performance and service:
  — Does the supplier bring to the job automated tools that support the maintenance team in analysis, documentation, and testing?

LEVEL OF SERVICE

An outsourcing arrangement, by definition, is different from typical contracting arrangements. The outsourcing supplier should assume greater responsibility for successful performance of the function being outsourced, sharing not only rewards but risks as well. The supplier should therefore be willing to provide services on a fixed-price basis.

First, however, the supplier and the contracting company need to agree on a level of service to be provided. The supplier can then guarantee the agreed-to level of service for a monthly fixed price.

The level of service should define minimal levels for each area; if additional services are needed, these can be contracted for at an additional fee. The service areas and some samples of service criteria include:

- Responsiveness to production rescue:
  — hours for providing production rescue
  — approach to off-hours coverage
  — speed of response to emergency maintenance
  — number of hours per month provided for production support

- Amount of work:
  — number of change requests completed
  — number of change requests by category
  — amount of work completed versus estimated
  — percentage of work completed on schedule
  — function points affected or changed
- Quality of work:
  — quality of delivered product (subjective)
  — meantime between failures
  — average number of incidents
  — average time to correct
  — failures per XXX lines of code

STEPS FOR INITIATING AN OUTSOURCING ARRANGEMENT

When initiating a maintenance outsourcing arrangement, a structured approach, with discrete predefined activities and events, is advised to ensure optimal results.

Identifying a Pilot System. In undertaking the first such initiative, it is prudent to begin with a pilot. The size of the pilot project has to be large enough to make it worthwhile for the outsourcing supplier, but from the standpoint of the user organization, starting with a pilot minimizes risk and allows the organization to devote the resources necessary to ensure success. A pilot system also provides enough information that can be used to evaluate whether the effort should be extended to additional systems.

Identifying Potential Suppliers. Although there are always advantages to soliciting several suppliers to bid, there may also be significant benefits in dealing with a single supplier. If there is a firm that meets the criteria (such as outlined previously), is familiar with the systems in question, and with whom there is an existing positive relationship, these benefits may override the advantages of competitive bidding.

Assessing the Systems Environment. A major activity is conducting an assessment of the existing environment. Some of the issues to be addressed during this assessment include:

- defining the scope and size of the system
- evaluating the quality (e.g., stability, maintainability) of the systems
- assessing service requests and backlog history and trends
- evaluating presence and quality of procedures
- determining current level of user satisfaction

This assessment provides the baseline for:

- defining (with the supplier) the level of service desired or required

- developing a fixed-price bid
- determining required staff levels (during transition and beyond)
- identifying opportunities for improving the environment

Determining Feasibility. Based on the results of the assessment, the feasibility of outsourcing can be evaluated. Are there opportunities for improvement? Is there reason to believe that an outside supplier with existing procedures, tools, and methodologies can be more successful? Are there issues that might preclude outsourcing?

Defining Level of Service. Using the findings of the assessment, a minimum level of service should be defined for each of the relevant categories (e.g., production support, enhancements, user support).

Soliciting and Evaluating Proposals. Using the qualitative and quantitative data uncovered during the assessment, the next step is to solicit proposals from the identified suppliers. These proposals should include the desired level of service and a fixed-price bid should be requested, based on this service level. In addition, the user organization must request pricing parameters for effort to be supplied over and above the minimum level of service. Proposals should also include plans for transition and the requirements to be imposed on the contracting firm, both during and after transition.

Reaching an Understanding. On the basis of the proposal of the selected vendor, the relationship with the vendor, and the benefits desired, the contractual agreement must be negotiated. (Pertinent issues relating to the contract are discussed in more detail in the next section.)

Initiating the Pilot Outsourcing Effort. In addition to the steps required to initiate and phase-in the outsourcing arrangement, monitoring and tracking procedures should be defined in advance. These procedures should be designed to allow an evaluation of the success of the effort and to support a decision on whether the desired benefits were achieved. This work will help the organization decide whether to continue the arrangement or even extend outsourcing to additional systems.

THE CONTRACT

Under a partnership approach, the contract should not be viewed as the sole means for holding each party to its obligations. A strong partnership relationship, in which each organization has incentives to strive for a common goal, is far more likely to yield successful results. That said, in the end, the contract is the vehicle for articulating and reviewing what each party expects from the other, and there are several key issues to review.

Thoroughness and comprehensiveness. As the vehicle for ensuring that everyone understands and agrees to the terms and obligations, the contract should be as comprehensive as possible, defining all pertinent issues. It must discuss the obligations of each party, costs, duration, terms, and conditions. Care should be given to anticipating future needs as well as those known up-front. Where it may be premature to resolve or even discuss an issue, the contract can include language on how and when the issue will be raised and resolved.

Flexibility. Although the contract should be explicit about issues known at the outset, it must provide flexibility for future situations. The contract can be viewed as a set of master terms and conditions, with details about the specific work required, and the compensation for that work, treated as additional components. Each system to be maintained could have a separate component defining its level of service and associated fixed price. Additional work to be defined during the course of the arrangement can be dealt with in additional components, without requiring renegotiation of the underlying contract. Unanticipated events can be treated the same way.

Duration. Although the supplier will require a minimum timeframe to make the effort worthwhile, there also needs to be some escape clause in case the effort does not work out as envisioned. This can be accomplished through objective criteria for termination (where possible), payments to the vendor to compensate for early termination, and lead time for termination.

Incentive. The contract should be structured so that the supplier has an incentive to improve the environment. When the supplier can share in the benefit, there is an incentive to improve the stability or maintainability of the systems through restructuring, reengineering, or improved documentation. Such improvements can provide benefits to the contracting organization through better customer service or reduced cost of processing.

RECOMMENDED COURSE OF ACTION

The use of maintenance outsourcing can help a user organization achieve its strategic objectives. Such an arrangement relieves management of many of the day-to-day burdens of maintenance and thus allows management to dedicate more attention to strategic activities. Redeployment of IS staff currently assigned to maintenance can enhance the size and quality of staff assigned to new development activities. Reduction of maintenance costs can support increased expenditures in strategic development activities.

To achieve these potential benefits, management should adhere to the following steps:

- *Developing a plan to guide the activities*. This involves identifying a set of activities to be pursued, responsibilities for all tasks, and key decision criteria. The benefits desired should be defined in advance so that ongoing monitoring can determine whether the desired benefits are being achieved.

- *Defining the baseline.* An outsourcing assessment is necessary to define the existing environment from both a quantitative and a qualitative perspective. When this is accomplished, key objectives can be defined.
- *Defining a desired level of service using the findings of the assessment.* Level of service is of paramount importance in selecting a supplier, in establishing a fixed price, and in evaluating ongoing performance.
- *Selecting a maintenance outsourcing supplier.* The selection must be made carefully and wisely, ensuring that the supplier has the required credentials, experience, and tools and resources. It may be best to select a firm with whom the organization is already comfortable or with whom it feels confident it can develop a partnership relationship.
- *Exercising due diligence in establishing contract terms and ongoing expectations.* At the same time, it is vital to recognize that a partnership approach or philosophy holds the greatest promise for success. Maintaining the concept of partnership during the contract process provides the opportunity to structure an arrangement that can foster an environment of shared risk as well as shared benefits.
- *Monitoring performance and results on an ongoing basis.*

Chapter 15
Support Services Outsourcing
William J. Beaumont

MANY IS ORGANIZATIONS STRUGGLE TO CONTROL the skyrocketing costs associated with desktop assets. Companies that have traditionally relied on large, distributed systems as the backbone of their information systems are increasingly dependent on desktop systems. Although the use of desktop computers has grown dramatically, only recently have PCs and LANs been entrusted with mission-critical tasks. This new dependence on PCs has created certain problems resulting from the fact that PCs and LANs do not have the centralized support infrastructure that data centers had.

GROWING UP WILD

Desktop systems have evolved in an undisciplined fashion, with few central controls and often with little central planning. This is not surprising, because most PCs started out as personal productivity tools — calculators were replaced by spreadsheets and typewriters by word processors. Computers became the tools of office task automation by virtue of the explosion of computing power, made possible through chip development and aided by sophisticated software.

Business managers purchased desktop computers without much coordination with legacy systems and often with only ad hoc guidance from the IS professionals running the data center. There was no standard PC platform, no standard for support, and usually little or no centralized management of desktop systems. Thus, the support underlying desktop technology has been a multilayered jumble in some organizations.

For years, everyone from technologists to business managers was preoccupied with buying equipment, installing it, integrating it with existing systems, and linking it with the necessary cabling and adapters. Often, PCs are not adequately administered, and this lack of coordination results in duplicated services, resources, and expertise, as well as difficulty in implementing standards and applying systems management tools.

THE TWO-HEADED MONSTER: COST AND CONTROL

As a business tool, a computer helps users increase productivity by performing tasks cheaper, better, and faster than alternate methods; if it does not, it is not worth buying. After all costs are counted — purchase, installation, operator training, and support — the computer should save the organization money. The purchase of desktop units must pass the same test that every business expenditure must pass: the purchase should generate a return on investment. Fortune recently reported that only 20 percent of all CIOs believe they are obtaining a return on their IT investment.

Total Cost of Ownership. Whether or not a piece of equipment is a sound investment depends partly on what the cost is and how it is measured. For the past decade, The Gartner Group has compiled data on a measuring concept now widely adopted by the IT industry known as Total Cost of Ownership (TCO). TCO is defined as the total cost of the computer asset, including the hard costs of purchasing hardware plus the soft costs of labor associated with supporting and maintaining the asset.

As much as 85 percent of a PC's total cost of ownership is associated with soft costs, which can be as much as $10,000 per machine, per year. The TCO of a typical desktop PC is now approximately $44,000 over the PC lifecycle (i.e., a period of five years).

Gartner has been tracking costs using its TCO model since 1987. In that time, five-year costs have jumped more than 135 percent. A fully networked PC is even more expensive at approximately $11,900 per node, per year for hardware, software, support, administrative services, and end-user operations.

Although processors are now extremely fast for a great deal less than before, increases in labor costs have been massive. Administrative expenditures have quadrupled and those for end users have doubled, prompting the urgent need to bring distributed computing costs under control.

INTEGRATION OF DESKTOP SUPPORT SERVICES

The only way to control the escalating costs of desktop computing is through greater coordination of desktop support services, since that is where the majority of corporate IT money is spent. Any company hoping to gain control of its IT environment must be able to measure and justify all of the expenses associated with end-user computing.

This justification can best be achieved with a fully integrated desktop management solution for identifying, controlling, and reducing TCO, which should include ways to analyze improvement plans, implement optimization plans, and audit results to ensure that reductions are being achieved.

Savings of several thousand dollars per PC can be achieved by organizations committed to a serious, companywide cost-reduction effort. Even greater savings are possible — from 25 percent to as much as 50 percent — when the effort is managed at the enterprise level.

Outsourcing Support Services

The need for third-party support services continues to grow at a rapid pace as companies struggle to keep up with growing user demands within multivendor, multiplatform environments. Soft costs are escalating beyond affordable rates, making outsourcing of support services a more efficient and practical way of supporting employees. In addition, outsourcing these services allows companies to focus on business issues at hand instead of addressing individual problems that could be handled more effectively by another party.

The increase in outsourcing support services can largely be attributed to complex processing environments. IT managers are challenged by the sophistication of today's networks and application software, the shortage of skills needed to support their users, and increased pressure from day-to-day business issues. It has become more difficult for even the largest in-house support center to stay abreast of new applications and technologies to support their own base of users and keep them satisfied.

Mixed PC/workstation environments spend more than $400 per user, per year on problem resolution. Multiplied throughout an organization with hundreds or thousands of users, the cost of providing effective support becomes prohibitive.

Third-party organizations that focus on support services can leverage their investments in technology and staffing across a broad base of clients to obtain economies of scale that allow them to provide cost-effective solutions. A single point of contact to handle multiple support issues, ranging from software applications through operating systems through hardware problems, has become a more cost-effective way to resolve problems on a per-user basis.

The most practical solution helps customers optimize their investments in IT by taking on some or all support tasks facing overwhelmed, under-budgeted IS staffs. This allows IS to focus on strategic functions such as developing new systems and introducing new technology that benefits their businesses.

The third-party service provider should be:

- **A single source to consult for product management.** The vendor should singlehandedly coordinate workgroup management across the enterprise.
- **Vendor neutral.** The third party should support all brands and harbor no product bias.

- **Simple to deal with.** The third-party service should be a virtual extension of in-house support.
- **Low risk.** The vendor selected should have an established track record.
- **Able to produce concrete, measurable benefits.** Third-party providers should be able reduce costs, enhance control, maximize systems availability, and increase end-user satisfaction.

A STRATEGIC, COMPREHENSIVE APPROACH TO CONTROLLING COSTS

Most customers need a strategy for controlling costs at the desktop, including the following integrated services.

Planning and Consulting Services. Planning support services help customers define their environments, set targets for improvement, and monitor progress against plans. These services should be offered either as a one-time service or used over the course of a project.

Consultants should be used on ad hoc projects. Sometimes the greatest value of outside consultants is having an independent, unbiased party review internal operational reports or organizational approaches to problems.

Hardware Services. Both remedial and preventive maintenance, with optional on-site staff support, should be provided for a variety of products. Almost every desktop unit undergoes at least one or two changes per year. Moves, adds, and changes to any system should be supported, providing a comprehensive solution.

Asset Management Services. Asset management contributes to service effectiveness in large organizations. Accurate information is vital to cost control. Companies that engage in IT asset management stand to reap significant savings and boost end-user productivity.

An effective asset management service inventories a customer's IT environment and creates an asset database through a combination of automated and manual data collection activities. Once completed, the database should contain information detailing the customer's IT assets from several perspectives including hardware, software, end users, location, and cost centers.

To ensure that all facts are up-to-date, it is a good idea for a client support team to apply specialized software to probe the network for new, moved, or changed devices and see that all changes are captured in the database. Periodic audits of the IT environment should be performed.

End-User Support Services (Help Desk). End-user support services, more commonly known as the help desk, aid users with the navigation and resolution of computer technology questions, as well as supporting hardware, software, and system-related activities. Services should meet the growing needs of multivendor processing environments, offering new solutions that are flexible to a customer's needs.

End-user support services should include:

- **Call management.** Support should include a problem triage service.
- **Basic end-user support.** The service should support popular shrink-wrapped applications.
- **Network end-user support.** Network operating systems should be supported.
- **Customized support.** The service should be able to support unique software packages often found in particular industries.
- **Advanced product support.** Complex software, such as Lotus Notes, should be supported.

Network Support Services. IS organizations spend approximately 40 percent of their time on networking issues and 60 percent of their tools budget on network management.

A customer's environment should be remotely monitored 24 hours a day, seven days a week, to improve costs, boost user productivity, and increase systems availability. Round-the-clock monitoring allows for the identification of potential trouble spots and enhances network performance by helping to highlight areas for improvement.

Program Management. Some customers need support for individual projects or complete management of their desktop environment. In either case, a tailored program should be designed, allowing companies to focus their resources on their core competencies.

Support Partner Services. When a customer requires additional services such as leasing, procurement, or disaster recovery, it is ideal if the vendor can respond with an integrated solution through support partners. These preferred vendor relationships offer quick, comprehensive responses to a customer's business requirements.

THE SOLUTION IS AT HAND

Technology is changing at a rapid pace, and companies are struggling to come to grips with managing their desktop assets. They are seeking innovative solutions to lowering the total cost of ownership of their IT environment.

To improve operational performance, service and support must be integrated. A tightly integrated suite of services to support desktop systems is the best solution for controlling the exploding costs of desktop computing.

Chapter 16
Outsourcing the Help Desk Function

Fritz H. Grupe

DESPITE THE DEBATE OVER THE PRODUCTIVITY PARADOX, corporate managers appear confident that their IT investments yield a significant return. They continue to acquire and use computers and their attendant peripherals and networks at an accelerating pace. Not surprisingly, investments in help desk-related goods and services are estimated to be increasing from 25 to 50 percent nationwide.

FACTORS DRIVING THE TREND TO OUTSOURCE THE HELP DESK

A major component of the IT outsourcing industry centers on the help desk arena. The following considerations drive this development:

- business size
- performance
- cost accounting
- service demands
- business needs
- staff development

Business Size. Some businesses are too small to provide adequate staff support. Although such businesses deploy as wide a variety of systems, software packages, and networks as their larger counterparts and encounter an equal number of related problems, they have fewer resources with which to resolve problems. Outsourcing offers these businesses a range of service options delivered in a professional manner. For example, an outsourcer specializing in help desk operations can acquire and implement expensive support tools that facilitate end-user support but are not cost-effective when implemented by small companies.

Performance. There is little doubt that outsourcing is sometimes viewed as an alternative to what are perceived as ineffective, unresponsive IS departments. Help desks are challenged by a host of difficulties, including high turnover, poorly trained staff, improperly motivated staff, staff recruitment problems, and unsatisfactory problem tracking. Understaffed help desks often service end users reactively and fail to offer proactive solutions through training and end-user documentation.

Cost Accounting. In-house help desk operations are frequently budgeted as general expense overhead. This form of budgeting does not encourage judicious use of help desk resources. An outsourcing arrangement developed around a chargeback system focuses attention on the cost of unnecessary services. Services must be priced realistically so that the so-called "underground network" does not shift the workload away from the help desk to unskilled and inefficient co-workers whose time does not appear on an expense sheet.

Service Demands. Some companies use outsourcing vendors to provide specific services for the in-house help desk, such as coverage for peak periods, nonbusiness hours, special constituencies, or specific problem areas.

Business Needs. Some companies need to downsize while focusing on their core specialties. Outsourcing the help desk function offers a means of transferring the funds committed to positions that are not highly valued to the acquisition of a higher quality service. The strategy of converting fixed costs into variable costs holds promise of reduced overall expenditures.

In addition, IS managers in companies experiencing a rapid growth curve may not have the time to properly staff, train, and equip a help desk. In spite of the help desk's importance in enabling end users to fully utilize mission-critical applications, the help desk is not a mission-critical function. Many companies that outsource the help desk function do so simply to avoid the necessity of staffing and managing such a unit while expanding their services. Considerable savings of management time are realized when scheduling, training, hiring, and coordination are offloaded to an outsourcing vendor.

Staff Development. Help desk positions are not considered a highly desirable career goal. An outsourcer can provide employees with more extensive training opportunities and establish career paths within its management structure. Outsourcers may also have more opportunities to move promising staff into positions unrelated to help desk operations.

OUTSOURCING OPTIONS

Managers reviewing their help desk needs and the best way to address them should consider four options in respect to outsourcing. Selection of the most appropriate model depends, of course, on individual company circumstances.

1. *Insourced help desk.* An organization with adequate resources or a high inventory of in-house developed systems may find it most effective to staff the help desk entirely with its own employees.
2. *Outsourced help desk.* In this model, a firm specializing in help desk operations provides all help desk services.
3. *Hybrid help desk operations.* In the hybrid model, the organization provides some of the help desk employees and the outsourcing firm provides others. This model offers several flexible service options. Companies can outsource support for shrinkwrap applications only and use the internal help desk for legacy and proprietary systems. Or, they can contract the first level of support and retain support for more substantial problems. The reverse strategy is also possible.
4. *Provision of supplementary support tools.* In this model, outsourcing vendors provide prebuilt expert systems, case-based reasoning tools, and automated text-retrieval systems (e.g., hypertext and indexing systems) to enhance the help desk staff's access to up-to-date information.

Substantial numbers of help desk outsourcing arrangements have been implemented. Following are some of the more illustrative examples.

Taco Bell. The Store Operations Support Project (SOS Taco) is a partnership between Taco Bell and PricewaterhouseCoopers. SOS provides assistance on inventory, staff scheduling, point-of-sale data gathering, and other back-office operations for more than 4100 sites in the United States. and abroad. PricewaterhouseCoopers provides nearly 20 part-time and full-time supplementary staff for the help desk during high demand periods and night shifts. This group augments a much smaller Taco Bell support group, creating an in-house core of people who can network with other Taco Bell employees on development activities. Pricewaterhouse Coopers provides each employee with four weeks of training. The help desk handles in excess of 20,000 calls each month.

Novell, Inc. This well-known vendor of networking and other software provides outsourced support services to Dallas-based CompuCom Systems, Inc. The agreement merged three help desk operations into one and serves some 6000 employees at four main sites.

Microsoft Corp. When Microsoft needed help in supporting new users of Windows 95, it contracted with Boston-based Keane, Inc., to set up a help desk with 350 support personnel. The Keane help desk group augmented Microsoft's existing telephone hot-line staff.

SELECTING A HELP DESK OUTSOURCER

Given the options for operating a help desk organization, the process of selecting an outsourcing vendor seems daunting. With forethought, proper information gathering, and careful planning, however, the process of identifying the right outsourcer becomes straightforward. The exercise of gathering requirements and current customer support information is both informative and the key to ensuring that the outsourcer provides the correct type and level of service. These requirements are specified in a request for proposal (RFP) and become the basis for evaluating outsourcing vendors and negotiating the service level agreement.

It is important to be honest with potential vendors about support requirements and company-specific idiosyncrasies. Working as a team with the vendor results in a win–win outsourcing arrangement. The following six steps provide guidance on how to achieve this arrangement.

Step One: Developing Help Desk Requirements

The critical first step of any help desk outsourcing venture is gathering the information needed to develop accurate requirements for the new or improved help desk facility. Clear objectives and accurate requirements greatly enhance the ability of the outsourcer to develop an offer that matches company expectations. Conversely, a lack of accurate information results either in an overpriced bid designed to ensure that the vendor's risks are covered or in an underpriced bid that inhibits the vendor from meeting service expectations. Experienced help desk consultants, who can quickly assess the current environment and facilitate goal development, can provide valuable assistance during this first step.

The process of developing help desk requirements involves determining outsourcing objectives, project scope, and in the case of an existing help desk, current performance.

Determining Goals and Objectives. An organization must determine the goals of its help desk and why outsourcing is under consideration. Is the goal to implement a new help desk, increase the efficiency of an existing operation, or follow the company's strategic plan to outsource nonmission-critical functions? After general goals are established, the following more specific objectives are set:

- level of coverage or hours of operation
- level of responsiveness
- customer-satisfaction criteria

Determining Project Scope. If the goal is to outsource an existing help desk operation, information on the scope and size of the outsourcing project is gathered by examining current resource use. The existing operation, particularly the procedures and tools used, should be thoroughly documented, and statistical information to determine call volumes and peak periods should be captured. If the goal is to implement a new help desk, outside assistance is particularly helpful during this phase. Specific scoping tasks include:

- describing current processes, software tools, and equipment
- calculating service capacity
- determining call volumes
- determining average length per call
- identifying peak-period support requirements
- describing the range of applications and products to be supported
- calculating current costs
- calculating support staff costs
- calculating facilities and equipment costs
- documenting skill requirements

Determining Current Performance. An accurate picture of the current level of performance is important for determining the service level agreement, especially if service level improvement is a goal of the outsourcing effort. Performance statistics should be captured as part of standard help desk operations. Key questions to ask include:

- What is the average wait in queue?
- How many calls are resolved on first contact?
- What are the average response times by category of calls?
- What is the call abandon rate?
- Is there a backlog of open problems?

Step Two: Determining the Appropriate Outsourcing Model

Once the goals, scope, and performance objectives are determined, the appropriate outsourcing model is selected. One fundamental question is whether to outsource the function or the solution. When an outsourcing vendor assumes the support function, the systems and processes currently in place are replicated. This approach has the advantage of appearing seamless to help desk customers. Outsourcing the complete solution allows the outsourcer to reengineer the operation as required to provide the optimum level of service. Other issues that must be decided include whether to outsource the entire help desk or only portions of the operation, to use on-site or off-site support, or to purchase support as part of a shared help desk function.

Step Three: Formulating a Request for Proposal

Once the groundwork has been completed, the next task is to create a request for proposal. This document is the prime communication vehicle used to solicit bids from outsourcing vendors. Although each situation is unique, experience has shown that an RFP should contain several basic sections:

- *Overview.* The overview section describes the objectives for the outsourcing project and lists the reasons for creating the RFP.
- *Background.* This section describes the company's business, mission, locations, and organizational structure.
- *General requirements.* The general requirements section, often the largest section of the RFP, describes guidelines for proposals, a time schedule for the evaluation, contract terms, and the logistical requirements for the project.
- *Required service levels and volume forecast.* This section is used to describe the expected quality results and projected volumes. It delineates current service levels and minimum acceptable service levels.
- *Selection method.* This section describes the criteria and method for choosing the outsourcing vendor. A partial list of possible selection criteria includes company stability, management organization, flexibility, facilities, service capabilities, training, price, implementation plan, and references. The selection criteria should be ranked by priority.

Step Four: Evaluating Vendors

The evaluation process begins as vendors respond to the RFP with their own proposals. If numerous vendors respond to the RFP, a cursory evaluation of the responses may be sufficient to eliminate marginal vendors. A more thorough evaluation of the remaining proposals is needed to determine the vendor's comprehension of company requirements and the quality of the proposed solution. This evaluation include several steps.

Reviewing Proposals. Proposals should be evaluated with an evaluation matrix containing the evaluation attributes, their weighting, and a column for each vendor. Each vendor's solution is ranked for each attribute on a scale of from 1 to 10. These scores are then adjusted by the appropriate weighting factor and added to produce an overall company score. Exhibit 16-1 depicts a sample evaluation matrix with recommended evaluation attributes. Key questions to ask include:

- Does the proposed solution meet the objectives described in the RFP?
- Does the vendor have the experience and resources to implement the solution?
- Does the vendor have a formal methodology for help desk support?
- What is the vendor's reputation for meeting service commitments?
- Does the vendor have a reasonable implementation or transition plan for phasing in the outsourcing service?
- Is the vendor's pricing in line with the level of services provided?

Visiting the Vendor and Checking References. It is prudent to evaluate the veracity of vendor claims by checking references and visiting one of the vendor's help desk facilities. Although references are helpful, a visit to an

Exhibit 16-1. Sample vendor evaluation matrix.

Category/ Attribute	Weight	Vendor 1		Vendor 2		Vendor 3	
		Raw Score	Weighted Score	Raw Score	Weighted Score	Raw Score	Weighted Score
Company							
Reputation	4	10	40	5	20	7	28
Financial Stability	5	10	50	6	30	7	35
Quality Programs	8	6	48	10	80	7	56
Flexibility	12	10	120	8	96	6	72
Location	4	3	12	5	20	10	40
Staffing Ability	8	10	80	6	48	8	64
RFP Compliance	4	6	25	7	28	7	28
Employee Practices	5	10	50	5	25	4	20
Total Company	50	65	425	52	347	56	343
Services							
Comprehension	6	7	42	8	48	9	54
Solution	4	8	32	7	28	6	24
Methodology	9	10	90	8	72	8	72
Management	3	7	21	6	18	5	15
Technology	1	7	7	7	7	5	5
Implementation Plan	2	8	16	5	10	5	10
Total Services	25	47	208	41	183	38	180
Price							
Price Score	20	5	100	10	200	8	160
Risk/Reward	5	7	35	0	0	2	10
Total Price	25	12	135	10	200	10	170
Total Score			768		730		693

operational help desk is the most effective way of gaining insight into the vendor's practices. IS managers should be sure to examine the support procedures in action and talk to help desk clients about their support satisfaction. Examining customer survey results is another good source of this information.

Step Five: Selecting a Vendor

Carefully following the selection process just described simplifies final vendor selection, because it is likely that one vendor more clearly meets requirements than others. IS managers should take care, however, not to let price alone determine the outcome of the selection process. Although price is an important consideration, lower price alone may not provide the highest value. Managers must carefully weigh price with other considerations, such as service levels, to identify the vendor that provides the highest value per support dollar.

Although precise criteria for evaluating outsourcing vendors depends on the nature of an individual contract, some general areas of evaluation common to all help desk outsourcing vendors are not covered by the contract. Weightings for each of these criteria should also be developed according to individual organizational needs. A list of such criteria follows:

- How much experience has the vendor had with help desk operations? How many other contracts has the vendor implemented? Does the vendor have positive references? How well has the vendor adhered to the letter and the spirit of previous ventures? Does the vendor use effective project management skills? When contractual problems have arisen, have they been handled smoothly and to each party's mutual benefit?
- Is the vendor's staff capable of providing the required support? Can the vendor's staff handle all of the application programs, programming environments, and networking systems present and implement sophisticated knowledge bases of previous problems solved, interactive voice response systems, call center operations, automated support tools, voice and e-mail, and statistical programs? Will the vendor be able to recruit, train, retrain, and retain qualified staff who have the depth of specialization to meet difficult, company-specific problems?
- Does IS know who the outsourcer's project manager will be? Are résumés of key players available? What is the degree of their involvement?
- Is the vendor stable financially and managerially? Does it have the funding and the managerial competence to survive? Does the vendor have some knowledge of the company's business and can its people adapt to the types of employees in the company? Does the vendor have the resources to remain competitive in the outsourcing arena?
- Will the relationship with the vendor be synergistic? In other words, will the vendor realize anything other than financial gain from the partnership? Will the vendor make the commitment to form a productive relationship that gives the company a competitive advantage?
- Can the outsourcer's personnel be trusted to exercise confidentiality regarding sensitive issues such as business objectives, technology plans, and business data? Is the vendor open to changing modes of operation to fit the corporate culture? Can the vendor's staff be seamlessly transitioned into the company's operations?

Step Six: Defining the Contract and Negotiating Terms

The final step in the outsourcing selection process is the definition and negotiation of the terms by which both parties in the outsourcing agreement function. It is crucial to ensure that all terms used to describe the help desk operation are clearly defined, because assumptions about the meanings of terms such as calls, problems, and incidents can lead to contractual nightmares.

A clearly defined contract helps control the costs of outsourcing by providing an accurate description of which cost items are included in the arrangement as well as the items that need to be assessed for demand measures. A distinctly outlined contract also provides vendors with a sharper definition of what services they have to provide and less opportunity for hedging cost estimates.

Despite the need for a clear contract, it is important that both parties be ready to modify their means and ends as the outsourcing relationship emerges and develops. Not all aspects of the contract are foreseeable. Following are some of the issues the contract should define.

Coverage Areas. The contract should specify which hardware and software is to be supported and whether support pertains to industrywide products and services or to company-specific legacy systems that require greater support.

Service Level Agreements. The evaluation criteria specified in the service level agreement include the types of response times and successful completion rates to be used to rate service as being above, at, or below average. Hours of operation should also be delineated, as should the expected volume of calls and any actions to be taken if the number exceeds or fails to meet expectations.

Other issues that need to be determined include which types of calls are considered top priority and which can be delayed, acceptable response times, and whether the calls/requests for assistance can be categorized by length of time needed for a response and by complexity. Finally, the predictability of the call distribution throughout the day must be considered.

Reporting. It is essential that explicit quality control measures be in place, such as periodic, planned review sessions. The group or individual overseeing the contract must address several questions, such as:

- What statistical and other types of reports are needed and what types of data will gathered for use in these reports?
- What logs and tracking systems must be in place? Must they track abandoned calls and the length of time spent waiting for pickup and response?

- Will calls be monitored on a selective basis?
- Who is able to conduct call monitoring?

Determination of Service Adequacy. It is important to delineate which measures will be used to determine whether the help desk is succeeding. Available methods include end-user satisfaction surveys and help desk statistics.

Staffing and Scheduling. The contract should address the issues of how many and what types of support personnel are expected to be available and the hours during which they will be available. Procedures for escalating problems to more experienced personnel when initial contacts are unable to provide resolution should also be specified.

The contract must obviously deal with issues relating to hybrid work situations, such as how personnel problems will be managed and whether the necessity for co-workers to function under two different salary schedules and personnel policies will prove problematic. Finally, the contract should stipulate whether and for how long the outsourcing vendor is expected to employ organizational staff.

Implementation. Service implementation should specify how the service will be initiated and how a transition to full operation should be accomplished. One vendor conducted a preliminary test of the outsourced help desk system by preparing several hundred calls that tested whether adequate escalation procedures, automated systems, consulting skills, and other processes were in place. Access to the help desk by corporate users was initiated only after adequate test results were achieved.

Location. The contract must specify whether calls can be received and assistance provided from a distance or on-site. If onsite support is provided, the number of sites needing such support must be specified. Finally, the availability and use of alternative means of communication such as fax or electronic bulletin boards should be included.

Equipment. The area of equipment involves numerous and broad issues relating to both hardware and software. For example, the contract must specify whether software for logging and tracking problem resolution is needed, on whose machine the software will reside, and who holds the license and owns the data. The availability of other software, such as e-mail, corporate groupware, proprietary software, and change management software, should be addressed.

Other issues include stipulation of needed telephone systems, use of artificial intelligence packages and whether their contents (e.g., rules, cases, and problems) will be provided immediately or built up over time according to the company's own experience, and use of interactive voice response systems. The contract should also address whether help desk staff will operate end-user equipment such as printers, training laboratories, or general purpose workstation facilities.

Termination and Renegotiation. In addition to stating an expiration date, the contract should cover mediation or arbitration procedures. It should also delineate the exit procedure following termination. Other items for consideration include where automated software used for accumulating knowledge will reside after the contract period.

Payment and Costs. The contract must delineate total costs as well as the payment method. If a chargeback system will be used, its costing structure should specify whether the chargeback is by call, size of the user base, problem category, or a blanket fee. Bonuses or penalties for the vendor's success or failure to meet objectives such as increased first-call problem resolution or degree of customer satisfaction must also be specified.

Change Service Orders. Workloads are rarely fixed or entirely predictable. The contract must therefore state how additional costs for a changing workload or the addition of new functions will be levied.

OUTSOURCING PROBLEMS AND PITFALLS

Several potential problems can derail a help desk outsourcing effort. The following sections discuss some of them.

Losing Track of Long-Term Goals. Outsourcing should be a long-term relationship. Short-term goals such as immediate cost savings or correcting a staff turnover problem may have a high initial profile but are misleading in the long run.

Selecting an Unqualified Outsourcer. As is the case with many technology-oriented firms, specialization exists in the help desk arena. Not all companies are equally equipped to effectively handle outsourcing. Some firms have extensive experience in selecting support tools, specialists who can address complex issues, and regularly trained staff. They also have a track record of building mutually beneficial partnerships with their clients based on financial stability, technical skills inventory, and management competence.

Failing to Consider All Contractual Consequences. An organization outsourcing its help desk cannot simply accept a proposed standard contract. Managers must fully understand the implications of the outsourcing decision and why specific services are being outsourced, as well as the effects of altered conditions such as corporate growth or stagnation, addition of functions, and other organizational changes on the help desk.

Assuming that a Contract Will Administer Itself. Signing an outsourcing contract does not end management responsibilities. A qualified contract manager or group is essential for overseeing the implementation of the contract and ensuring that the vendor handles personnel issues appropriately, corrects problem areas, and provides appropriate reports.

Omitting Items from the Contract. When it comes to contracts, the sins of omission are at least as serious as the sins of commission. What is left out of a contract can be expensive to add on later.

Losing Staff Control. The offset of having the outsourcer do the hiring and firing is that the contractee has to work through the outsourcer to correct problems. Because the outsourcer may choose or be forced to reassign people in its organization, the contractee may suffer from a higher turnover of trained staff.

Encountering Resistance from IS Departments. Not only does the outsourcer replace IT staff, new staff members become part of the IT operation. As external observers become aware of internal problems, response rates, user attitudes, and backlogs, a great potential for conflict is created. When a hybrid arrangement is in effect, differences in pay scales, leave policies, and other personnel policies may become points of contention.

Setting Unrealistic Goals. Contract goals, however measured, should be realistic. Overly ambitious expectations of improvement may prove illusory and negate chances for improvement. For example, one vendor reported that an emphasis on first-call resolution hampered upper-level executives and their aides from receiving the help they needed. These people did not want to wait on the telephone while an answer to a help desk query was being developed. When the answer was ready, or when assistance could be provided on-site, the executives wanted to be contacted again.

CONCLUSION

As the number of end users has increased, so has the demand for help desk services. Although keeping end users productive is essential, organizations are finding it difficult to provide the breadth of support needed. Outsourcing all or part of the help desk function offers one alternative for providing services economically and effectively. Selecting an appropriate vendor and preparing a detailed contract are critical to the eventual success of such a partnership. Following the steps presented in this chapter will help IS managers accomplish both of these processes.

Chapter 17
Outsourcing Data Center Performance
John R. Vacca

TODAY'S DATA CENTERS ARE CHALLENGED to find highly flexible and manageable solutions to meet the quickly increasing demands, both financially and architecturally, of enterprise computing. As these external pressures to expand hardware and software services quickly increase, sites require a server solution that can grow flexibly to achieve these goals. Such a solution like outsourcing a data center's performance would generate larger revenues, improve response time and quality, expand customer services, and provide overall competitive advantages.

DATA CENTER PERFORMANCE ECONOMY OF SCALE ASSUMPTION

Often, economies of scales are used to determine outsourcing a data center performance decision. They do exist in a data center performance environment, as shown in the cost comparison chart in Exhibit 17-1. However, it is not safe to make quick or simple assumptions. A well-run 400 million instructions per second (MIPS) data center can outperform an 800 MIPS shop in an average monthly cost per MIPS comparison. In fact, over the last eight years, there have been some small data centers, on a unit cost basis, that can outperform data centers six to seven times their size. In theory, this should not occur; but in practice, better management can win out. Armed with this fact, the decision to outsource should not simply be a matter of data center size. The real trick is being armed with where your enterprise stands in a cost comparison. It should be noted that *best-of-breed* enterprises in each category outperformed anywhere from 6 to 36 percent below the average costs, as shown in Exhibit 17-1.

In addition, one should be aware of the trend existing in data center performance where average costs are declining overall by 16 to 21 percent annually. In light of this and the knowledge of the economies of scale, it is recommended that small data center clients (150 MIPS or less) should:

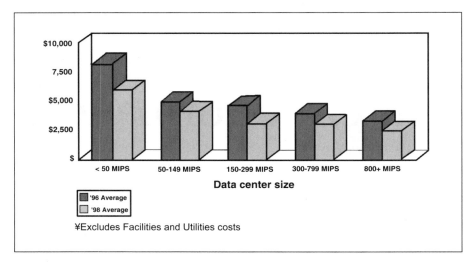

Exhibit 17-1. Monthly average cost per MIPS comparison.

1. be growing in size
2. consider changing platforms to reduce costs
3. consider outsourcing their center

It should be noted that enterprises must find a way to compare out-sourcing all functions of data center performance. Likewise, individual sub-process functions can be examined against costs at other similar-sized data centers. Many enterprises now are simply seeking to determine whether or not to outsource one or more functions such as enveloping, laser or impact printing, microfiche, tape operations, and help desk.

So, how good do you want your data center performance to be? Take a brief look.

HOW GOOD DO YOU WANT TO BE?

A recent PricewaterhouseCoopers survey of 539 high-growth enter-prises revealed some disquieting news. Over half of the enterprises sur-veyed were dissatisfied with the overall results of their outsourcing agree-ments. Things, they said, just did not get *better*.

As previously asked, how good do you want the data center perfor-mance to be? How much *better* does your data center performance need to be in order to stay competitive? One should know the answers to these questions before starting to plan an outsourcing relationship with data center's performance.

To measure what is *better*, one needs to understand what exists. To stay competitive, one needs to measure the enterprise against the *best of breed* of data center performance in the industry. This is where comparative analysis comes in. It allows one to determine the enterprise's own internal costs, quality, and performance levels, and compare those levels against the best of breed. If a wide gap is found, one has plenty of company. Out of all the four-years-and-longer-in-place outsourcing arrangements reviewed by Compass in 1998, only two were close to providing best-of-breed performance levels.

Armed with the comparative analysis information, one can determine whether outsourcing data center performance makes sense. If it does, one has what one needs to select an outsourcer and develop a win–win relationship.

How do you identify *best of breed?* By definition, best of breed:

- are identified by name, industry type, national or international location
- are among the top 11 percent of enterprises analyzed in terms of unit costs
- do not achieve efficiencies at the expense of clients or good enterprise practices
- have had analyses performed
- have high production quality
- are included regardless of industry or geographical location

With the comparative analysis, in hand, one knows the size of the gap between your enterprise and the best of breed. Now come the big questions. How much *better* can the situation be? Is there a true opportunity for an outsourcer to deliver cost and quality improvements to data center performance?

Then look at the question that goes straight to the bottom line. Can one negotiate an outsourcing agreement based on identified and achievable levels? The information gathered can serve as a guide. For example, if the current data center performance costs are $20 million a year, but an outsourcer offers a services contract for $18 million annually, that may seem like a good deal — unless one's information indicates that best-of-breed costs are only $16 million a year. Then it becomes obvious that one is leaving money on the table at the $18 million figure.

The baseline also serves another need. It can provide a record of any outsourcer's claims of achievements in performance, production, quality, or costs after the contract is established. Many relationships fail because of issues that arise when no accurate baseline was established in the beginning.

Comparative analysis is not a one-time process. A outsourcing data center performance contract should allow one to compare performance against the best of breed annually and provide recourse if the results stray beyond a defined acceptable level. This measurement can also establish bonus arrangements for outsourcers achieving better than best-of-breed levels.

Knowing how good one wants the outsourcing for the data center performance to be, what about planning for outsourcing beyond data center performance?

PLANNING FOR OUTSOURCING BEYOND DATA CENTER PERFORMANCE

Ah, the honeymoon stage of an enterprise relationship: that early stage when everyone is enthusiastic, when one envisions benefits that will continue to multiply, when one celebrates each small increment of success. One is focused on the objectives of the agreement. One talks frequently. One nips and tucks and shapes exactly the relationship needed.

Then, too often, time erodes the enthusiasm, and the excitement turns to exasperation. An outsourcing data center performance relationship, like every other enterprise relationship, runs that same risk of deterioration. Communication breaks down. Turnover eliminates key individuals from both the outsourcer and the client, and the original mission is lost. Amnesia sets in on both sides of the equation, and the frustration level grows dramatically.

The problem can be avoided. Outsourcing data center performance relationships can flourish long past the honeymoon stage if the dangers are anticipated and dealt with in the planning process. Communication and incentives for success are key to growing those long-term relationships.

The enterprise's outsourcing data center performance account team should focus daily on the mission at hand. The enterprise communicates clearly with the outsourcers throughout the evaluation and selection process, but that is only the beginning. Each month, both groups should convene to discuss last month's performance and what changes are anticipated for the next month.

These discussions provide a short-term measurement to monitor ongoing behavior. Benefits expected to be achieved over the length of the contract are reaffirmed, and progress toward delivering those benefits is measured. Just as each employee knows the price of company stock, everyone should know the status of the data center performance criteria.

Candid discussions are based on trust, and trust is essential in an outsourcing data center performance relationship. The outsourcer must be instrumental to success, so give their team the information they need. Drive home what the enterprise is all about. Be frank with issues facing the industry, both short and long term. Give them the tools they need to achieve or maintain the company's position as an industry leader.

Be clear about respective roles in the relationship. The enterprise determines *what* it wants to achieve. The outsourcer's primary focus is on *how* to achieve those goals. It is recommended that out-of-the-box thinking be encouraged for creative solutions.

That creative approach should also apply to the financial arrangements. It is a critical success factor that the outsourcer share in the benefits. The win–win relationship allows the outsourcer to increase their revenues when the company increases its revenues. That is what business is all about.

One recent trend is offering the outsourcer stock or stock options, so that they are truly rewarded and motivated to improve the company's bottom line. Another example of how the revenue sharing could work would be if the primary goal is lowering the cost of data center operations by reviewing budget versus actual costs at the end of the fiscal year. Establish a stair-step formula that allows the supplier to increase its share of revenue based on the overall savings.

Service level objectives are another critical parameter in this gain-sharing equation. If the annual surveys indicate that data center performance is satisfactory, then the cost reduction efforts did not hamper service and the supplier performed in an optimum fashion.

With awareness of the pitfalls and careful long-term planning to avoid them, one can keep the spark in the outsourcing data center performance relationship. Moreover, one can bring the outsourcer on board as an integral member of your team.

The message is clear. To turn an outsourcer into an asset, put them in the boat with you. Constantly provide them with the proper insight and concise enterprise objectives of why they were selected in the first place. And if one cannot turn the outsourcer into an asset, then one should not have outsourced the data center performance in the first place.

With that in mind, why outsource in the first place anyway?

WHY OUTSOURCE?

Some enterprises find that switching does not lower costs. Enterprises that are considering outsourcing to cut the cost of their IT operations may want to think again. A growing number of enterprises are finding that outsourcing data center performance does not necessarily lead to lower IT costs.

For example, Mobil Corp. and Ryerson Tull, Inc., decided there were no compelling financial reasons to outsource their data center performance. The comparative-analysis consulting firm, Compass America, Inc., has seen costs increase at 18 enterprises that have outsourced their data center performance for at least three years.

Reasons for the increases include vagueness in contracts, resulting in users getting nickel-and-dimed to death. In other cases, there is no mechanism in place to keep the vendor in line with the declining cost of computing.

Recently, none of the outsourcers that have been analyzed matched the performance of the best IT enterprises, especially in data center operations. Over the past six years, Compass client Mobil, for example, automated operations, reduced staffing, and improved work practices to cut costs by 79 percent — even as workload increased by 94 percent.

In data center performance, it is clear that Mobil is one of those enterprises that has been very successful in outsourcing. The oil enterprise also tapped GartnerMeasurement[1] (a division of The Gartner Group, Inc.) to benchmark Mobil's wide area networking and desktop computing.

Similarly, Ryerson Tull, Inc., found its IT operations very competitive when it considered outsourcing its data center performance to Computer Sciences Corp., EDS, IBM, or Lockheed Martin. Ryerson Tull, Inc., used analyses from G2R, Inc., an IT consulting firm in Mountain View, California, plus advice from Technology Partners, Inc., an outsourcing consulting firm in Houston, and from the law firm of Shaw, Pittman, Potts & Trowbridge in Washington.

Ryerson Tull, Inc., also considered outsourcing its data center performance because so many of its competitors — including Bethlehem Steel and British Steel — have outsourced. But after analysis, Ryerson Tull, Inc., concluded the outsourcers couldn't offer a competitive advantage.

Still, cost is not the only factor in IT data center performance outsourcing, and the outsourcing enterprise continues to thrive. For example, DuPont & Co. (based in Wilmington, Delaware) found that it would have to pay an outsourcer $60 million a year more than it spent internally to run its data centers. But DuPont's enterprise strategies demanded greater flexibility and speed from its IT enterprise than it could deliver alone.

Recently, DuPont (a chemicals and energy enterprise) signed off on outsourcing data center performance contracts valued at $6 billion with Computer Sciences and Andersen Consulting. While measurements of DuPont's data center performance and networking operations showed high levels of cost efficiency, the same could not be said for desktop computing and applications development. More importantly, DuPont was embarking on a major overseas expansion, and it did not seem that DuPont's IT groups would be able to support the expanded enterprise alone.

CONCLUSION

In conclusion, before deciding on an outsourcing data center performance agreement, conduct a comparative analysis of the enterprise against the *best of breed* in the industry. Determine whether a true opportunity exists for an outsourcer to deliver cost and quality improvements to the operation. Also, if one decides to go ahead with an outsourcing data center performance relationship, use the information gathered as a baseline for negotiating the agreement. One should also do a comparative analysis annually.

Furthermore, one should also avoid relationship deterioration by planning for the pitfalls. Next, schedule monthly meetings to reaffirm objectives and measure data center performance. Also, give the outsourcer financial incentives to succeed.

The final advice for enterprises looking to outsource: do not look to make quick or simple evaluations or decisions. Remember that outsourcing data center performance negotiations usually take a minimum of 14 months to finalize. The real trick is knowing where one's enterprise is in terms of *best-of-breed* performance and what the actual functional costs are. Armed with that knowledge, one will have an established baseline from which to negotiate should the enterprise decide to outsource the data center performance.

Notes

1. GartnerMeasurement's proven benchmark methodologies /provide quantitative and qualitative assessments of IT costs, data center performance, efficiency, and quality. It contains three units: Measurement Services, Benchmarking, and Best Practices. GartnerMeasurement enables continuous IT improvement by providing clients with measurement-related insight on the IT environment. This insight provides the opportunity for enhanced IT data center performance, by improving the bottom line and increasing enterprise value. The opportunity starts with an understanding of why, what, and how to measure IT, followed by comparative analyses, both internally and externally with peers, as well as exchanges for best practices in IT topics.

Addresses of Companies Mentioned in This Article

1. Compass America, Inc., 12007 Sunrise Valley Drive, Reston, VA 20191, 1999.
2. PricewaterhouseCoopers, 630 Fifth Avenue, 5th Floor, New York, NY, 10111, 1999.
3. Compass America, Inc., 12007 Sunrise Valley Drive, Reston, VA 20191, 1999.
4. Mobil Corporation, 3225 Gallows Road, Fairfax, VA 22037, 1999.
5. Ryerson Tull, Inc., 2621 W. 15th Place, Chicago, IL 60608, 1999.
6. Gartner Group Corporate Headquarters, 56 Top Gallant Road, Stamford, CN 06904, 1999.
7. Computer Sciences Corporation, 3170 Fairview Park Drive, Mailcode 242, Falls Church, VA 22042, 1999.
8. EDS Headquarters, 5400 Legacy Drive, Plano, TX 75024-3199, 1999.
9. International Business Machines Corporation, Corporate Offices, New Orchard Road, Armonk, NY 10504, 1999.
10. Lockheed Martin Corporation, 6801 Rockledge Dr., Bethesda, MD, 1999.
11. Bethlehem Steel Corporation, 1170 Eighth Ave., Bethlehem, PA 18016-7699, 1999.
12. British Steel plc, 9 Albert Embankment, London SE1 7SN, U.K., 1999.

Chapter 18
Application Service Providers

Leilani Allen

FOR THOSE WHO HAVE BEEN IN THE TECHNOLOGY FIELD FOR SOME TIME, the phrase "everything old is new again" is particularly meaningful today. One of the current hot concepts for managing information resources is that of the ASP (application service providers). This notion hearkens back literally to the early 1970s, when it was known as "time sharing." In those days, computers were expensive, and the expertise required to program and maintain them was scarce. Also, companies were not as dependent on computers as they are today. They might only have needed the computer to run month-end payrolls or inventory reports. So, rather than purchase an entire configuration, they purchased part of one. Much like the borrower who does not need a vacation home at the beach all year-round, but rather for two weeks in July, and decides on a time-share, so too could companies purchase just the computer power they needed when they needed it.

The time-share concept eventually diminished as computers dropped in price, and, especially, as companies went from batch to online processing. Once most users were accessing computers during most of the day, it became cost-effective to have one's own data center with one's own computer staff. That was the heyday of mainframe computing, as companies built proprietary applications designed for their specific needs.

Along came client/server, which helped decentralize computing and, in many cases, turned over the development of software and the management of computer hardware to the business units. Instead of a $20 million mainframe, a department could now buy a minicomputer, or server, for prices that easily fit into their budget. Everyone was gung-ho to create the latest and greatest client/server applications.

So what about the mainframe applications? Over time, a majority of industries standardized on a couple of operating system/subsystem choices, with IBM's MVS/ESA and CICS being the leading combination. Once this was accomplished, the care and feeding of the operating environment became largely generic. This meant that knowledge of the particular business was presumably no longer essential.

Thus began the era of *outsourcing*, when companies large and small outsourced their data center and their core applications to companies such as IBM, EDS, CSC, and a host of system integrators. Outsourcing was particularly welcome in the 1980s, when organizations sought to become "lean and mean," and eliminate all "unnecessary" headcount. How much easier it was to turn over the whole responsibility to someone else.

Outsourcing took at least three forms. The first model was to outsource all of information technology (IT) — network, hardware, and software development — keeping only a skeleton staff to manage the contract with the vendor, and do strategic technology analysis. The most common approach was to outsource the first two components but keep software development in-house, and thus more responsive to the particular business. A third approach was to turn to outsourcers (service bureaus) for specific applications such as accounting or payroll.

As usual, no technology solution is completely satisfactory. Companies soon found that the outsourcers often underbid the contract for the first one or two years of operation, but that, over time, the cost exceeded the original in-house installation. Also, many employees who really knew the applications were lost in the shuffle, making maintenance and enhancement a real challenge. Indeed, one of the reasons that the cost for Year 2000 (Y2K) remediation was so large was that so many people who had built the applications in the first place were no longer available.

Unfortunately, one of the downsides of outsourcing for the technology industry was that innovation in mainframe technology largely disappeared. The last thing an outsourcer wants is new and different technology to migrate their clients to.

Thus, outsourcing gave an indirect boost to client/server technology. Firms found that, with their core production (legacy) applications safely in the hands of outsourcers, the remaining IT staff was free to focus on strategic systems that utilized the newest technology. Significant innovation occurred at the level of departmental applications. True, with innovation came a lot of failures that gave client/server a bad reputation for awhile. As time passed, however, the client/server architectures became more stable and reliable, and IT became more skilled and knowledgeable in this technology as well.

Thus, today, there is a whole new layer of mission-critical production systems that are now built on client/server technology. They are often very complex, involving multiple servers and network connections. They are usually built upon databases that require special expertise to design and maintain. And, as before, there has been a good deal of standardization in the languages and tools used to create these systems.

This is another opportunity to outsource. Oracle Corporation President Larry Ellison has declared his firm to be the world's largest and fastest-growing ASP. He says, "The software industry is in the process of a huge change, a tectonic change. Software is on its way to becoming a service." And software companies are becoming service providers.

DEFINITION OF AN ASP

An ASP can be defined as a firm that implements and provides ongoing support of application software for customers on one or more computer platforms and networks. The term "ASP" was supposedly coined by International Data Corp. of Framingham, Massachusetts, in 1998 in a study on the future of outsourcing. By May of 1999, 25 companies had joined a newly formed ASP Industry Consortium. By November, 178 companies had joined. At the Consortium's first conference in Denver, almost all of the technology industry heavyweights spoke in favor of the concept.

For example, Compaq and Cable and Wireless (a United Kingdom-based telecommunications firm) announced a global network of data centers that would host applications, and provide help desk services, systems integration, and market strategy. On the software side, Microsoft unveiled Office Online to deliver its popular suite of productivity products to users across an Internet connection. Corel already rents WordPerfect for $9.95 per user per month, while Sun Microsystems began giving away its StarOffice suite last year. Indeed, Gene Banman, a Sun executive, says, "Hosted application services will replace boxed software sales altogether in the next decade."

Hardware vendors are equally enthusiastic. IBM is repositioning its venerable AS/400 minicomputer as an ASP platform. Hewlett-Packard and KPMG are working to build CyberCenters to host data warehouses. Novell, Inc. recently acquired Just-On, Inc., a Web-based file management business. PC maker Acer, Inc., in Taiwan is partnering with software giant Computer Associates in Islandia, New York, to offer ASP services. Cisco Systems and Sun Microsystems are developing standards and practices guidelines for ASPs, including a certification program.

The latter point is particularly important. Just as there were no strict rules about the services that an outsourcer once offered, there is no strict definition of an ASP. Many firms do not yet have documented contracts in place, and have not really worked through their economic model. Services, performance, and availability of applications are also fairly restrictive.

There are at least three models of ASPs, in descending order of popularity:

1. **Internet service providers (ISPs)** provide access to individuals and firms for Internet services. ISPs vary widely in terms of services provided, but most are still confined to hosting Web sites and providing e-mail capabilities. Market researcher Input in Mountain View, California, expects Internet management outsourcing to grow 76 percent annually between 1998 and 2003. A recent *Computerworld* (October 25, 1999) survey of IT managers found that 22 percent of firms were already using an ISP for Web hosting, although 47 percent said they had no such plans.

2. An emerging group of companies are what this author refers to as **bundled service providers (BSPs)**, essentially service bureaus hosting a handful of interrelated applications. The most popular are enterprise resource planning (ERP) systems from such firms as SAP, PeopleSoft, or Baan; or customer relationship management (CRM) systems that bind together telephone, computing, and Internet technologies to support telemarketing sales and service centers.

3. Finally, there is the **proprietary service provider (PSP)**, usually a software firm that will make its software available on a shared basis. Instead of paying for the software outright and running it on their own computers, customers contract with the PSP to connect to the vendor's architecture. PSPs vary widely on the ancillary services available to customers.

WHY ASP?

There are already a number of ASP success stories from firms as varied as Monsanto, Volvo, Fleetwood Retail, Robert Mondavi Winery, and Barnes & Noble. Cynthia Morgan, writing in *Computerworld* (October 25, 1999), finds that ASPs make sense for larger firms when:

- the application requires expertise lacking in the existing IT staff
- IT has more pressing projects
- a neutral party is needed to merge and centralize services
- an application needs extremely rapid deployment
- users will be widely scattered, often with only a handful at a particular site
- users are outside the firewall

Almost all experts agree that the ASP solution is primarily for smaller companies that want to use a world-class application but cannot afford the upfront costs of acquisition, or the ongoing personnel burden of maintenance. Because they are most susceptible to swings in market conditions, smaller companies like the fact that ASPs usually charge on a variable price basis. If volume diminishes, the monthly bill declines, although the actual cost per transaction (or loan) may increase because volume discounts no longer apply.

Not surprisingly, the cost-effectiveness of ASPs is similar to that of any leasing arrangement. The longer one expects to keep a given vehicle, the less it makes sense to lease, because the cost of ownership can be amortized over a longer period of time. On the other hand, in the world of technology, long-term relationships are not the norm, and a firm can expect to change its technology every three to five years.

Continuing with the car analogy, leasing a car requires the dealer to be responsible for maintenance and repairs, recalls, and model obsolescence. Similarly, it is the ASP that must worry about system maintenance and performance, capacity, and technology obsolescence. The ASP must contend with vendors, dealing with bugs and sweating through the installation of new releases and issues of system compatibility.

Most important, the ASP must worry about recruiting and retaining knowledgeable staff. At the moment, there are an estimated 300,000 technology jobs going begging. Even small firms are finding that the cost of IT professionals is beyond their means, with a typical programmer/analyst earning as much as senior managers in the business units, and specialists such as database administrators or Webmasters earning the same as executive vice presidents. It is almost impossible for many firms today to find these people, provide sufficient technical challenges and financial incentives to keep them, and have appropriate management to make sure they are doing the right things. Thus, ASPs are an attractive alternative.

Another factor fueling ASPs is the fact that implementation times can be a lot quicker. The organization need not build an infrastructure to handle the application; the infrastructure is already in place. A firm's representatives can visit the service bureau, see the servers and network configurations already in place, presumably happily serving other customers. More and more, ASPs are also providing an electronic commerce (E-commerce) infrastructure for companies that want a fast path to Internet viability.

The argument in favor of ASPs is neatly summed up by Craig Kinyon, CFO for Reid Hospital and Health Care Services, Inc., in Richmond, Indiana, "The ASP model takes care of what I call the 'Tylenol factors' of applications — the maintenance, support, upgrades, and hardware. And we don't have to find and pay for staff to handle the applications." (*Information-Week*, February 21, 2000).

A CASE EXAMPLE

A small mortgage company (with less than 300 employees) has offered government (FHA/VA) and conventional (Fannie Mae/Freddie Mac) loans, primarily to first-time homebuyers in the northeastern United States. Its loan origination and servicing technology was written by a third-party provider to run on a DEC platform. Two or three staff members were hired to work with the third party to run the hardware and maintain the software.

Mortgage lending is an industry where there are a great number of regulatory changes. Not exciting work, but necessary. The IT staffers who were brought on board quickly became bored and left. Maintenance of the hardware was outsourced to a contractor; maintenance of the software largely ceased because it was too difficult to find the right technical skill set. The third-party provider (essentially a one-man shop) moved on.

To compound matters, this is a period when mortgage lenders are fundamentally reexamining their processes and approach to the marketplace, wishing to include such facilities as workflow and Internet lending. To stay competitive, the firm must update its technology. Needless to say, the existing platform will not accommodate such profound enhancements.

The firm evaluated third-party mortgage lending packages and found three that had the functionality it desired. All the packages used relational database technology and ran on NT servers.

However, there would still be some customization required. So, once again, the firm was confronted with the task: who would customize and maintain the software on a go-forward basis? Where would they get the NT expertise to run the hardware?

One of the software firms raised the concept of ASP. It offered to customize the software and maintain it, as well as operate the hardware (the database server from its own data center, and the application server on-site). In addition, the vendor could provide database, help desk, security, and disaster recovery services. The cost? A set-up charge, as well as a fee per user per month.

To the mortgage lender, it seemed an attractive alternative. The firm would overcome its personnel problem by having the vendor's staff perform the work. Recruiting, training, management, and retention would all be someone else's problem. The vendor would be responsible for regulatory and other software modifications, as well as keeping abreast of technology changes.

The executives liked the idea that they would not have to pay the full cost of the hardware and software upfront (approximately $1 million), but rather could "lease" the technology on a pay-as-you-go basis. This is especially important in a highly cyclical industry such as mortgage, where interest rate fluctuations bring feast or famine volumes. Assuming that the number of users generally reflects the volume of work, the firm could translate its technology cost from fixed (if it owned the technology) to variable.

Not everyone was pleased with the proposal. Some of the managers were concerned about not having support on-site. They also did not like the fact that the firm would not own the software, but merely lease it. The hardware contractor began a campaign of denigrating NT's supposed reliability and performance.

Moreover, the vendor's sales representative was only lukewarm about the concept. Part of this was lack of familiarity; part of it was the impact on their wallet. After all, salespeople are traditionally paid commission based on the value of the signed contract. In an ASP mode, the total amount of the sale is unknown; commission would be calculated on an amount to be paid out over time based on usage. Not as attractive a proposition. This is a factor software-companies-cum-ASPs will have to consider.

Thus, a firm that would appear to be an ideal candidate for an ASP still has hesitations about whether the model will work for it. And the vendor still has some homework to do on selling its own people.

THE FUTURE

Will every technology company become an ASP, or call itself one? Probably — for a while. However, a number of software firms will undoubtedly find that running reliable "data (cyber) centers" is more difficult than imagined. For one thing, the ASP concept calls upon a different set of expertise than what they have used to develop whiz-bang applications. Many of today's current software developers have little understanding of, or appreciation for, such issues as performance analysis, tuning, and capacity planning. In the past, if the application grew too big or obstreperous, the solution was simple — buy a bigger box. To maintain profitability, ASPs will not be able to simply resort to this practice. They will need to have a rigorous program of configuration management that is constantly evaluating and improving the reliability and performance of their hardware and networks.

And, as recent experience has shown, the software firms-cum-ASPs will have to take the same rigorous approach to security management that was the norm for the big outsourcers, with multiple layers of security and disaster recovery. After all, an individual firm's computer center was not much of a target for hackers; however, an ASP handling business for dozens or hundreds of firms is far more inviting. Indeed, the *Computerworld* poll referred to above found that 96 percent of respondents had concerns about security. On the other hand, an ASP is more likely to have access to security experts than a typical small company.

Also, as anyone who has ever endured the torture of calling a software provider's customer support line knows, these firms have a dismal record in post-market support. Staffing a competent help desk is no easy task, but will be mandatory for a successful offering as an ASP. The firms are hosting mission-critical applications, and users will need quick and accurate answers. Yet finding the source of a problem will prove very difficult for those ASPs who try to integrate software from several different vendors.

Another key problem for an ASP firm is finding the appropriate price model. For example, CenterBeam, Inc., in Santa Clara, California, is offering a Lucent Technologies-based network, a PC running Windows 2000 and Microsoft Office applications, a wireless LAN service, a public Web site, a company intranet, high-speed DSL Internet access, daily data back-up, and 24×7 technical support for less than $200 per user. BSP firms will have price tags must higher than this because they must incorporate.

Still, Forrester Research of Cambridge, Massachusetts, expects the ASP market to jump from $150 million in 2000 to $6 billion the next year. Dataquest in Redwood City, California, is far more optimistic, predicting $22 billion in revenues by 2003.

EVALUATING ASPS

Not every ASP will be successful. How to know if one is dealing with the right firm? Generally speaking, it is better to deal with an ASP that offers a focused group of applications. This will be a learning experience; and the greater the number of variables, the greater the chances of failure. It is important to find an ASP that has developed the offering as part of a natural evolution of its product or industry, rather than one that is just a case of "me too." The range of issues to consider is lengthy, but a preliminary list includes:

1. **Expertise.** Just what are the provider's qualifications? Has it built infrastructures before, or is it simply a software developer? Has it run a 24×7 operation? What is its motivation in doing this? How does it expect to make money? Will the provider be in it over the long haul? Obviously, the greater the expertise, the better. Also, the financial expectations should be realistic and include an honest assessment of the costs. And it is essential that the provider has an understanding of system performance and capacity planning.
2. **Service.** When is the system available? What response time is guaranteed? What happens if service degrades? What happens if there is a system failure? The more competent the ASP, the more guarantees of service it will offer, and the more likely it will be to offer compensation for its errors.
3. **Help desk.** How are people trained on the help desk? What questions do they handle — technical only or application specific? What is the allowable wait time for a response? Is the response received over the phone or via e-mail? What hours does the help desk work? What happens after-hours? The help desk will be the only real con-

tact most of a client's users have with the ASP, so support must be of the highest possible caliber.

4. **Security**. How is this handled? Will one's auditor be comfortable? What happens in the event of a security breach, and who is accountable for damages?

5. **Special services**. Does the ASP provide database administration, disaster recovery planning/testing, project management? Is some of this built into the standard contract, or is each service separate? The former method is preferred. Otherwise, one gets the "nickel-and-dime" effect.

6. **Licensing**. Who pays, and on what basis? Can software be made "rent to own?" If the intention is to utilize the ASP for less than three years, then negotiating to own the licenses at the end of the contract is important.

7. **Scalability**. Can the infrastructure grow to handle one's needs? Who decides when upgrades are necessary, and how is payment handled? This is especially important if a number of clients are sharing a configuration.

8. **Software maintenance/enhancement** (especially for BSPs). How are new releases handled? What if one does not want to move to the new release? How does one request enhancements, and who gets a vote on setting priorities? How are enhancements tested? It is important that the ASP have a rigorous system life-cycle methodology, and a careful method of deciding which enhancements will be part of the standard release, and which are truly custom. Otherwise, the costs can be prohibitive.

9. **Pricing**. Is the charge per user per transaction? Is there a charge for storing data? Are there separate charges for reports? Which factors most affect the monthly bill? The ASP should provide guidance in helping the client get the most bang for the buck.

10. **Implementation**. What is the process for getting up and running? What does the provider do; what does the client do? Is there a sample contract? Is there a significant choice of offerings, and the ability to negotiate a customized deal? Flexibility is good, but beware the ASP that claims to provide all things to all people. Part of the deal in sharing a resource is learning to live with limitations; both the client and the ASP must understand this. And that will be the most difficult lesson of all.

11. **Administration**. How is billing done? One may wish to pay on a quarterly or monthly basis; can the provider accommodate this? Ask to see a variety of performance reports each month — availability, response time, help-desk call resolution times, etc. The ASP should have a mechanism in place to routinely survey its customers, and it should be willing to share the results of internal audits. There should be a user group or advisory council in place where

customers can routinely influence the ASP's direction. The more willing the ASP is to shine a light on its own operation, the more confident one can feel in its capabilities.

12. **Termination.** There is no point in maintaining a relationship if one partner is unhappy. As much as the ASP will want to lock one in for the long term, there should be a relatively painless and graceful way of terminating the contract if expectations are not met. Look for provisions that provide reasonable notice (no more than 90 days) and reasonable penalties (no more than the equivalent of six months' lost revenue, but try for something even better).

CONCLUSION

ASPs offer clear advantages to firms large and small that are contending with the problem of too many initiatives and too little talent. They offer an efficient way to utilize hardware, software, network, and human resources. However, a shared platform often ends up catering to the lowest common denominator. Therefore, the more different or innovative a firm wants to be, the less likely it will be comfortable with the ASP as a long-term solution.

The best advice? Perform due diligence with particular care, and find a vendor that has good solid business reasons for being an ASP, as well as a plan that makes it a long-term player. If one decides to take the plunge, take advantage of being an early customer by ensuring that one has a voice in how the ASP is run, and how it develops its products, prices, and services over time. And monitor, monitor, monitor the ASP's performance — not only in the reports it provides, but by surveying one's users. Remember that, outsourced or insourced, to one's business peers, technology is still YOUR responsibility.

Section V
Managing Outsourcing

Chapter 19
Managing Outsourcing through Metrics

Howard A. Rubin

AS OUTSOURCING EXPANDS INTO MORE AREAS, its dimensionality is changing as well. At first, outsourcing activity focused on the data center, followed by networks, the telecommunications infrastructure, help desks, and workstation support. The latest area of heightened activity appears to be in the area of applications development and support.

It is safe to say that outsourcing is exploding. Yet because outsourcing is also imploding in some cases, it is critical to leverage lessons learned from the dynamics of outsourcing agreements now in progress.

The most startling lesson is that good intentions and a 600-page contract are not enough to ensure the success of outsourcing agreements. The corollary to this lesson is that a successful agreement requires that all parties to it be successful. In other words, squeezing the last dollar out of a provider by negotiating a tough contract is not in the best interests of the overall success of the deal.

Another key lesson stems from the propensity for change. Although outsourcing agreements are typically specified in multiyear terms, flexibility must be built into the arrangement. In addition, most agreements contain backward-looking performance measures that specify penalties and rewards after the fact; if predetermined targets are not hit by the end of some time period, money changes hands. Such systems are, by design, sources of frustration and friction. The true lesson is that no organization wants to end up in the penalty box. An agreement is successful if objectives are met, not if penalties are paid.

Quite simply, outsourcing agreements must specify results and expected outcomes in basic business terms and contain the tools for continuous assessment of whether the agreement is operating in a zone that provides expected levels of performance and value. From this perspective, the age of outsourcing oversight through metrics has definitely arrived.

THE BASICS OF METRICS

IS managers and their organizations need to become aware of the potential to use measurement not only as a mechanism for looking backward to determine if outsourcing performance targets have been met, but also as a proactive navigational tool to support the achievement of performance improvements. In addition, the success of an outsourcing agreement goes beyond technical improvements in performance; in some manner, gains in productivity, quality, and service must be linked to business results.

Companies embarking on outsourcing should apply measurement through the following types of activities:

- **Contract-initiation actions.** These actions include baselining today's performance and benchmarking current performance against industry performance.
- **Contract goal-seeking activities.** Such activities include designing and implementing a measurement system that provides the necessary telemetry (i.e., metrics collected as part of natural work processes) to enable the parties involved in the agreement to actively monitor, manage, and navigate to performance targets from both technical and business perspectives.
- **Performance target-attainment actions.** These actions involve:
  — continuous measurement support for the duration of the agreement in the form of real-time updates of performance data as it is generated; in other words, creating a continuous, forward-moving baseline
  — real-time monitoring of position relative to the attainment and movement toward contractual goals
  — periodic (i.e., monthly) formal management reviews on progress
  — quarterly benchmark analysis against external industry performance
  — production of an annual baseline/benchmark report as required by the contract

This action-oriented approach focuses on five principle activity areas or workstreams targeted at:

1. rapidly establishing a baseline
2. providing an external calibration benchmark comparison
3. designing an overall measurement system that supplies the parties to the agreement with the measures to both assess contractual conformance and proactively manage performance in real-time toward contract targets

4. implementing the measurement system
5. providing continuous support, monitoring, reporting, and coaching for the duration of the agreement

Workstreams one and two comprise the contract-initiation actions and are executed concurrently with workstream three.

Workstream three focuses on the contract goal-seeking activities. By maximizing the concurrency between workstreams one, two, and three, short-term metric needs are met while the development of a more complete, long-term measurement system is under way.

Workstream four puts the measurement system into action, and workstream five makes use of it to steer the organization toward its goals while providing contractually dictated reporting and analysis.

Exhibit 19-1 depicts the design methodology for outsourcing oversight. The approach is neither universal nor a boilerplate, but designed instead to focus a forward-looking process of determining and enacting the metric elements critical to the success of an outsourcing agreement. By incorporating technical measures and their business linkages into the overall management structure, all parties to the agreement better position themselves to harvest the benefits of their outsourcing strategy. The methodology's synergistic use of multiview metrics (i.e., IT, internal business, external business, and external benchmarks)and flight-deck approach provide a model for effective outsourcing management.

THE OUTSOURCING OVERSIGHT CONTROL PANEL

The basic oversight control panel contains gauge clusters addressing nine critical areas of outsourcing oversight. These areas are equally applicable to all dimensions of IT outsourcing, from the data center to desktop management to applications development and support. The nine clusters are as follows:

1. **Finance/budget.** The focus here is on cost management and on-cost delivery of services and work products.
2. **Customer satisfaction.** This area focuses on the critical attributes that generate satisfaction with IT services and work products among internal business customers.
3. **Work product delivered.** Here, the focus is on quantifying the amount of service or work product provided in a given time period.
4. **Quality.** This area focuses on the objective and measurable aspects of quality of services and products.
5. **Time/schedule.** The time/schedule cluster focuses on critical service, product, and project time frames and the ability to deliver on-time.

Exhibit 19-1. Design methodology for outsourcing oversight metrics.

Workstream	Activities	Outcome(s)
Rapid Baselining	Construct list of measures needed as perceived by both parties. Inventory currently available data/assess data quality. Analyze contractual agreement in terms of business value and goals/assess measurement coverage. Create baseline.	Metric baseline of current performance established in minimum time frame.
Benchmark Analysis	Identify industry groups/company types to be included in benchmark. Construct benchmark analysis by overlaying baseline data on external performance data. Analyze and report on current performance vs. external performance.	Assessment of degree of stretch of contractual goals; potential for identification of additional performance improvement opportunities.
Measurement System Design	Link internal IT measures to business outcome measures. Identify progress/navigational measures. Create overall measurement system incorporating contractual performance measures, progress/navigational measures, linkage to internal business measures, linkage to external business measures. Identify and define all measures, data sources, collection and analysis tempos, and end uses. Create systems dynamic simulation (optional).	Organizational IT flight deck designed for monitoring and managing contractual performance parameters from both technical and business perspectives; expectations of business outcomes of the agreement fully charted; simulation environment available for what-if analyses (optional).
Implementation	Define roles and responsibilities for enacting measurement system. "Wiring" the organization.	Mechanism for contractual reporting and proactive performance management in place.
Continuous Support	On-going acquisition of data based on required data collection tempos. On-going tracking against contract targets and trajectory; assessment (using model) of impacts of deviations from performance expectations. On-going comparison against benchmark database. Data-driven performance coaching. Monthly analysis of progress/performance. Quarterly management briefings. Annual assessment/report.	Continuous third-party analysis, assessment, and coaching in support of contractual objectives.

6. **Business value.** This area measures the outsourcing agreement's outcome attainment from the financial/shareholder view, external customer/marketplace view, organizational learning and improvement view, and internal process improvement view.
7. **Operational service levels.** The focus here is on critical service tempos, availability, and delivery of work products.
8. **Human resources.** The human resources cluster focuses on changes to the skill inventory and internal job satisfaction.
9. **Productivity.** Here, the focus is on the efficiency of the production and delivery of work products.

Two classes of measures are associated with each gauge cluster in the control panel.

First, as a direct by-product of the creation of an outsourcing agreement, each gauge cluster must have target or destination measures that indicate the goals of the agreement. The measures may focus on a single value or on multiple values each linked to a point in time.

Second, each gauge cluster must have rate measures that focus on the direction and rate of movement toward the targets. These direction and rate measures are, in fact, the navigational measures essential for monitoring.

These ideas can be applied in the context of applications development outsourcing. More specifically, they can be applied to measuring the throughput performance of an IT organization.

MEASURING THROUGHPUT PERFORMANCE IN APPLICATIONS OUTSOURCING

Measuring the amount of work done by an applications development and support organization and the amount of product produced or delivered by such an organization has proved to be both difficult and elusive. Such measures are critical to outsourcing, however, because the most commonly asked executive questions in the world of IT are related to them. Examples of these questions include:

- Are we using our IT organization effectively?
- Is the IT organization efficient?
- Are we spending the right amount on IT?
- Are we getting value for our IT dollars?
- Are we doing more work than last year?
- Are we doing more with less (or less with more)?
- Are we doing the right work?

Suppose the CEO of an organization asks the IT director or CIO whether the outsourced IT organization did more work than last year or how much more work it expected to do next year versus this year. How does an IT executive obtain a quantitative answer to these questions?

Many executives typically attempt to solve the problem by applying function points. Although function points may be useful for quantifying the work product size and change in size for a particular set of classes of systems, they do not cover all aspects of work. IT organizations provide user support, for example, as well as help desks. They may also be using technologies (e.g., object orientation) for which function points do not apply. Function points do not even pick up small maintenance tasks that involve computation changes. In addition, technology updates (e.g., moving from one database or operating system to another) also pose a challenge.

Clearly, function points have a low capture ratio; in other words, the amount of coverage of IT work types accurately counted by function points is low. Lines of code (LOC) as a metric faces similar problems. Finally, in the world of objects, specialty metrics such as metrics for object-oriented systems environments (MOOSE metrics) do not capture all the territory either.

There does not seem to be a way to use a single metric to express the amount of work done by an IT organization. There also does not seem to be a way to express the amount of work product produced by an IT organization. If neither of these two aspects of work can be computed, then overall efficiency cannot be computed and analysis of effectiveness is problematic.

By accepting the nature of the problem, however — that an IT organization performs many different work types, each of which may have its own natural sizing measure — the problem can be solved.

WORK AND WORK PRODUCT MEASUREMENT

Focus for the moment on the notion of throughput. Throughput is defined as the amount of material put through a process in a given period of time. It can be viewed as something that is discernible or visible to the customer or user of a process in terms of process inputs and outputs. From the customer's vantage, these inputs and outputs are really requests and results (i.e., work product delivered in some form to the customer).

Exhibit 19-2 expresses this view of IT throughput similarly to the way that an application boundary is drawn around an application in traditional function point analysis. What the customer sees represents only a portion of what goes on. Inside-the-box internal work invisible to the customer (who may be paying for it) is also performed.

From a customer perspective, this internal work should not be measured. From an IT organization's perspective, however, the ratio of customer-visible work (i.e., throughput) to internal work clearly relates to the IT organization's efficiency and its overall process yield.

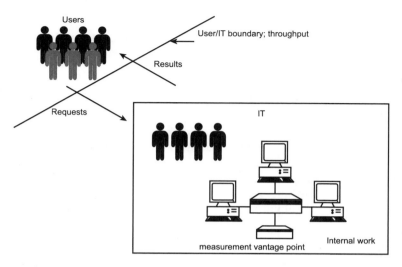

Exhibit 19-2. IT throughput from the perspective of the applications delivery function.

Returning to the definition of throughput shows that the amount of material put through the process in Exhibit 19-2 is essentially the total volume of work performed. The volume of work performed is a function of the types of work requested and the size of the requested work expressed as some sort of units.

Possible work types or categories of work that may be requested by a customer include new systems development, platform migration, adding of new functionality to existing systems (i.e., adaptive maintenance), improving existing functionality (i.e., perfective maintenance), fixes/repairs (i.e., corrective maintenance), report generation, preventive maintenance, support functions, and production support. It is important to note that work types are not static. New ones may emerge over time.

Internal work types include release-control activities, technology upgrades, and disaster recovery. This list too may grow over time.

Using this simple work type-based model yields two equations.

Total work performed equals:
volume of work requested (executed) + volume of internal work.

Throughput (as viewed by the customer) equals:
volume of work requested (executed).

COMPUTATIONAL ASPECTS OF THROUGHPUT

The previous equations are unsatisfactory because they are at too high a level to be useful. More detail is needed to compute volume of work requested.

It is worthwhile to review this proposal. First, draw a box around IT and called it the IT/user boundary. Then identify all work types (i.e., requests and results) that move across the boundary and also those that do not.

Using insight gained from the function point measure, it appears that a logical next step and parallel would be to be able to count the number of occurrences of each work type and multiply that number by a weight to get an overall throughput score or volume. This is essentially what is done in function point counting; each function type is identified, multiplied by a weight, and the overall volume computed.

The example, however, lacks weights, and counting the number of occurrences of each work type does not do justice to the varying size of each type requested.

This dilemma is remedied by the function point method, particularly the work of Charles Symons on MK II Function Points. This method provides the insights necessary to complete the computation framework for throughput measurement.

The problem should be tackled backwards, by first concentrating on the weights. In the traditional function point measure, the weights used were determined by trial and error. In Symons' method, the weights are calibrated.

For each work type, however, the weight used should be the average delivery rate per size unit of the work type. This, of course, raises the problem of having a size unit for each work type.

The concept of a natural size unit is used to deal with this issue. In simple terms, this is the size unit that best fits the work type: it is discernible and measurable and can be audited. For some work types, the size unit is function points. In other cases, it may be lines of code. In still another case, such as the help desk, it may be the number of hours spent on serving the request.

In essence, computing throughput involves, at a high level:

- identifying all the natural work types
- establishing a size unit for each work type
- establishing a delivery rate for each work type to be used as a weight (e.g., hours per size unit)
- computing the weighted sum of all the work volumes (i.e., size times rate)

Exhibit 19-3 depicts this process.

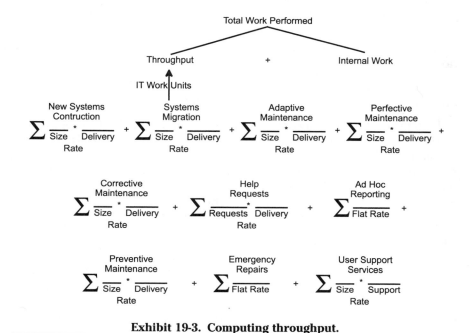

Exhibit 19-3. Computing throughput.

Readers who have followed this analysis carefully are aware that the weighted sum is essentially total work hours performed. This should not be alarming.

THE WORK UNIT CONCEPT

Throughput can now be defined as the sum of all the work associated with requested work types. From this point on, throughput is expressed as ITWUs (IT work units).

Work units for each natural work type are either:

(size of work requested) * (baseline delivery rate)

or

(number of requests for the work type) * (flat rate delivery rate for the work type).

Rates in both these cases are expressed as work units per unit of request size.

Consider the work unit to be an elemental measure of IT work similar to a calorie or the gold standard before currencies could float.

Although a work unit can be defined as virtually anything, for the purposes of this analysis, it is defined as the number of hours needed to convert one function point to operational code. Using the results of the 1995 Worldwide Benchmark Project, which calibrated the productivity of the average U.S. IT developer as 88 function points per person year and 1,824 hours per person year, a work unit is equal to 20.7 hours.

Although almost any number can be used as a basis for work units, there are advantages in relating work units to function points.

Using this concept, any piece of work requiring one hour to perform is the equivalent of .05 work units or ITWUs. In this way, the ITWU measure is applied as sort of an exchange rate. Using this concept, an organization that performs a volume of work equal to 10 ITWUs (or 207 hours) could have either performed that particular work or had an average US IT professional implement a system with 10 function points.

Exhibit 19-4 provides a sample application of the ITWU computation. In this chart, the metric column identifies the natural sizing metrics used, the size requested column shows the total size of requests for the year, the natural rate size unit shows the baseline rate used for the weight, the work unit/size unit column shows the rate expressed as work units, and the work unit column shows the work units computed for the work type. The last figure in the exhibit is the total ITWUs performed by the organization for the period, which is one year.

Exhibit 19-4. Computing throughput for a sample IT organization during the baseline year.

Type of Work Requested	Natural Size Metric	Size Requested	Natural Rate/Size Unit	Work Unit/Size Unit	Work Units
New Development	FP	5,000	6.56	.3169	1,585
Platform Migration	FP	2,000	8	.3865	773
Enhancements (large)	FP	1,000	6.56	.3169	317
Minor Enhancements (small)	FP	500	6.56	.3169	158
Minor Enhancements (computational)	LOC	250	.0656	.0032	1
Adaptive Maintenance	FP	1,000	14.45	.6981	698
Computation Adaptive Maintenance	LOC	250	.067	.0032	1
Repairs (large)	FP	500	7	.3382	169
Repairs (small)	LOC	250	.07	.0034	1
Ad Hoc Reports	FP	500	.28	.0135	7
Operations Repairs	Flat rate	200	2.21	.1068	21
Preventive Maintenance	FP	1,000	4	.1932	193
User Support	Flat rate	175,000	1.23	.0594	10,399
Total ITWUs		14,322			

BENEFITS OF WORK UNITS AS AN OUTSOURCING MEASURE

Using the work unit form of throughput analysis forces an organization to define its work from the customer's vantage point. This is essential in an outsourcing agreement. The work types themselves are used as a basis for discussion, and the IT work units are used as a basis for planning and resource allocation.

Work-type analysis allows for multiple metrics to be used concurrently. There is no need to search for a single metric to size all work. If a single metric cannot be found for an individual work type, the work type probably needs to be split. In addition, as new work types emerge, they are added to the computation process.

Productivity/efficiency analysis is simple. When this technique is applied on a year-to-year basis, three things are apparent:

1. A catalog of relevant work types has to be developed for each year, along with a sizing of the amount of each. This part of the analysis allows shifts in work to be easily tracked.
2. For each work type, a baseline rate is established each year to use as a weight. In this way, determining if productivity has changed for a given work type from year to year becomes an easy task.
3. Most important, the question of overall efficiency is easily answered. For any given year, the baseline rates from the previous year are substituted in the computation to answer the question of how much work (ITWUs) it would have taken to perform this year's work at last year's level of productivity. Alternatively, last year's requests can be recomputed at this year's baseline rates.

The most intriguing potential application of the throughput concept has to do with benchmarking IT organizations and making outsourcing decisions. This process is analogous to hardware benchmarking. Suppose a mix of work is picked. In other words, a set of work types and their associated sizes is selected. If the delivery rates of various organizations are obtained and inserted into the ITWU computation, the total amount of work required for each to execute the mix can be determined. This means that the amount of work each of them needs to perform a standard set of requests can be compared. This is true benchmarking. In addition, organizations using this framework can benchmark themselves on the distribution of work across work types; these differences can even be compared within and across industries.

Throughput analysis also provides a basis for outsourcing agreements involving applications development and support. The methodology has the advantage of being able to quantify exactly what is being committed to in terms of work and acts as a scorecard for contractual performance changes.

CONCLUSION

The success of outsourcing agreements is fundamentally based on the ability of the involved organizations to place themselves in a win–win situation. Doing so requires that all goals and objectives — technical, business, and otherwise — be visible and agreed to.

By codifying outsourcing objectives using measurement and control panels that include the business value measures, technical performance measures, and underlying change rates and targets in all areas, IS managers position their organizations for success. If they do not use these panels, they are launching their organizations into outsourcing like unguided missiles.

Chapter 20
Managing the Risks of Outsourcing Systems Development: Part I

Ken Doughty
Franke Grieco

THE INFORMATION TECHNOLOGY (IT) OUTSOURCING STRATEGY is usually associated with the contracting out of an organization's entire Information Services (IS) function to an external service provider. There are a number of organizations that are not outsourcing the whole IT function, but only those functions considered to be non-"core" competencies. Systems development is a function often considered to be non-core and therefore outsourced.

Arguably, the decision to outsource should be based on a detailed analysis of the organization's Strategic IT Plan and Corporate Plan. From this analysis it can be determined whether outsourcing conforms with the organization's strategic direction or if it is required to facilitate the organization's IT strategies. The main arguments for outsourcing are the minimization of the risks associated with systems development and the maximization of return on investment in information technology (more value for money). Therefore, outsourcing the systems development function is considered by many a risk reduction and cost minimization strategy.

The more sobering argument is that outsourcing systems development does not eliminate the risks associated with it. However, it transfers some risks to the contractor and exposes the outsourcing organization to new risks.

The factors that may contribute to an outsourcing decision include:

- the development of the Strategic IT Plan, resulting in identification of the systems development function as no longer being a "core competency"
- the dramatic increase in the availability of "off-the-shelf" parameter driven software (e.g., SAP, Oracle Financials, People Soft, BAAN, MAN/MAN/X)
- previous systems development experience by the organization (especially failures)
- access to "best-practice" software development organizations (ISO9000 certification)
- lack of credibility in the organization's Information Systems (IS) Department
- accelerated realization of reengineering benefits
- the rising cost of in-house systems development
- reduction in and better control of systems development costs
- lack of adequate infrastructure or resources and skills to develop systems to meet the organization's requirements on time and within budget
- the opportunity to free the organizations resources for other purposes
- business venture with developers in marketing a product

THE AUDITOR'S ROLE

Executive management is demanding that their IS Auditors, as part of their mandate, ensure that the risks associated with systems development are being minimized. To facilitate this, the Information Systems Audit and Control Association (ISACA) recently released a document titled "Control Objectives for Information and Related Technology (COBiT)."[1] This document replaces the Control Objectives, which was the ISACA standard for auditing information technology. COBiT has been developed with a business orientation as the main theme and designed not only to be utilized by auditors, but also, and more importantly, as a comprehensive checklist for business process owners.

COBiT provides a framework for ensuring that an organization has a strong internal control environment for its information technology business processes. COBiT Section Planning and Organization PO9 — Assess Risks states that:

> *Control over the IT process of assessing risk that satisfies the business requirement of ensuring the achievement of IT objectives and responding to threats to the provision of IT services is enabled by the organization engaging itself in IT risk-identification and impact analysis, and taking cost-effective measures to mitigate risks ...*

COBiT clearly details the requirement for IS Auditors to review the risk management of any information technology project, including systems development. However, limited audit resources and other business-related priorities can restrict the ability of the IS Auditor to adequately cover the development process (i.e., when systems development is outsourced). Therefore, an IS audit framework is required to ensure that the IS auditor complies with the professional association's requirements and assists the organization in the risk management of its systems development. This includes managing the risks associated with outsourcing systems development.

This chapter defines risk management and how it should be applied to the system development. Additionally, a detailed risk model and IS audit approach for the risk management of outsourcing software development, utilizing COBiT, is demonstrated.

The IS audit model discussed in this chapter provides the IS auditor with a control approach that identifies systems development risk, risk factors, risk rating, and risk reduction strategies in outsourcing the systems development process.

RISK MANAGEMENT

To develop the IS audit approach and the application of the COBiT requirements, the IS Auditor is required to have a sound understanding of risk management concepts and the application of these concepts to IS auditing.

The majority of IS Auditors do not realize that they have been using risk management techniques in auditing their organizations. For example, risk management techniques are utilized in the preparation of the organization's Audit Plan, particularly in the identification of those business functions/processes that are to be audited according to predetermined criteria or depending upon the level of the auditor's "comfort."

Ideally, the auditor should use a proven and documented methodology in the application of risk management techniques. For example, the Australian/New Zealand Standard AS4360[2] defines the first generic standard on risk management in the world. The standard defines the following terms:

Risk. "The chance of something happening that will have an impact upon objectives. It is measured in terms of likelihood and consequences."

Risk Management. "The systematic application of management policies, procedures, and practices to the tasks of identifying, analyzing, assessing, treating, and monitoring risk."

Risk Treatment. "Selection and implementation of appropriate options for dealing with risk."

The standard also provides guidelines in its appendices for the following areas:

- Application of risk management
- Steps in developing and implementing a risk management program
- Generic sources of risk and their areas of impact
- Examples of risk definition and classification
- Examples of quantitative risk expressions
- Risk management documentation
- Identifying options of risk treatment

The IS Auditor can utilize this standard not only in gaining a sound understanding of the risk management concepts, but also in its application.

The IS Auditor should also be aware of the other tangible risks associated with project management that may contribute to the failure of the outsourcing software development project. The following risks are project risks irrespective of whether outsourcing is utilized or not; they are included here to provide a checklist of issues to consider during the contract negotiation phase with the preferred outsourcing contractor and during the planning for, and initial set-up of any project.

1. Failure to have a clear business objective for the project that is well understood by all participants and stakeholders in the project.
2. Having too large a scope for the project or not having the scope of the project clearly defined.
3. Ineffective project management, which is demonstrated through factors such as:
   — Either no or poor project management methodology or procedures.
   — No project management charter or it is unclear in specifying the role, duties, and responsibilities of the project manager or project team members.
   — Multiple project managers, with responsibility for the management of the project not clearly defined.
   — Lack of a formal, and regularly updated, project plan.
   — Failure to adhere to the project plan.
   — The project plan not covering all stages of the project from its initiation through to the post-implementation review.
   — Irregular project progress reporting or progress reporting that imparts little real information to the project sponsor and steering committee.
   — The authority of the project manager may be implied rather than stated and communicated to all the stakeholders by executive management.

— Project team members may be working independently without any overall coordination, resulting in wasted resources and contributing to the failure of the project.

— Project reporting lines may either be not established, not clear, or be to inappropriate management.

— Project monitoring systems may not have been established or developed at the outset of the project.

— Monitoring standards or benchmarks to measure the performance of project management may not be established or may be inappropriate.

— Project reports may not be sufficiently detailed to assist executive management to monitor the progress of the project in terms of work completed against milestones and budgets.

— Insufficient knowledge of project management software to effectively use the software.

4. Not having a clearly defined project structure:
   — no clearly defined sponsor/owner for the project at the senior management level
   — not having the right mix of IT and user staff (stakeholders) on the project team
   — project team members not having appropriate levels of technical skills and experience

5. The Project Manager or project team may not have the skills or training to undertake the role. Often, the Project Manager is user appointed because he or she "knows" the current system.

6. Long lead times between project deliverables.

7. Uncontrolled or high levels of requests for modifications to the design specifications during the development and implementation phases of the project.

8. Failure to control the change management aspects of the project, such as:
   — maintaining user involvement and commitment
   — redesign of business processes and work practices
   — changes in the organization structure
   — training
   — post-implementation support

SYSTEM DEVELOPMENT METHODOLOGY

For the purposes of this paper it is assumed that the executive management of the organization has made a strategic decision that systems development is no longer a core competency. This decision was based on a detailed analysis in developing the organization's strategic IT model. It is also assumed that the organization's IS Auditor has reviewed the Strategic

IT Plan (refer to "Auditing the Strategic IT Plan," K. Doughty, *EDP Auditing,* March/April, 1997. Auerbach, New York).

The strategic IT plan details the IS department's strategic direction from being a systems developer and maintenance provider to adopting a "caretaker role" with regard to the organization's current legacy systems. This means that systems development of new systems, including the purchase of off-the-shelf software solutions, will be outsourced.

It is important that the organization's executive management "manage" this change in strategic direction from internal systems development to outsourced development. A key point to note is, an organization's processes have a greater influence on the culture of the organization than behavior. Therefore, a competent change management process must be undertaken to ensure that there is a cultural and business change that will be accepted by the organization as a whole. If the executive management does not manage the process competently, it may result in the rejection of the outsourcing concept and also cause dysfunctional activities by stakeholders (e.g., system owners, users, and the IS department).

Today, systems development methodologies address the issue of risk management, whereas previously, risk management in systems development was often inferred in the process rather than a project task item that had to be addressed, actioned, and signed off. Previously, IS management was recommending to executive management to develop or redevelop systems without the support of a risk analysis being undertaken. This exposed the organization to unidentified and unmanaged risk that may have led to business objectives not being attained.

Systems development methodologies (for example, APT[3]) address risk management in the following terms :

Project Initiation.

> Responsibilities of all parties involved in the project
> Deliverables and delivery schedule
> Acceptance criteria
> Risk, problem, and change management
> Standards and procedures to be used

Identify System Risks. Document the risks at the system level. These risks include loss of systems and data caused by hardware malfunctions, human errors, malicious damage, fraud, viruses, unauthorized use, hacking, theft, or sabotage.

Assess Probability of Risk Occurring. Examine each identified risk and estimate the potential for its occurrence.

Determine the compounded probability of risks identified occurring. (For example, if there are 200 risks with a possible 1 in 100 chance of occurrence per annum, then there is a probability of two risks per annum.)

Assess Risks.

Identify the critical system consequences of each of the risks occurring and place monetary values upon them.

Assess strategic risks and consequences for the business.

Review the results of the exercise with management and rank the risks.

Document damage potential, the costs associated with the occurrence of the risks, and the overall probability.

Document the risk management strategies and the likely costs.

Review Current Risk Management Processes.

For each risk, identify the counter measures currently in place and their annual costs.

Examine each risk and estimate its probability.

Examine the effectiveness of the counter measures.

Document the current counter measures, their costs, the risk probability, and the potential costs to the organization.

Determine Overall Risk Management Strategies. Document potential risk management techniques that could be used in place of current practices.

The IS Auditor should ensure that the organization's system development methodology not only addresses the risk management process, but also the consistent application of the process throughout the system development life cycle.

Further, the IS Auditor has to ensure that the results of the risk analysis are complete and accurate and they are to be conveyed to the organization's executive management before the outsourcing of systems development is approved.

CONCLUSION

Controlling the oursourcing of software development is an essential element of managing risk in an organization today. This chapter explains why and what the IS Auditor can do to help in this process.

Notes

1. COBiT: "Control Objectives for Information and Related Technology (COBiT), Systems Audit and Control Association (ISACA), 1996.
2. AS4360: Risk Management. Standards Association of Australia.
3. APT: APT Methodology, EXECOM, Perth, Western Australia, 1993.

Chapter 21
Managing the Risks of Outsourcing Systems Development: Part II

Ken Doughty
Franke Grieco

INADEQUATE RISK ASSESSMENT AND MANAGEMENT may lead to software development projects going "off-the-rails" due to unidentified risks eventuating and being poorly managed. The associated extra costs and time escalations can:

- detrimentally impact the viability of a software development project
- lead to failure in achieving strategic business objectives
- in a worst-case scenario, cause an organization to go out of business

The IS Auditor can assist the organization in developing a risk framework by utilizing the COBiT[1] PO9 Assess Risk Guidelines. By adopting and appropriately applying the COBiT PO9 Guidelines, the IS Auditor ensures a comprehensive coverage of the risks associated with outsourcing software development.

A risk assessment framework should be an intrinsic part of a business continuity plan. The framework would require an assessment of risks that could impact on the organization reaching its business objectives on a regular basis. The assessment should also identify the residual risk (the risk the organization's management is willing to accept). Ideally, it should provide risk assessments for the organization as a whole and for the separate processes, including major projects.

0-8493-0875-5/00/$0.00+$.50
© 2000 by CRC Press LLC

The COBiT PO9 Assess Risk Guideline refers to a number of control objectives that need to be addressed in its application. The control objectives are:

1. Business risk assessment
2. Risk assessment approach
3. Risk identification
4. Risk measurement
5. Risk action plan
6. Risk acceptance

Business Risk Assessment

The organization's management needs to identify its role in contributing to the organization's objectives, policies, and strategies when making decisions about risk. These must be clearly understood as they help to define the criteria as to whether a risk is acceptable or not, and the basis of control. COBiT states that management should establish a systematic risk assessment framework.

The organization needs to have policies and standards in place to provide guidance to the staff responsible for risk management. Responsible staff need to be aware of the instances where risk assessment needs to occur and the desirable criteria that should be used.

For example, the size (i.e., monetarily, timeframe, impact on the business) a project must be for a risk assessment to be mandatory. Guidelines for the context that should be used, (e.g., strategic context, organizational context or project/process context). In some instances, it may be necessary to assess risk at both the global and project levels.

Risk-Assessment Approach

To ensure a consistent and acceptable standard of risk assessment, an approved approach needs to be in place. It should outline the process for determining the scope, boundaries, methodology, responsibilities, and required skills.

There has been a considerable amount of research performed in the area of risk management and assessment. Therefore, management does not need to reinvent the wheel in establishing an approach. In many instances, management only needs to determine what approach is best suited for the business. For example, in developing a risk measurement approach, the Australian/New Zealand Standard AS/NZS 4360:1995 "Risk Management" can be utilized.

Exhibit 21-1 outlines the steps to be followed in developing the risk action plan template for outsourced system acquisition/development projects. It is at a high level and simply follows the COBiT control objective steps.

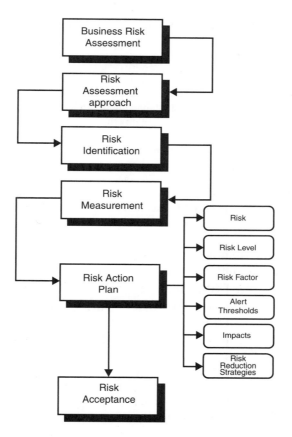

Exhibit 21-1. IS audit risk approach.

The AS/NZS 4360:1995 "Risk Management" Standard was used as the basis for developing the risk action plan template found in Chapter 22. A matrix approach was utilized, as shown in Exhibit 21-2.

Exhibit 21-3 is an example extracted from the template.

Risk Identification

There are number of methods of identifying risks, for example :

- surveys, questionnaires, interviews
- workshops, discussion groups
- past history failure analysis
- S.W.O.T analysis
- documentation and analysis of flows (data, physical, etc.)
- modeling
- analysis of local and overseas experiences, etc.

Exhibit 21-2. Excerpt from the risk action plan template.

Title	Description
Risk	The risk being addressed
Risk level	A measure of likelihood and seriousness of a risk's impact; it is calculated using the A/NZS 4360 Risk Management Standard
Risk factors	A list of the elements that collectively contribute to the risk
Alert thresholds	The symptoms or events that indicate the risk is likely to occur
Impacts	The specific effects if the risk occurs.
Risk treatments	The strategies that can be implemented to minimize the likelihood or impact of the risk

If a workshop method is used, then the attendees should consist of the project team representatives, project stakeholders, and if possible, individuals who had previous experience in developing a risk framework.

The auditor's role in the workshop is one of a facilitator. The facilitator's role is to ensure that all the workshop participants clearly understand the project's strategic business objectives and requirements, and that a comprehensive list of risks are identified. The following template provides a good basis for the list. However, it is only a basis and not a complete list suited for every type of outsourced systems development project. The risks, risk measurement, and risk treatments will vary depending on the type of project, type of organization, and type of industry.

Exhibit 21-3. An example extracted from the risk action plan template.

Title	Description
Risk	Inability of Outsourcing Contractor to fulfill contract requirements
Risk level	H (High)
Risk factors	Outsourcing Contractor loses the capability to continue satisfying contract requirements due to excessive demands placed on its resources (e.g., Customer base grows too fast or the Company loses key resources)
Alert thresholds	Expanding client base (winning new project contracts and soliciting large new clients)
Impacts	The organization's requirements become low priorities for the Outsourcing Contractor
Risk treatment	Monitor contract schedule/contract performance; link incremental payments with successful completion of project milestones within a set timeframe

Exhibit 21-4. A ranking of the likelihood of a risk occuring.

Level	Description	Description
A	Almost certain	The event is expected to occur in most circumstances
B	Likely	The event will probably occur in most circumstances
C	Moderate	The event should occur at some time
D	Unlikely	The event could occur at some time
E	Rare	The event may occur only in exceptional circumstances

The risk identification workshop should attempt to identify all possible risks associated with the project, both within and outside the control of the organization. Areas to be included are:

- threats
- vulnerabilities
- strategic directions
- relationships

Risk Measurement

This risk measurement phase requires the analysis of the likelihood and consequences of each risk identified. The guidelines provided by AS 4360 suggest that the risk level is a function of the likelihood of a risk occurring and the possible impact of the risk if it eventuates. Once the likelihood and impact of a risk are estimated, the results are incorporated into a matrix to give the final risk level a value.

The rankings for the likelihood of a risk occurring are detailed in Exhibit 21-4.

Exhibit 21-5 is an example of likely events.

The rankings for magnitude/impact of consequences if a risk occurs are described in Exhibit 21-6.

Exhibit 21-7 exemplifies the different categories of risk impact.

Exhibit 21-5. An example of likely events.

Level	Description	Description
A	Almost certain	Unauthorized entry through use of poor passwords
B	Likely	Corruption of backup media due to poor storage conditions
C	Moderate	Theft of equipment due to visitors being unsupervised
D	Unlikely	Flooding on the top floor of a high-rise building
E	Rare	Physical damage to facilities due to terrorist attack

Exhibit 21-6. Ranking of the consequences of a risk occurring.

Level	Description	Description
1	Insignificant	Low financial loss; minimal reduction in customer service, staff morale or operational efficiency; minor impact on cash flow or ability to plan business activities; no or low political impact.
2	Minor	Medium financial loss; medium reduction in customer service, staff morale or operational efficiency; medium impact on cash flow or ability to plan business activities; medium political impact.
3	Moderate	High financial loss; high reduction in customer service, staff morale or operational efficiency; high impact on cash flow or ability to plan business activities; high political impact.
4	Major	Major financial loss; major reduction in customer service, staff morale or operational efficiency; major impact on cash flow or ability to plan business activities; major political impact.
5	Catastrophic	Total financial loss; huge reduction in customer service, staff morale or operational efficiency; catastrophic impact on cash flow or ability to plan business activities; total political impact.

Combining the estimated rankings for likelihood and impact from the above tables into another matrix provides a measurement of risk. The final risk measurement rankings are defined as follows and depicted in Exhibit 21-8.

Therefore, if a risk is likely to occur and the possible impacts are considered major, then the risk level is regarded as High (H).

Exhibit 21-7. Categories of risk impact.

Level	Description	Description
1	Insignificant	Non-stakeholders protesting their lack of involvement in the project
2	Minor	High staff turnover in project teams, requiring an increase in training expenditure and lost productive time due to new project team members familiarizing themselves with the project requirements
3	Moderate	Failure to reach milestones within planned timeframe, causing overruns in expenditure and key strategic objectives not being achieved
4	Major	Failure of a major IT project to provide the expected results (i.e., the project not yielding expected returns on investment)
5	Catastrophic	Halfway through the project, the outsourcing contractor goes into receivership, bringing the project to a halt until all legal issues are resolved and expertise and resources are again organized to continue the project

Exhibit 21-8. Measurements of risk.

	Consequences				
Likelihood	**Insignificant** **1**	**Minor** **2**	**Moderate** **3**	**Major** **4**	**Catastrophic** **5**
A (almost certain)	S	S	H	H	H
B (likely)	M	S	S	H	H
C (moderate)	L	M	S	H	H
D (unlikely)	L	L	M	S	H
E (rare)	L	L	M	S	S

H = High risk: Detailed research and management planning required at senior levels

S = Significant risk: Senior management attention needed

M = Moderate risk: Management responsibility must be specified

L = Low risk: Manage by routine procedures

Risk Action Plan

In developing a Risk Action Plan, the following categories should be covered.

Risk Factors. Risk factors are the basic elements that collectively contribute to the risk. These can be identified, for each risk, during the risk identification phase (e.g., during the workshop).

For example, Risk: The selected outsourced software developer may lose the ability to satisfy its contractual obligations.

The risk factors that may contribute to this risk include:

- financial difficulties
- taken over by another company, or broken up and sold off
- change in the outsourced software developer's strategic direction
- the outsourced software developer decides that there are no longer any benefits to be obtained in continuing with the outsourcing contract arrangement

Alert Thresholds. Alert thresholds include events or trends that indicate the probability of a risk occurring is becoming more likely.

For example, for the risk identified in Section 5.5.1, rumors of cash flow problems could be an indication of financial difficulties. A ratio analysis of the outsourced software developer financial statements could indicate possible financial difficulties.

Impacts. The impacts represent the likely result if a risk eventuates.

For example, for the risk identified in Section 5.5.2, if the outsourced software developer is bankrupted, then the organization has the task of picking up the pieces (i.e., continuing the software development of the strategic business system). This would require either building in-house teams to continue with the project or finding another suitable contractor. Either way, the organization would incur losses in time and money.

Risk Treatments/Risk Action Plan. The risk treatments are risk management strategies for minimizing the likelihood of occurrence or the impact on the organization if the risk eventuates.

For example, to minimize the impact of the outsourcing contractor going into liquidation, the outsourcing firm can ensure that an escrow agreement is entered into by all relevant parties. This will provide the outsourcing firm with access to all source code and documentation if such an event occurs.

Alternatively, the outsourcing firm could foster a partnership working relationship. Depending on how critical the system development is, it could provide financial support to the outsourcing contractor, if required.

Risk Acceptance

Once the risk management strategies have been identified, a number of steps are required.

The first step is the identification of what risks executive management are prepared to accept (i.e., residual risk). The residual risks are usually those events that have a very low likelihood of occurrence or very low material impact. For example, there is a very low likelihood that the earth will be struck by an asteroid 1 cubic kilometer in size and the impact on the operations of the organization if the petty cash float of $20.00 being stolen is very low.

The remainder of the risks need to be addressed. The implementation of the relevant risk strategies need to be planned and costed. If viable (i.e., cost-effective), then the strategies should be implemented. However, if not, alternative strategies need to be developed.

Most importantly, the responsibility for the implementation of the risk reduction strategies needs to be assigned to a manager with the appropriate skills, commitment, and authority.

CONCLUSION

The risk management of outsourcing software development is an essential element of managing risk within an organization today. Without implementing a risk management strategy for outsourcing software development, the organization will not only fail to achieve its strategic business objectives, but may expose the organization to the possibility of going out of business.

Executive management is looking toward its IS Auditors to assist in minimizing the risks associated with the development and implementation of the outsourcing strategies.

COBiT provides the IS Auditor with guidelines to achieve the executive management objectives. However, the IS Auditor still needs to utilize/develop a risk management methodology in the application of COBiT.

Note

1. COBiT: Control Objectives for Information and Related Technology (COBiT) Systems Audit and Control Association (ISACA), 1996.

Chapter 22
Managing the Risks of Outsourcing Systems Development: Part III

Ken Doughty
Franke Grieco

THE APPLICATION OF THE RISK AUDIT APPROACH involves a developer (the organization) requiring a new application system for one of its core business functions. The organization had determined that it lacked the skills internally and that the software development was not one of its core businesses. Therefore, executive management decided to outsource the development.

USING THE TEMPLATE

The successful contractor's responsibilities included:

- the selection of the development tools
- the development of a fully functional system that meets the user's requirements and complies with the strategic IT architecture
- the effective management of the change management process
- the acquisition and installation of the hardware platform and operating system

The hardware and software maintenance was not included within the scope of the development project.

The following is a list of definitions relevant to the template.

Developer: The organization acquiring the product or service.

Outsourcing contractor: The prime contractor, the organization responsible for delivering the product or service.

Application developer: The organization providing the skill and resources to design the application, write the code, and build the data base.

Hardware provider: The organization that will provide the computer equipment.

DBMS provider: The organization that provides the database development products.

Change management contractor: The organization responsible for the change management required to make the implementation of the new system a success.

Middleware provider: The organization that provides the software tool products for the development of the application.

CONCLUSION

In 1996, the Systems Audit and Control Association (ISACA) issued Control Objectives for Information and Related Technology (COBiT) to aid the IS Auditor in applying COBiT in controlling the risks inherent in outsourcing the development of software systems. However, the IS Auditor still needs a risk management methodology for applying COBiT. This chapter provides such a methodology and the template is given in Exhibit 22-1.

Exhibit 22-1. The risk audit assessment template.

Risk	Risk Level	Risk Factors	Alert Thresholds	Impact	Risk Treatment
Inability of Outsourcing Contractor to fulfill contract requirements.	H	Outsourcing Contractor loses the capability to continue adequately satisfying contract requirements due to excessive demands placed on its resources (e.g., customer base grows too fast or the Company loses key resources). Outsourcing Contractor is no longer commercially viable (e.g., goes into receivership or liquidation.) Outsourcing Contractor changes ownership. The new owners break up and sells off the Contractor's assests and it ceases to exist. The new owner may take action that would reliquish its contractual obligations to the Developer. Outsourcing Contractor is or becomes fundamentally incapable of delivering (e.g., they lied about their ability).	Expanding client base. (Winning new projects and soliciting new customers.) Analysis of financial performance indicates that Outsourcing Contractor will go or goes into receivership. News of takeover threats by a corporate raider. Deliverables are constantly not met.	The organization's requirements become low priorities for the Outsourcing Contractor. Restricted access to hardware, source code, and documentation that has been paid for but is still in the possession of the contractor. Loss of Contractor for system development, maintenance, support, and enhancement. Incur costs associated with finding replacement contractors or organizing resources internally. If Outsourcing Contractor goes into receivership ownership of hardware and software license may revert to subcontractors. (This is sometimes a contract condition between prime and subcontractors.)	Monitor schedule/contract performance. Monitor acceptance criteria compliance. Prioritize the Developer business with Vendor. Contract condition requiring contractor to provide certified financial information on a regular basis for the purpose of evaluating financial performance. Ensure that the Developer has the ability to take over or acquire critical Outsourcing Contractor's resources in order to keep the project going. Contract condition that contractor-supplied equipment becomes the Developer's property on payment, and that transfer of ownership is confirmed by the subcontractor. View software acquisition documentation to determine extent of licence/copyright ownership by Outsourcing Contractor to see if it may have a detrimental effect.

Exhibit 22-1. The risk audit assessment template. (continued)

Risk	Risk Level	Risk Factors	Alert Thresholds	Impact	Risk Treatment
					Ensure that Outsourcing Contractor indemnifies the Developer over any action that may arise between Outsourcing Contractor and its subcontractors (e.g., copyright ownership claims, etc.).
Risk of Outsourcing Contractor losing interest in meeting contractual obligations.	H	Outsourcing Contractor decides to change its strategic direction and no longer wishes to support, maintain, or enhance the product the Developer acquired. The product provided matures to a point that it would no longer be financially viable for the Contractor to continue enhancing it. The product fails in the market place and Outsourcing Contractor loses interest.	Outsourcing Contractor is sold/taken over. Change in profile of Contractor's client base. Sunset clause of facilities support/maintenance. Relationship deterioration between Developer and Contractor.	Loss of Contractor for system development or diminished service. Loss of Contractor for system maintenance, support and enhancement, or diminished service. Incur costs associated with finding replacement Contractors or organizing resources internally. Loss of Contractor for system development or diminished service.	Ensure that the Developer has the ability to veto the transfer of software copyright ownership to a third party (i.e., the Developer should have the ability to stop the sale of copyright ownership to a small unknown company). This should also apply to the transfer of support and service contracts. Retender or complete project with internal resources. Details of personnel involved in developing and maintaining system. The Developer has access to Outsourcing Contractor's marketing strategy and market research material for assessment purposes.

Ensure that the Developer has the ability to approve key personnel for the project, including those employed by subcontractors as well as Outsourcing Contractor.

Ensure that the Developer has the ability to veto the transfer of software copyright ownership to a third party.

Ensure that contracts between Outsourcing Contractor and subcontractors are in place, and the Developer has access to the contracts.

Outsourcing Contractor should commit to providing support for the product for a minimum of 5 years. (The Developer should not be committed to acquiring Outsourcing Contractor's support for more than 1 year at a time.)

Performance guarantees from Contractor signed by a guarantor.

Ensure that the Developer has the ability to veto the transfer of software copyright ownership to a third party.

Exhibit 22-1. The risk audit assessment template. (continued)

Risk	Risk Level	Risk Factors	Alert Thresholds	Impact	Risk Treatment
Risk of Application Developer losing capacity or interest for meeting contractual obligations.	H	Application Developer is no longer commercially viable (e.g., goes into receivership). Application Developer decides to change its strategic direction and no longer wishes to support, maintain, or enhance the product. Application Developer changes ownership. The new owners break up and sell off the Contractor's assets and it ceases to exist.	Analysis of financial performance indicates that Application Developer will go into receivership. Application Developer goes into receivership. Change in management or ownership. Application Developer is sold/taken over.	Time blow outs, increased costs, and loss of expertise. Increased costs in product maintenance and support. Increased costs in maintenance and support, and a possible loss of access to expertise.	Outsourcing Contractor must have the ability to acquire ownership of source code copyright in the event that Application Developer goes out of business. This should be evidenced by the Developer. Contract condition that permits the Developer unencumbered access to source code and related documentation if Outsourcing Contractor goes out of business. Ensure that there are no legal restrictions preventing the Developer from employing key personnel that worked for the outsourcing contractor. (The above three treatments apply to all three risk factors listed in this section.)

Risk	L				
Risk of Hardware Provider losing capacity or interest for meeting contractual obligations.	L	Hardware Supplier is no longer commercially viable (e.g., goes into receivership). Hardware Provider decides to change its strategic direction and no longer wishes to support, maintain, or enhance the hardware the Developer acquired. Hardware Provider changes ownership. The new owners break up and sell off the Contractor's assets and it ceases to exist.	Hardware Supplier goes into receivership. Change in management or ownership. Hardware Supplier is sold/taken over.	Hardware no longer supported. Increased costs in supporting and maintaining. Costs associated in porting to another platform. (The above three impacts may apply to all or some of the risk factors listed in this section.)	Provide support internally. Port system to a new platform. Ensure that hardware satisfies open systems standards. (The above three treatments apply to all three risk factors listed in this section.)
Risk of DBMS Provider losing capacity or interest for meeting contractual obligations.	L	DBMS Provider is no longer commercially viable (e.g., goes into receivership). DBMS Provider decides to change its strategic direction and no longer wishes to support, maintain, or enhance the product the Developer acquired. DBMS Provider changes ownership. The new owners break up and sell off the Contractor's assets and it ceases to exist.	DBMS Provider goes into receivership. There is a change in management or ownership. DBMS Provider is sold/taken over.	DBMS Provider DBMS no longer supported. Costs associated in porting to another DBMS. (The above impacts may apply to all or some of the risk factors listed in this section.)	Port to another DBMS. Ensure that DBMS satisfies open systems standards. (The above two treatments apply to all three risk factors listed in this section.)

Exhibit 22-1. The risk audit assessment template. (continued)

Risk	Risk Level	Risk Factors	Alert Thresholds	Impact	Risk Treatment
Risk of Change Management Contractor (Change Management Contractors) losing capacity or interest for meeting contractual obligations.	H	Change Management Contractor is no longer commercially viable (e.g., goes into receivership). Change Management Contractor loses the capacity to provide.	Change Management Contractor goes into receivership. Analysis of financial performance indicates that Change Management Contractor will go into receivership.	Time loss. Time loss.	Find some one to replace Change Management Contractor. Perform change management function internally. Select a Change Management Contractor with sound financial and performance backgrounds. (The above treatments apply to all risk factors listed in this section.)
Risk of Middleware Provider losing capacity or interest in meeting contractual obligations.	L	Middleware Provider is no longer commercially viable (e.g., goes into receivership). Middleware Provider decides to change its strategic direction and no longer wishes to support, maintain, or enhance the product the Developer acquired. Middleware Provider changes ownership. The new owners break up and sell off the Contractor's assets and it ceases to exist.	Middleware Provider goes into receivership. Change of management or ownership. Middleware Provider is sold/taken over.	Middleware Provider product no longer supported. Cost of changing product. (The above impacts may apply to all or some of the risk factors listed in this section.)	Replace Middleware Provider with alternative product. Ensure that product satisfies open systems standards. (The above three treatments apply to all three risk factors listed in this section.)

The risk of relationship deterioration between the Developer and Outsourcing Contractor.	H	A dispute between the Developer and Outsourcing Contractor.	A high degree of disputes/unresolved disputes. Disputes can occur while trying to reach a compromise over a system functionality; payments; and product/service quality.	Extended delivery times. Cost over runs. Diminished deliverable quality.	Ensure that relationship is built on the basis of partnering, not an adversarial contract. Neither party should be too restrictive in its demands or lack flexibility in accepting solutions. Good project planning can contribute to a healthy relationship between Vendor and Purchaser. The project plan should clearly stipulate: • The roles and responsibilities of all parties • Who the key personnel are for both the Developer and Outsourcing Contractor • Project time plan • Channels of communication • Risk management approach and quality planning Dispute resolution procedures in contract (i.e., escalation, arbitration, etc.). Nominate an independent mediator, agreeable to both parties, to decide on unresolved disputes.

Exhibit 22-1. The risk audit assessment template. (continued)

Risk	Risk Level	Risk Factors	Alert Thresholds	Impact	Risk Treatment
The risk of having to pay for modifications to the application.	L	Outsourcing Contractor maintains that all modification requests are Developer-specific. Therefore, the Developer must pay. This may be the case early on in the project life as the Developer will be one of a few customers, if not the only one.	Being billed by the Contractor for any modifications requested.	Cost overruns and disputes.	Commitment from Outsourcing Contractor that they will provide software version support for, say, at least 18 months for each release. To have access to support, the Developer should not be committed to upgrade each time there is a new release of the product. Hourly rates should be stipulated in a contract schedule to cover requested services that are outside the contract. Rate increases should be negotiated and specified in the contract. Ensure that there is a formal process for handling modification requests. The process should ensure that quotes are provided, in accordance with schedule rates, and that the request is formally approved by the Developer before Outsourcing Contractor performs any work on the request. Dispute resolution clause in contract.

Nominate an independent arbitrator to decide on unresolved disputes.
Contract conditions and monitoring.

Risk	S	Cause	Symptom	Consequence	Recommendations
The risk of there being misinterpretation of system specifications	S	Outsourcing Contractor's interpretation of functional specifications may differ from that of the Developer's.	Disputes between the Developer and Outsourcing Contractor. Outsourcing Contractor wishing to renegotiate contract requirements.	Cost overruns and disputes.	Ensure that the specifications are adequately defined (use an accepted methodology, etc.). Adequate planning and partnership fostering, as for previous risk, to ensure that issues never escalate to a dispute stage. Dispute resolution clause in contract. Nominate an independent arbitrator to decide on unresolved disputes.
Lack over control of deliverable quality.	S	Outsourcing Contractor loses its QA accreditation. Inadequate QA acceptance criteria is specified in the contract. Lack of escape clauses in the contract. Detailed design specifications are inadequate.	Lack of QA accreditation proof. Constant failure of deliverables to meet design review or acceptance criteria.	Diminished deliverable quality.	A the Developer agent should be appointed to evaluate Contractor quality assurance systems. The contract or project plan should detail quality requirements and acceptance standards. Acceptance criteria should be clearly defined and based on the detailed design specifications. Payments should be tied to performance. The contract should contain dispute resolution procedures.

Exhibit 22-1. The risk audit assessment template. (continued)

Risk	Risk Level	Risk Factors	Alert Thresholds	Impact	Risk Treatment
					Contract condition that Outsourcing Contractor maintains its quality accreditation. Contract condition to rectify faults, "bugs" in system that were not found during the course of reasonable testing. (The above treatments may apply to all risk factors listed in this section.)
Product licenses restricting the Developer's use of facilities.	S	Changes in legal structure and relationships of the Developer entities.	Business Units become independent corporations. The Developer Units establishing one-stop shops or similar. The Developer extending its network through agents and other facilities. Separate the Developer Entities (Developer gets broken up into more than one Developer).	Facilities licenses restrain use of facilities by other entities. Business or organizational development opportunities constrained.	Contract condition that will allow for the Developer entities and agencies to utilize systems. Contract to indicate that the Developer does not pay for additional costs for extra site licenses or user licenses. Alternatively, the contract could contain formulae for calculating costs associated with obtaining site licenses and user licenses.

Risk Factor	Rating	Risk	Impact	Treatment
Ongoing availability of key contractor personnel (HR plan for key project personnel succession).	H	Outsourcing Contractor may have an inadequate staff training and replacement strategy. Outsourcing Contractor's knowledge base may be sensitive to staff loss. Inadequate system documentation maintained by Outsourcing Contractor.	High staff turnover for Contractor. Inability of Contractor to meet deadlines. Time blow outs. Inability to obtain product support, etc.	Identify key resources and implement strategies to maintain their availability (e.g., ensure that Outsourcing Contractor plans to train and maintain at least four people that are adequately familiar with the product). Outsourcing Contractor to provide information, on a regular basis, of their key project personnel, detailing their skills, experience, and background. Ensure that the contract does not restrict the Developer from employing key staff that leave Outsourcing Contractor. (The above treatments may apply to all three risk factors listed in this section.)
Risk of adequate performance criteria and KPIs not clearly specified in contract.	H	Inability to define KPIs. KPIs artificially set too high or too low.	Lack of Contractor accountability. Software deficiencies diminished data integrity. Disputes with Contractor. Detrimental impact on deliverable quality. *(The above impact applies to both of the risk factors listed in this section.)*	Base KPIs on detailed system specifications. Use industry standards for setting KPIs. Expert assistance in defining KPIs. Mutually agreed KPIs. Ability to modify KPIs during course of project. (The above treatments may apply to all risk factors listed in this section.)

Exhibit 22-1. The risk audit assessment template. (continued)

Risk	Risk Level	Risk Factors	Alert Thresholds	Impact	Risk Treatment
Viability of equity interests (funding the development but not owning the product).	S	No intellectual property rights.		No royalty streams for the Developer, and potential loss of revenue. Competitors can easily negate any competitive advantage provided by the technology via acquisition.	Informed executive or policy decision on whether to partake in royalties or not. An affirmative decision could result in a long-term relationship between the developer and the outsourcing contractor.
No apparent risk sharing arrangement with contractor.	S	The contract price does not adequately account for the risks taken and the returns forgone by the Developer.		Contract price too high.	Competitive tenders.

Outsourcing Contractor may demonstrate the product to prospective customers and use the Developer as a demonstration site. Therefore, there is a risk that a business partnership agreement with the Outsourcing Contractor may cause too much disruption in the Developer.	M	The Developer becomes a beta site. There are frequent new releases of the product (every 6 months).	Testing beta releases of the product on a frequent basis. Too many visits from prospective customers. Staff complain that they cannot complete their own work due to customer visits.	Down time due to failure of beta software. Costs associated with staff time taken up demonstrating the product. Overtime costs associated with catching up on work backlogs.	Restrictions on beta testing. Stringent testing before allowing any beta versions into the Developer production environment. Restrictions on product demonstrations. Contract condition indicating that liabilities rest with Outsourcing Contractor for any costs or losses incurred by the Developer during testing or product demonstrations.

Exhibit 22-1. The risk audit assessment template. (continued)

Risk	Risk Level	Risk Factors	Alert Thresholds	Impact	Risk Treatment
Risk of inaction or delay in making decision on project supply contract.	S	Long periods for decisions to be made.	Evaluation and decision to appoint a Contractor takes too long. Complaints received from tenderers.	Damage to the Developer image. On cost factor added into tenders by any party tendering for jobs with the Developer. Tenders withdrawn. Tender price may be revised upward.	Streamline process for future decisions. Improve process for briefing tenderers.
Risk of developing Project in-house.	H	The Developer not currently geared up for developing a system for project-type project (inadequate internal skills base and resources).	No Suitable Contractors. Inability to reach agreement with tenderers.	Schedule and budget overruns. Requirements unsatisfied. High costs.	Detailed performance measures for all contract deliverables. Detailed planning and an adequately skilled project team. Follow recognized methodology. QA and audit reviews. Employ or contract into the organization the required skill base and expertise. Performance-based payment.

| The risk of failure in the change management processes | H | System not meeting stakeholder expectations. System not being used to its fullest potential. System considered a failure and a hindrance to business processes. Decreased level of service. No realized productivity or performance gains. Increased customer complaints. | Inadequate stakeholder involvement or ownership. Poor promotion and selling of new system to users/stakeholders. Lack of adequate staff training and documentation. Poor redeployment and retraining planning. Change Management Contractor becomes unavailable. | Nonacceptance of the system. | Ensure adequate stakeholder involvement and encourage ownership of system. Monitor processes. QA acceptance of change management. Develop a change management plan that includes communication of issues to all stakeholders and training. (The above treatments may apply to all or some of the risk factors listed in this section.) |

Exhibit 22-1. The risk audit assessment template. (continued)

Risk	Risk Level	Risk Factors	Alert Thresholds	Impact	Risk Treatment
Risk of over control by the Developer.	S	Relationship between the Developer and Contractor is not one of partnership, but confrontational. Multiple project managers.	The contract is too restrictive. The Developer's organizational culture is not conducive to a partnership with the Outsourcing Contractor. Too many groups established to review Contractor progress and performance. No formal communication channels established between the Contractor and the Developer.	Diminished quality in service and deliverables.	Obtain expert advice to ensure that the contract is not too restrictive. Ensure that undue pressure is not placed on the Outsourcing Contractor (i.e., it is not the Developer's main objective to force the Outsourcing Contractor into receivership). Ensure that communications with the tenderer are through one point. Ensure that there is a Charter that contains the explicit authorities defined. It should also contain procedures on how the Developer will deal with Outsourcing Contractor during modifications and after the contract is set. (The above treatments may apply to all the risk factors listed in this section.)

The Developer's inability to address changing customer needs across a wide range of business processes.	S	Contractor cannot address modification requests quickly so that the Developer processes can adjust to meet customers' changing needs.	Modifications requests are not addressed in a timely fashion by the contractor.	Cost increases. Time blow outs.	The project functional specifications require that many parameter changes can be performed by the user. This will minimize dependency on the Outsourcing Contractor for implementing system modifications. Adequate acceptance testing to ensure functionality.

Exhibit 22-1. The risk audit assessment template. (continued)

Risk	Risk Level	Risk Factors	Alert Thresholds	Impact	Risk Treatment
Security Risks					
• Unauthorised access to the Developer data and equipment.	H	Poor security culture.	Poor access controls at Outsourcing Contractor premises.	Cost overruns. Time deadlines not met. Project failure or termination.	Outsourcing Contractor must have a disaster recovery capability. It should have insurance to cover any Developer equipment on their premises. Backup processes should be in place, with at least one set of copies going off-site to the Developer-designated premises. Evidence of above requirements must be provided on demand during course of contract.
• Malicious intent to undermine project.	H		Poor access controls on the Developer premises.		
• Disaster recovery planning and risk management during development and implementation on phases.			Poor Industrial Relations policies or their poor implementation. Lack of business continuity planning and risk minimization strategies by Outsourcing Contractor.		

Risk					
Risk that the Developer's data provided for development and test purposes or even residing in the production environment could be accessed and used for unauthorized purposes.	H	The Developer not having access to or control over its own data, leading to unauthorized access or usage of the data.	Ownership clauses not included in contract.	Damage to the Developer's image. Possibility of missed income. Costs incurred to access data or use data in different ways.	Contract to indicate ownership of all data and its usage. Independent audit review of Outsourcing Contractor's logical and physical security.

Exhibit 22-1. The risk audit assessment template. (continued)

Risk	Risk Level	Risk Factors	Alert Thresholds	Impact	Risk Treatment
The risk of functionality changes during the course of the project.	H	Initiation of change requests.	The Developer decides on new types of fees, taxes, and rebates. Payment requests from Outsourcing Contractor for unauthorized change requests.	Increases in contract cost. Time blow out for project completion.	Ensure that there is a formal process for handling modification requests. The process should ensure that quotes are provided, in accordance with schedule rates, and that the request is formally approved by the Developer before Outsourcing Contractor performs any work on the request. The project functional specifications require that many parameter changes can be performed by the user. This will minimize dependency on the Outsourcing Contractor for implementing system modifications. Acceptance testing to ensure functionality.

Chapter 23
Audit and Control of Information Systems Outsourcing

S. Yvonne Scott

OUTSOURCING IS CONTRACTING WITH AN OUTSIDE VENDOR for the performance of a function that was previously performed by an employee of the company. It is a practice that organizations have been engaged in for some time. For example, most large companies collect payments through a bank lock box rather than having employees receive them at home offices. Similarly, many companies have chosen to have an outside firm process and distribute payroll. These practices are both examples of general accounting outsourcing. Outsourcing is a reality and is an industry force that warrants the audit community's attention. Any significant change in the established control environment indicates security issues that should be closely examined. In addition, information (and the systems used to generate it) can differentiate a company from its competitors; therefore, information is a valuable asset worthy of protection.

Previous Misconceptions

Outsourcing IS is not a new trend. The use of service bureaus, contract programmers, disaster recovery sites, data storage vendors, and value-added networks are all examples of outsourcing. In addition, such functions as time-sharing, network management, software maintenance, applications processing, limited facilities management, full facility management, and EDI services are now considered potentially outsourced functions. For example, Eastman Kodak entered into a ten-year agreement to outsource its entire IT function in 1989, a deal worth an estimated $100 million. As a result of increased reliance on outsourcing by organizations, a new area of audit responsibility has been created.

Outsourcing is not a transfer of responsibility. Tasks and duties can be delegated, but responsibility remains with the organization's management.

Therefore, outsourcing does not relieve the organization or management of the responsibility to provide IS services for internal operations and, in some cases, customers.

Outsourcing is not an excuse for substandard customer service, regardless of whether the customers are internal or external to the organization. Customers do not care how or by whom services are provided. Their concern is that they receive the quality services they need, when they are needed.

The most successful outsourcing deals are tailored relationships that are built around specific business needs and strategies. There has been a definite shift from an all-or-nothing approach to a more selective application of outsourcing. In many cases, deals have been structured to more closely resemble partnerships or alliances rather than service agreements. For example, some of these deals include agreements to share in the profits and products that result from the alliance.

In the internal audit profession, outsourcing is not an elimination of the need to audit the outsourced services. It is the auditor's responsibility to safeguard all of the assets of an organization. Therefore, because information is clearly an asset, the auditor must ensure that its confidentiality, integrity, and availability are preserved.

Types of Outsourcing Services

As previously discussed, any agreement to obtain services from an outside vendor rather than providing them internally meets the definition of outsourcing. The following list includes the types of IS outsourcing service contracts that the audit community is being required to address:

- time-sharing and applications processing
- contract programming
- software and hardware maintenance
- contingency planning and disaster recovery planning and services
- electronic data interchange services
- systems development and project management
- network management
- reengineering services
- transitional services
- limited facilities management
- full facility management
- remote LAN management

It should be noted that the first six services in this list have been outsourced for at least a decade. The remainder of the list represents expansions of the other services. For example, facilities management is the use of time-sharing on a broader basis, and remote LAN management is hardware maintenance on a distributed basis.

Implementation Reasons

Outsourcing should be specifically tailored to the business needs of an organization. It appears to be most viable for those organizations with the following characteristics:

- **Organizations in which IS is not a competitive tool.** If there is little opportunity for an organization to distinguish itself from its competition through systems applications or operations, there is less concern over entrusting the execution of these services to a third party.
- **Organizations in which short-term IS interruptions do not diminish the organization's ability to compete or remain in business.** An outsourcing vendor should be able to recover operations in one to two days. It is probably not reasonable to rely on a third party to recover complex systems within one to two hours. Contracts can be structured to specify that the outsourcer must recover within a one- to two-hour timeframe or incur severe penalties. However, if the outsourcer fails to comply with the contract, it is unlikely that the penalty adequately compensates the organization for the long-term effects of losing customers. Therefore, the shorter the tolerable window of exposure, the less viable outsourcing becomes.
- **Organizations in which outsourcing does not eliminate critical internal knowledge.** If outsourcing eliminates those internal resources that are key to the future innovations or products of the organization, the risk may be too great to assume.
- **Organizations in which existing IS capabilities are limited or ineffective.** If this is the case and the organization is considering outsourcing, management has probably determined that additional investments must be made in the area of IS. In this situation, it may make more sense to buy the required expertise than to build it.
- **Organizations in which there is a low reward for IS excellence.** In this case, even if the organization developed and operated the most effective and efficient information systems the payback would be minimal. Because every organization must capitalize on its assets to survive, the effort that would be expended could probably be spent more wisely in other areas.

Motivating Factors

Companies have various reasons for outsourcing. Just as the outsourcing agreement itself should be tailored to the individual circumstances, the factors that cause an organization to achieve its objectives through outsourcing are unique.

Because more and more auditors are becoming involved in the evaluation of IS solutions before they are implemented, it is important to understand these motivating factors when evaluating whether a particular solution meets an organization's objectives. In addition, as in all cases in which the auditor has an opportunity to participate in the solution of a business problem (e.g., systems development audits), it is important to understand the overall objectives. In order to add value to the process, these objectives and their potential shortcomings should be considered when evaluating whether the outsourcing agreement maximizes asset use and maintains the control environment. For this reason, the motivating factors often cited by management, as well as some of the reasons why these objectives may not be readily met, are discussed in the following sections.

Cost Savings

As the global economy grows, management faces increased competition on reduced budgets. The savings are generally believed to be achievable through outsourcing by increasing efficiency (e.g., staff reductions, shared resources). However, several factors may preclude cost savings. Comparable reductions in service levels and product quality may occur, and comparable staff reductions may be achievable in-house. In addition, vendors may not necessarily achieve the economies of scale previously gained through shared hardware because many software vendors have changed their licensing agreements to vary with the size of the hardware.

Fixed Cost versus Variable Cost. In some cases, management has been driven to a fixed-cost contract for its predictability. However, service levels may decrease as the cost of providing those services increases. In addition, should business needs dictate a reduction in information systems, the company may be committed to contracted fees.

Flexible IS Costs

Management may have indicated that outsourcing is preferred because it allows management to adjust its IS costs as business circumstances change. However, necessary revisions in service levels and offerings may not be readily available through the vendor at prices comparable to those agreed on for existing services.

Dissatisfaction with Internal Performance

Dissatisfaction is often cited by senior management because it has not seen the increases in revenue and market share nor the increased productivity and cost reductions used to justify projects. Many outsourcing agreements, however, include provisions to transfer employees to the outsourcer. The net result may be that the personnel resources do not change significantly.

Competitive Climate

Speed, flexibility, and efficiency are often considered the keys to competitive advantage. By outsourcing the IS function, personnel resources can be quickly adjusted to respond to business peaks and valleys. However, the personnel assigned to respond to the business needs that determine the organization's competitive position may not be well acquainted with the company's business and its objectives. In addition, short-term cost savings achieved through reactive systems development may lead to long-term deficiencies in the anticipation of the information systems needs of both internal and external customers.

Focus on Core Business

Such outsourcing support functions as IS allows management to focus on its primary business. If IS is integral to the product offering or the competitive advantage of the organization, however, a shift in focus away from this component of the core business may lead to long-term competitive disadvantage.

Capital Availability and Emerging Technologies

Senior management does not want to increase debt or use available capital to improve or maintain the IS function. If IS is proactive and necessary to support the strategic direction of the organization, however, delaying such investments may result in a competitive disadvantage. In addition, precautions must be taken to ensure that the outsourcing vendor continues to provide state of the art technology. Obsolescence can be tempered without the use of capital by negotiating hardware leases that afford some flexibility.

Staff Management and Training

Outsourcing eliminates the need to recruit, retain, and train IS personnel. This becomes the responsibility of the vendor. But regardless of who these individuals report to, IS personnel need to receive training on the latest technologies in order to remain effective. After control over this process is turned over to a vendor, provisions should be made to ensure that training continues. In addition, the cost of this training is not actually eliminated. Because the vendor is in business to turn a profit, the cost of training is included in the price proposal. In addition, this cost is likely to be inflated by the vendor's desired profit margin.

Transition Management

As mergers and acquisitions take place, senior management views outsourcing as a means to facilitate the integration of several different hardware platforms and application programs. In addition, some managers are utilizing outsourcing as a means to facilitate the organization's move to a new processing environment (e.g., client/server). However, knowledge of strategic information systems should not be allowed to shift to an outside vendor if the long-term intention is to retain this expertise within the organization. In such cases, the maintenance of existing systems should be transferred to the outsourcer during the transition period.

Reduction of Risk

Outsourcing can shift some of the business risks associated with capital investment, technological change, and staffing to the vendor. Because of decreased hands-on control, however, security risks may increase.

Accounting Treatment

Outsourcing allows the organization to remove IS assets from the balance sheet and begin to report these resources as a nondepreciable line item (e.g., rent). The organization should ensure that outsourcing is not being used as a means of obtaining a capital infusion that does not appear as balance sheet debt. This can be achieved if the outsource vendor buys the organization's IS assets at book (rather than market) value. The difference is paid back through the contract and, therefore, represents a creative means of borrowing funds.

All of these driving forces can be valid reasons for senior management to enter into an outsourcing arrangement. It should be noted that the cautions discussed in the previous sections are not intended to imply that outsourcing is undesirable. Rather, they are highlighted here to allow the reader to enter into the most advantageous outsourcing agreement possible. As a result, these cautions should be kept in mind when protective measures are considered.

Protective Measures

Although it is desirable to build a business partnership with the outsource vendor, it is incumbent on the organization to ensure that the outsourcer is legally bound to take care of the company's needs. Standard contracts are generally written to protect the originator (i.e., the vendor). Therefore, it is important to critically review these agreements and ensure that they are modified to include provisions that adequately address the following issues.

Retention of Adequate Audit Rights

It is not sufficient to generically specify that the client has the right to audit the vendor. If the specific rights are not detailed in the contract, the scope of an audit may be subject to debate. To avoid this confusion and the time delays that it may cause, it is suggested that, at a minimum, the following specific rights be detailed in the contract:

- Who can audit the outsourcer (i.e., client internal auditors, outsourcer internal auditors, independent auditors, user controlled audit authority)
- What is subject to audit (e.g., vendor invoices, physical security, operating system security, communications costs, and disaster recovery tests)
- When the outsourcer can or cannot be audited
- Where the audit is to be conducted (e.g., at the outsourcer's facility, remotely by communications)
- How the audit is conducted (i.e., what tools and facilities are available)
- Guaranteed access to the vendor's records, including those that substantiate billing
- Read-only access to all of the client company's data
- Assurance that audit software can be executed
- Access to documentation

Continuity of Operations and Timely Recovery

The timeframes within which specified operations must be recovered, as well as each party's responsibilities to facilitate the recovery, should be specified in the contract. In addition, the contract should specify the recourse that is available to the client, as well as who is responsible for the cost of carrying out any alternative action should the outsourcer fail to comply with the contract requirements. Special consideration should be given to whether these requirements are reasonable and likely to be carried out successfully.

Cost and Billing Verification

Only those costs applicable to the client's processing should be included in invoices. This issue is particularly important for those entering into outsourcing agreements that are not on a fixed-charge basis. Adequate documentation should be made available to allow the billed client to determine the appropriateness and accuracy of invoices. However, documentation is also important to those clients who enter into a fixed invoice arrangement. In such cases, knowing the actual cost incurred by the outsourcer allows the client to effectively negotiate a fair price when prices are open for renegotiation. It should also be noted that, although long-term fixed costs are beneficial in those cases in which costs and use continue to increase, they are equally detrimental in those situations in which costs and use are declining. Therefore, it may be beneficial to include a contract clause that allows rates to be reviewed at specified intervals throughout the life of the contract.

Security Administration

Outsourcing may be used as an agent for change and, therefore, may represent an opportunity to enhance the security environment. In any case, decisions must be made regarding whether the administration (i.e., granting) and the monitoring (i.e., violation reporting and follow-up) should be retained internally or delegated to the outsourcer. In making this decision, it is imperative that the company has confidence that it can maintain control over the determination of who should be granted access and in what capacity (e.g., read, write, delete, execute) to both its data and that of its customers.

Confidentiality, Integrity, and Availability

Care must be taken to ensure that both data and programs are kept confidential, retain their integrity, and are available when needed. These requirements are complicated when the systems are no longer under the physical control of the owning entity. In addition, the concerns that this situation poses are further compounded when applications are stored and executed on systems that are shared with other customers of the outsourcer. Of particular concern is the possibility that proprietary data and programs may be resident on the same physical devices as those of a competitor. Fortunately, technology has provided us with the ability to logically control and separate these environments with Virtual Machine (e.g., IBM Corp.'s Processor Resource/System Management). It should also be noted that the importance of confidentiality does not necessarily terminate with the vendor relationship. Therefore, it is important to obtain nondisclosure and noncompete agreements from the vendor as a means of protecting the company after the contract expires. Similarly, adequate data retention and destruction requirements must be specified.

Program Change Control and Testing

The policies and standards surrounding these functions should not be relaxed in the outsourced environment. These controls determine whether confidence can be placed on the integrity of the organization's computer applications.

Vendor Controls

The physical security of the data center should meet the requirements set by the American Society for Industrial Security. In addition, there should be close compatibility between the vendor and the customer with regard to control standards.

Network Controls

Because the network is only as secure as its weakest link, care must be taken to ensure that the network is adequately secured. It should be noted that dial-up capabilities and network monitors can be used to circumvent established controls. Therefore, even if the company's operating data is not proprietary, measures should be taken to ensure that unauthorized users cannot gain access to the system. This should minimize the risks associated with unauthorized data, program modifications, and unauthorized use of company resources(e.g., computer time, phone lines).

Personnel

Measures should be taken to ensure that personnel standards are not relaxed after the function is turned over to a vendor. As was noted earlier, in many cases the same individuals who were employed by the company are hired by the vendor to service that contract. Provided that these individuals are competent, this should not pose any concern. If, however, a reason cited for outsourcing is to improve the quality of personnel, this situation may not be acceptable. In addition, care should be taken to ensure that the client company is notified of any significant personnel changes, security awareness training is continued, and the client company is not held responsible should the vendor make promises (e.g., benefits, salary levels, job security) to the transitional employees that it does not subsequently keep.

Vendor Stability

To protect itself from the possibility that the vendor may withdraw from the business or the contract, it is imperative that the company maintain ownership of its programs and data. Otherwise, the client may experience an unexpected interruption in its ability to service its customers or the loss of proprietary information.

Strategic Planning

Because planning is integral to the success of any organization, this function should be performed by company employees. Although it may be necessary to include vendor representatives in these discussions, it is important to ensure that the company retains control over the use of IS in achieving its objectives. Because many of these contracts are long-term and business climates often change, this requires that some flexibility be built into the agreement to allow for the expansion or contraction of IS resources. In addition to these specific areas, the following areas should also be addressed in the contract language:

- definition and assignment of responsibilities
- performance requirements and the means by which compliance is measured

- recourse for nonperformance
- contract termination provisions
- warranties and limitations of liability
- vendor reporting requirements

Protective Measures During Transition

After it has been determined that the contractual agreement is in order, a third-party security review should be performed to verify vendor representations. After the security environment has been verified, the contract can be signed. After the contract has been signed and as functions are being moved from internal departments to the vendor, an organization can enhance the process by performing the following:

- meeting frequently with the vendor and employees
- involving users in the implementation
- developing transition teams and providing them with well-defined responsibilities, objectives, and target dates
- increasing security awareness programs for both management and employees
- considering a phased implementation that includes employee bonuses for phase completion
- providing outplacement services and severance pay to displaced employees

Continuing Protective Measures

As the outsourcing relationship continues, the client should continue to take proactive measures to protect its interests. These measures may include continued security administration involvement, budget reviews, ongoing reviews and testing of environment changes, periodic audits and security reviews, and letters of agreement and supplements to the contract. Each of these client rights should be specified in the contract. In addition, the continuing audit effort typically includes the following types of audit objectives:

- establishing the validity of billings (IBM Corp.'s Systems Management Facility type-30 records can be used)
- evaluating system effectiveness and performance (IBM Corp.'s Resource Management Facility indicates the percentage of time the CPU is busy. As use increases, costs may rise because of higher paging requirements.)
- reviewing the integrity, confidentiality, and availability of programs and data
- verifying that adequate measures have been made to ensure continuity of operations
- reviewing the adequacy of the overall security environment
- determining the accuracy of program functionality

Audit Alternatives

It should be noted that resource sharing (i.e., the sharing of common resources with other customers of the vendor) may lead to the vendor's insistence that the audit rights of individual clients be limited. This is reasonable. However, performance of audits by the internal audit group of the client is only one means of approaching the audit requirement. The following alternative measures can be taken to ensure that adequate audit coverage can be maintained.

Internal Audit by the Vendor

In this case, the outsourcing vendor's own internal audit staff would perform the reviews and report their results to the customer base. Auditing costs are included in the price, the auditor is familiar with the operations, and it is less disruptive to the outsourcer's operations. However, auditors are employees of the audited entity; this may limit independence and objectivity, and clients may not be able to dictate audit areas, scope, or timing.

External Auditor or Third-Party Review

These types of audits are normally performed by an independent accounting firm. This firm may or may not be the same firm that performs the annual audit of the vendor's financial statements. In addition, the third-party reviewer may be hired by the client or the vendor. External auditors may be more independent than employees of the vendor. In addition, the client can negotiate for the ability to exercise some control over the selection of the third party auditors and the audit areas, scope, and timing, and the cost can be shared among participating clients. The scope of external reviews however, tends to be more general in nature than those performed by internal auditors. In addition, if the auditor is hired by the vendor, the perceived level of independence of the auditor may be impaired. If the auditor is hired by each individual client the costs may be duplicated by each client and the duplicate effort may disrupt vendor operations.

User-Controlled Audit Authority

The audit authority typically consists of a supervisory board comprised of representatives from each participating client company, the vendor, and the vendor's independent accounting firm and a staff comprised of some permanent and temporary members who are assigned from each of the participating organizations. The staff then performs audits at the direction of the supervisory board. In addition, a charter, detailing the rights and responsibilities of the user controlled audit authority, should be developed and accepted by the participants before commissioning the first review.

This approach to auditing the outsourcing vendor appears to combine the advantages and minimize the disadvantages previously discussed. In addition, this approach can benefit the vendor by providing a marketing advantage, supporting its internal audit needs, and minimizing operational disruptions.

Recommended Course of Action

Outsourcing arrangements are as unique as those companies seeking outsourcing services. Although outsourcing implies that some control must be turned over to the vendor, many measures can be taken to maintain an acceptable control environment and adequate audit coverage. Some basic rules can be followed to ensure a successful arrangement. These measures include:

- Segmenting the organization's IS activities into potential outsource modules (e.g., by technology, types of processing, or businesses served)
- Using analysis techniques to identify those modules that should be outsourced
- Controlling technology direction setting
- Treating outsourcing as a partnership, but remembering that the partner's objective is to maximize its own profits
- Matching the organization's business needs with the outsource partner's current and prospective capabilities (e.g., long-term viability, corporate culture, management philosophy, business and industry knowledge, flexibility, technology leadership, and global presence)
- Ensuring that all agreements are in writing
- Providing for continuing review and control

The guidelines discussed in this chapter should be combined with the client's own objectives to develop an individualized and effective audit approach.

Chapter 24
Audit Guidelines for IT Outsourcing

Wim Van Grembergen
Daniel Vander Borght

THE OUTSOURCING OF INFORMATION SERVICES has recently received a great deal of attention. Today, IT management can form contracts with third-party vendors for almost all IT services ranging from data center operations to acquiring packaged software and systems development. IT outsourcing literature provides some reasons why outsourcing is popular:

- Because of the economies of scale, companies' costs are reduced.
- Companies are able to purchase expertise that is not otherwise available.
- IT staff is available for projects that may have a greater strategic value.

The popularity of IT outsourcing has also been promoted by success stories, such as British Petroleum (BP). Now, BP has only 150 people employed in IT instead of 1,400 five years ago. Their data center is delegated to outsourcing companies, and most of the development of applications is replaced by packages or contract work. However, risks and pitfalls also come with IT outsourcing. Major risks are: being locked into a long-term contract, inflexible contracts for supplying data center services, and being totally dependent on outsourcing for the development and maintenance of applications. Therefore, a company can only harvest the benefits of IT outsourcing if proper control measures are in place; in other words, if the right structures, procedures, and practices are implemented.

It is management's responsibility to control IT outsourcing. To do this, managers need a framework of standardized and generally accepted IT outsourcing control practices to benchmark their existing approach for the outsourcing of information services. This kind of framework has recently been provided by members of the Information Systems Auditor's and Control Association (ISACA),the leading professional IT audit organization.

THE OUTSOURCING OF INFORMATION SERVICES

In examining the topic of IT outsourcing, these questions should be raised and answered:

- What can be outsourced?
- What are the reasons for outsourcing?
- What processes should be outsourced

WHAT CAN BE OUTSOURCED?

Outsourcing can be applied to all IT activities and processes. The best known and most recurring forms are contracts with software houses to develop applications and with firms to handle daily IT operations. Some typical IT processes for outsourcing include:

- Expert advice regarding the corporate strategic IT plan
- The specification of the requirements for applications development and hardware acquisition
- Formulating descriptions of the detailed functional and technical requirements, design, and implementation of information systems
- The development, maintenance, and production of specific applications (e.g., a payroll application)
- The complete or partial responsibility for day-to-day data center operations, including hardware maintenance, logical and physical security, and disaster recovery
- The education and training of IT staff and end users
- Support regarding the development and implementation of quality systems (e.g., following ISO 9000 guidelines for the systems development process)
- A source for new personnel

Recently, the outsourcing business experienced a big growth surge, and international companies like Andersen, Computer Sciences Corporation, EDS, and IBM are very active in both the U.S. and European markets. Locally, outsourcing vendors can be found that offer packaged software and customized applications.

WHAT ARE THE REASONS FOR OUTSOURCING?

The most important reasons for outsourcing are the freeing up of IT professionals and cost reductions. The IT staff can then be appointed to more crucial and strategic projects like the development of business systems that support and even shape the business objectives. Outsourcing vendors may have a functional and technical specialization that may result in lower costs. Some vendors advertise savings up to 50 percent. However, cost savings of 15 to 30 percent seem to be more realistic. Other benefits of outsourcing include:

- The increased quality of deliverables
- Fixed prices
- Increased flexibility of resources
- Fixed costs (i.e., overhead) become variable costs

External providers may deliver a higher quality of work because they recognize that they are working for clients and that they will lose future assignments if their clients are not satisfied. Outsourcing contracts also have the advantage of flexibility. For short-term contracts, companies can opt for new and emerging technologies, and temporary personnel can be hired to accommodate peak work situations.

On the other hand, IT outsourcing has some disadvantages, mainly in the areas of control and audit risks. Major IT outsourcing risks include:

- Dependence on outside vendors
- The loss of control, including inadequate control of data integrity
- The disclosure of strategic and confidential information
- Hidden or additional costs
- Applications and packages not meeting company requirements or needs
- The vendor-supplied documentation or training is inadequate or not provided
- No guarantee of the continuity of services

Furthermore, IT literature often gives a too optimistic view of IT outsourcing when, in fact, internal IT departments may also achieve similar results through a well-considered reorganization and reengineering of their services. There may be an insourcing response to the question of outsourcing. Internal IT departments must have the opportunity to submit a new bid against an outside vendor's offer. This may lead to an insourcing decision because general and IT management is usually threatened by outsourcing and will, therefore, be creative and introduce further cost-reduction strategies.

WHAT PROCESSES SHOULD BE OUTSOURCED?

The crucial question is undoubtedly: which IT processes are suitable for outsourcing and which IT processes must be carried out internally? The answer is simple: the processes that are strategic must stay in-house, and those that are not can be outsourced, particularly if it is at less cost.

Industry experts recommend outsourcing when the applications have little or no strategic value, when the interruption of the information systems service is not a problem, and when the internal functional and technical expertise is low and can be upgraded by bringing in specialists from the outside. For example, cafeteria-style accounting processes can be easily outsourced, but airline reservations systems typically have to be kept internally.

THE MANAGEMENT OF IT OUTSOURCING

IT outsourcing does not mean having to commit to long-term contracts over five or even 10 years. The objective should be to maximize flexibility and control through maximizing competition. IT outsourcing is not a once-only decision. A procedure should be implemented whereby external providers and internal IT departments must compete for delivering the different IT services.

Companies, like British Petroleum, already have gone through a long learning process and have moved from total and long-term outsourcing contracts to selective outsourcing based on yearly renewable assignments. In the 1980s, BP outsourced selectively some IT services, such as the maintenance of desktop computers, the help desk function, and the maintenance and support of some production applications, to external vendors. Most of these contracts gave the expected benefits of cost reduction, better service, and the introduction of new ideas and emerging technologies. However, there was an underestimation of the intercontract problems. The different outsourcers managed their processes quite well, but they did not cooperate with one another. As a result, BP searched for another, more effective approach.

The solution of retaining a single outsourcer was rejected because they did not want to be dependent on one supplier, and it was believed that a single external vendor can never excel in all IT areas. Moreover, BP did not believe in a long-term contract because it did not guarantee that the outsourcer would bring in new technologies as they emerged. Finally, they opted for a selective approach, having three complementary vendors that were also responsible for managing any intercontract difficulties. With these three suppliers, a long-term partnership was established, and each year the delivered services were evaluated and the contract terms were renegotiated.

This method implies that the performance of the outsourcers has to be measured, for example, in terms of client satisfaction, software development productivity, on-time delivery of applications, online availability, acceptable response times, and throughput. On the basis of the BP case, distinct alternatives regarding IT sourcing can be summarized:

- A single vendor for most IT services
- Selective outsourcing involving multiple vendors
- Selective outsourcing involving multiple vendors that share the responsibility for the whole contract
- Insourcing or the internal IT department remains responsible for all IT processes

Some interesting quantitative data on the different outsourcing forms is available from a sample containing the outsourcing decisions of 40 organizations. Approximately 25 percent of the sample organizations have long-term contracts ranging from five to 10 years, 25 percent decided to keep the IT services in house, and 50 percent opted for selective outsourcing.

IT OUTSOURCING CONTRACTS

Effective management of outsourcing contracts is of primordial importance. Using a standard contract is not advisable, because it often leads to endless discussions and supplementary costs for items that apparently were not originally included in the contract. It is possible that suppliers may try to maximize their benefits and will charge high prices for extra deliverables.

An outsourcing contract has to be established and executed on the basis of bargaining in good faith. The contract has to stipulate the responsibilities and tasks of the outsourcing party and of the internal IT department. It is very important that internal IT staff are involved in the outsourcing project. During the project, the internal staff must acquire the necessary functional and technical knowledge so that, in an emergency, they can continue the project and maintain the application after completion. It is obvious that maintaining control over the outsourcer involves more than checking the invoice. The internal IT professionals have to be a participating partner in the outsourcing project.

THE COBiT MODEL

Control Objectives for Information and related Technology (COBiT) have been developed as a generally applicable and accepted standard for good practices for information technology control. The authors, ISACA, of this control model position their model as a bridge between business control models like the Committee of Sponsoring Organizations of the Treadway Commission (1994) and the more focused control models for information technology, like the Department of Trade & Industry (1993). The COBiT model focuses on specific and detailed control objectives associated with 32 IT processes that, as shown in Exhibit 24-1, can be classified into four major domains: planning and organization, acquisition and implementation, delivery and support, and monitoring. An added feature of this list is that it contains all IT processes that can be outsourced. The COBiT control objectives related to the IT process No. 19, managing third-party services, are:

- **Supplier Interfaces** External vendors have to be properly identified, and technical and organizational interfaces with suppliers have to be documented.

- **Owner Relationships** A relationship owner, an individual who is responsible for ensuring the quality of the relationship, should be appointed.
- **Third-Party Contracts** A formal contract should exist and be agreed to.
- **Outsourcing Contracts** The contracts should be based on required processing levels, security, monitoring, and contingency requirements.
- **Continuity of Services** The business risks related to the third party should be considered.
- **Security Relationships** Security agreements, such as nondisclosure, should be identified and explicitly stated and agreed to.
- **Monitoring** A continuous monitoring process should be implemented to ensure adherence to the contract stipulations.

COBIT AUDIT GUIDELINES

COBiT describes the audit guidelines that enable auditors to review specific IT processes against the preceding control objectives. The value of this publication is the support that it provides in establishing an effective audit plan as shown in Exhibit 24-2.

CONCLUSION

This chapter has described an approach to controlling and auditing the process of IT outsourcing. The approach is based on COBiT, a recently developed IT audit and control model. IT outsourcing has become popular for these main reasons:

- because of the economies of scale, companies' costs are reduced
- companies are able to purchase expertise that is not otherwise available
- IT staff is available for projects that may have a greater strategic value

Exhibit 24-1. IT processes identified by COBiT.

PLANNING AND ORGANIZATION

1. Define a strategic plan
2. Define the information architecture
3. Determine technological direction
4. Define organization and relationship
5. Manage the investment
6. Communicate management and direction
7. Manage human resources
8. Ensure compliance with external requirements
9. Assess risk
10. Manage projects
11. Manage quality

ACQUISITION AND IMPLEMENTATION

12. Identify automated solutions
13. Acquire and maintain application software
14. Acquire and maintain technology architecture
15. Develop and maintain procedures
16. Install and accredit systems
17. Manage changes

DELIVERY AND SUPPORT

18. Define service levels
19. Manage third-party services
20. Manage performance and capacity
21. Ensure continuous service
22. Ensure systems security
23. Identify and allocate costs
24. Educate and train users
25. Assist and advise customers
26. Manage the configuration
27. Manage problems and incidents
28. Manage data
29. Manage facilities
30. Manage operations

MONITORING

31. Monitor the process
32. Obtain independent assurance

Exhibit 24-2. An audit plan for IT outsourcing adapted from COBIT.

- Obtaining an understanding by:
  - interviewing chief information officer, administrator of IT contracts, project leaders, and end users.
  - obtaining policies relating to purchased services, vendor selection procedures, contract content of third-party relationships, list of all current external vendors, and minutes of meetings and copies of correspondence with contract people.
- Evaluating controls by:
  - considering whether IS policies and procedures relating to third parties exist.
  - reviewing contract contents, ensuring that the necessary stipulations and penalties for nonperformance are included.
- Assessing compliance by:
  - testing for the following: the list of contracts is accurate, providers are actually performing the necessary stipulations, and appropriate independence between vendor and the organization exists.
- Substantiating the risk of control objectives that are not being met by:
  - comparing similar organizations or appropriate standards.
  - identifying third-party invoices to ensure that they reflect accurately charges for the performed services.
  - determining the reasonableness of those charges.

Chapter 25

An Audit of IT Outsourcing: A Case Study

Wim Van Grembergen
Daniel Vander Borght

THIS CHAPTER PRESENTS A CASE STUDY of an organization that does not have outsourcing contracts the size of BP. The organization under review is more typical, at least in the European economic market. The procedures, findings, and conclusions drawn from this case can also be applied to many organizations in the United States.

A DESCRIPTION OF THE COMPANY UNDER REVIEW

This company is a multinational organization active in the food industry. It conducts business in more than 50 countries. Its IT department is staffed at 147, of which 60 are employed in foreign branches.

Exhibit 25-1 displays the organization chart of the IT department. The Corporate IT Director reports directly to the Chief Financial Officer. Special Projects handles infrastructure projects such as the merging of data centers and electronic data interchange (EDI). IT International personnel manage the decentralized IT services in the different subsidiaries. Technical Services is responsible for managing networks, midrange computers, personal computers, and the support of end-user computing. Central Data Production Services manages the central data center, which encompasses 1,600 terminals distributed over all of Europe. Development is responsible for the procurement, development, and maintenance of applications. The total IT budget for the year under review was more than 25 million ECU. Exhibit 25-2 shows the four budget items related to IT outsourcing.

The three cost items totaled 1.5 million ECU, 85 percent of which was for contractors' fees. IT investments reached 1 million ECU, for a total IT outsourcing budget of 2.5 million ECU or 10 percent of the companywide IT budget. The ratio between external and internal IT personnel was 16 percent.

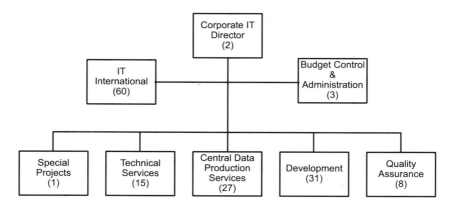

Exhibit 25-1. Organization chart of the IT department.

THE AUDIT PROJECT

The IT outsourcing audit project was carried out over a 12-month period. At that time, although the Control Objectives for Information and related Technology (COBiT) model was still in development, the authors already knew about its framework and discussed it with two members of the COBiT project team. Thus, COBiT ideas were already applied to this case, and the case was rewritten and adapted in 1996 after the publication of the two COBiT volumes.

The audit objective was the analysis and evaluation of the internal control system for IT outsourcing. The execution of this audit program took 342 hours: 50 hours (15 percent) for the preparation of the study (i.e., interviewing, obtaining documentation, and detailing the audit program), 216 hours (63 percent) for the execution of the audit, and 76 hours for discussing the findings with the auditees and writing the audit report with observations and suggestions.

Interviews

Interviews were held with the Corporate IT Director, IT personnel involved in the outsourcing projects, the procurement department, and accountants.

Exhibit 25-2. IT outsourcing budget.

Cost Budget
1. Contractors fees: costs for hiring IT professionals (body shopping)
2. Outside services: costs for services provided by external vendors
3. Consultancy fees: costs for consultancy and studies provided by externals

Investment Budget
4. IT investments accomplished by third parties (i.e., investments for items 1, 2, or 3)

Obtaining the Audit Sample

The following projects were evaluated:

- Ten outsourcing situations with interim personnel hired for a limited time
- Eight IT investment projects
- Fifteen consultant assignments
- Seven leasing or maintenance contracts for hardware

Each of the outsourcing contracts were in different phases of the outsourcing life cycle. Some were in the definition phase, and some were already completed and invoiced. In others, the suggestions for improvement had been implemented. The sample also contained cases directly managed by end-user departments. The selected cases represented the five IT functions described in the organization chart. Because of its specificity, the purchasing process for packaged software was not audited.

Evaluating the Controls, Compliance Testing, and Substantiation

The evaluation of controls, the compliance testing, and Substantiation steps were performed on each facet of the following IT outsourcing model:

- Specification of the requirements
- In- or outsourcing decision (i.e., a make or buy decision)
- Vendor selection
- Contract negotiations
- Execution of the services and management of the contract
- Payment of the delivered services

Specification of the Requirements. Evaluating the controls was performed by considering these questions:

- If the IT outsourcing project was in line with the IT strategic plan
- If there was an economic evaluation of the project
- If procedures regarding investment applications were applied
- If detailed specifications of the requirements existed
- If the project had been approved by end-user management, IT management, and the project sponsors

Findings of Compliance Testing and Substantiation. The Quality Assurance department had established rules for IT projects with a cost higher than 12,500 ECU. For these projects, a detailed written project proposal and project definition was required. In most of the outsourcing contracts, this was done by the project leader or end user with the cooperation of IT colleagues. These documents and, by consequence, the project, were usually approved by the project sponsor.

In case of an investment, the prevailing rules were mostly followed. However, a serious problem occurred in a number of cases; end users directly managed the IT outsourcing contracts without the intervention of the IT department. In many cases, this resulted in badly managed contracts, additional costs, and the implementation of systems that were not compatible with the existing installation or were very difficult to integrate. As a consequence of this finding, a new IT solution acquisition policy was established and distributed with the stipulation that each outsourcing contract first had to be evaluated by IT management.

In- or Outsourcing Decision (Make or Buy). Evaluating the controls was performed by considering these questions:

- If there was a formal procedure regarding the outsourcing decision
- If there were appropriate standard application forms for outsourcing
- If the IT budget had taken into account the outsourcing alternative
- If the outsourcing expenditures were in line with the budget
- If there were sufficient internal human and technical resources to manage and control the outsourcing project
- If the general procurement rules and procedures are applied

Findings of Compliance Testing and Substantiation. The analysis of different documents revealed that, in most cases, the choice between insourcing and outsourcing was not made on the basis of explicit criteria. It was impossible to detect why, for one project, it was decided to outsource and, for another project, it was kept in house. A new procedure was therefore proposed. Following this procedure, the project's sponsor had to specify for each outsourcing project its advantages and disadvantages and the motivation for the outsourcing decision. It was also suggested that, for example, for hiring external staff, the necessity had to be formally investigated: would the requisite internal staff be able to execute the assignment, and, if not, was there an actual deadline?

Vendor Selection

Evaluating the controls was performed by considering these questions:

- If there were at least three suppliers, when possible, involved in the selection procedure
- If each supplier was evaluated
- If the different offers were compared
- If the different items (i.e., price, expertise, and references) were investigated
- If the organization was not too dependent on some suppliers
- If the vendor decision was approved by those with approval authority
- If the appropriate staff was involved in the selection process
- If the companywide vendor selection procedure was applied

Findings of Compliance Testing and Substantiation. The necessity of contacting several suppliers is best illustrated with one of the projects that had been audited. The project was to convert a UNISYS/VM environment to an IBM/MVS environment. The highest bid was more than 1.5 million ECU, whereas the lowest and selected bid was less than 0.5 million ECU. Several serious shortcomings were detected:

- The procurement department was not involved in the IT outsourcing decision.
- The selection of providers was not formalized and, in many cases, only a single vendor was consulted.
- The selection criteria were determined by the project leader.
- Long-term contracts were never renegotiated.
- The same providers were always used in the case of body shopping, and these providers were directly contacted by the project leaders.

To overcome these problems, it was recommended that Corporate Purchasing had to be involved in the vendor selection:

- The existing companywide purchase procedures must be implemented for IT outsourcing.
- Purchasers had to support the vendor selection and be held responsible for the economic and financial negotiations.
- All existing long-term contracts must be investigated and possibly renegotiated.

Contract Negotiations. Evaluating the controls was performed by considering whether contract contents included the necessary stipulations as illustrated in Exhibit 25-3.

Findings of Compliance Testing and Substantiation. On the basis of the checklist in Exhibit 25-3, each contract of the sample was inspected. Compliance was evaluated through scores from 0 to 4. A score of 0 indicated that a contract item was not included, and a score of 4 indicated that the contract item was fully described. The main conclusions reached about the quality of the contracts were:

- The absence of standard contracts and standard checklists. (Exhibit 25-3 was compiled by the authors on the basis of existing literature.)
- On the average, 36 percent of the checklist items in Exhibit 25-3 were not included in the audited contracts.
- The most common items not included were:
  — documentation
  — maintenance
  — security and confidentiality
  — legal measures
  — quality assurance

Exhibit 25-3. Evaluation criteria for IT outsourcing contracts.

- In General
  - Subject of the contract
  - Name and address of parties
  - Duration of the contract
  - Annulment of the contract
  - Possible extensions to the contract
  - What-if case of breach of contract
- Technical Requirements
  - Detailed description of required services or products (i.e., requests for proposal)
  - Service level agreements, both qualitative and quantitative
  - Terms of delivery
  - Description of execution phases
  - Place of execution
  - Planning of different activities and phases
  - Testing: plan, place, and responsibilities
  - Temporary and final delivery
  - Level of support
  - Supply of material
  - Roles between contracting parties during the life of the contract
  - Reporting of service
  - Milestones and control points
  - Portability of the solution
  - Integration in the existing installation
- Financial Requirements
  - Unit prices (per hour, per day, or fixed) and additional costs
  - Index wages and overtime
  - Invoicing: date of maturity and invoicing address
  - Instrument of payment and currency
  - Bank guarantee
  - Maintenance costs
  - Invoice basis
  - Contents of the invoices
- Documentation
  - Kinds of documentation and contents
  - Language
  - Number of copies
  - Delivery time
- Education and Training
  - Kinds of education and contents
  - Languages
  - Number of courses
  - Delivery time

Exhibit 25-3. Evaluation criteria for IT outsourcing contracts. (continued)

- Maintenance
  - Subject
  - Term of validity
  - Intervention time
- Disputes
  - Way of determination (i.e., when is there a dispute?)
  - Settlement of disputes: arbitrage or court
  - Penalties for nonperformance
- Security and Confidentiality
  - Nondisclosure guarantees
  - Level of access given to vendor personnel
  - Rules and procedures to use internal IT resources
- Legal Measures
  - Access to the tools used by the vendor (e.g., development software)
  - Access to and availability of end products (e.g., source codes)
  - Dissolution process
  - Subcontracting
  - Multiple providers and mutual responsibility
- Quality Assurance
  - Use of standardized methods and methodologies
  - Specification of quality norms
  - Quality control process
- Vendor Personnel
  - Names and resumes of personnel assigned to the project
  - Continuity and replacement of personnel
  - Trial assignments
  - Availability

Some contracts were not signed. It was strongly recommended to establish a standard contract, especially for the process of hiring external IT personnel and to apply the checklist in Exhibit 25-3 to other contracts.

Execution of Services and Management of the Contract. Evaluating the controls was performed by considering these questions:

- If sufficient internal IT professionals were involved in the execution and management of the outsourcing contract
- If security measures were not violated by the outsourcing staff
- If the necessary reporting and documentation was supplied
- If the quality was measured and assured
- If the monthly performance records of the outsourcing staff was controlled

- If all modifications to the original agreement were formally written, approved, and agreed to

Findings of Compliance Testing and Substantiation. In this case, the management of IT outsourcing projects was the responsibility of the project leaders. This was undoubtedly an effective practice. However, two major shortcomings were detected: the development process was not standardized within the company, which made it very difficult to manage the external outsourcing projects; and, there was no tradition regarding service level agreements (SLAs)between IT operations and end users, which lead to the nonapplication of SLAs to outsourcing assignments. As a result of this audit, more effective practices were introduced in both areas, development and operations.

Payment of the Delivered Services. Evaluating the controls was performed by considering these questions:

- If the principle of separation of duties was implemented regarding the procurement and payment of the IT outsourcing contract
- If the traditional invoice controls were implemented (e.g., whether only delivered services or products were invoiced and paid)
- If the companywide procedure for the reception of goods was also implemented for IT
- If there was a correct accounting imputation of the IT outsourcing costs (investment or costs)
- If the invoicing addresses were correct

Findings of Compliance Testing and Substantiation. A detailed analysis was made for all invoices greater than 25,000 ECU. These problems were reported:

- In some cases (4 percent of a sample of 87 invoices), IT products were not reported to IT Budget Control and Administration.
- In 30 percent of a sample of 87 investigated invoices, an incorrect imputation was detected, resulting in incorrect depreciation rates.
- Some outsourcing contract with a value greater than 250,000 ECU were incorrectly imputed as costs.
- In 13 percent of a sample of 87 invoices, the invoice was sent to the end user and not to the official invoice address.

It was recommended that the Department of Budget Control and Administration should implement the necessary procedures regarding the completion and payment of the delivered services.

CONCLUSION

It is the authors' experience that the IT outsourcing process reported in this case has to be a more controlled process to overcome major short-comings. Detected problems were:

- The specification of the requirements by end users without the intervention and support of IT personnel.
- The choice between outsourcing and insourcing was not made in a systematic manner.
- The vendor selection was not formalized and, in many cases, only a single vendor was consulted.
- The lack of standard contracts and checklists for requests for proposals.
- Service level agreements were not uniformly required.
- The lack of or only partially the application of companywide procedures for procurement and payment.

This IT outsourcing audit was performed on the basis of a standardized control model: the COBiT model developed by ISACA. This model proved to be a good framework for establishing IT outsourcing controls and for planning and carrying out an audit. However, this model has to be more detailed and should be adapted to the particular environment. Finally, based on other cases, the authors conclude that these shortcomings are generic and can be found in other organizations and that IT outsourcing in general has to be a more controlled process.

Section VI
Long-Term Strategies for Becoming an Outsourcing Champion

Chapter 26
Outsourcing and Long-Term Strategy

William R. King

A SENIOR BUSINESS EXECUTIVE JUSTIFIED A $1 BILLION, DECADE-LONG IS OUTSOURCING CONTRACT on two grounds. "First," the executive said, "the vendor buys our IS assets and pays us money upfront; the annual contracted expense is less than we incur now; the vendor hires all of our people and guarantees them jobs for at least a year; and there's no learning curve, because the people who used to do the work will still be doing it, they'll just be working for the vendor."

"Second," the executive continued, "we decided that IS is not a core competency, so we could afford to make this judgment strictly on economic grounds. In fact, it was a no-brainer."

The executive might have added that outsourcing is currently a major trend in U.S. business: 85 percent of banks have outsourced their IS function, and up to 50 percent of the firms in other major industries have done so as well.

If he were not avoiding insulting his IS people, the executive might well have said that IS is notorious for the enormous demands it places on scarce capital investment budgets, for its cost and schedule overruns, for its inability to clearly demonstrate its direct impact on the bottom line, and for its arcane content and language. If a business manager can outsource the function, reduce costs, improve the balance sheet, and avoid or reduce the need to deal with Millions of Instructions Per Second and Computer-Aided Software Engineering and UNIX and the like, why not?

There was a time when business managers wanted to tightly control everything. They vertically integrated and created many small inefficient functions. Now they are doing an about-face. They are not even pretending to be able to do everything well in-house, thus outsourcing is popular.

0-8493-0875-?/00/$0.00+$.50
© 2000 by CRC Press LLC

But, of course, in an era in which quality and customer service are paramount, there is grave danger of outsourcing functions that can directly affect either quality or service. Who wants to depend on outsiders in dealing with customers or in retrieving data that is crucial to servicing customers?

OUTSOURCING IS A STRATEGIC ISSUE

Decisions regarding outsourcing significant functions are among the most strategic that can be made by an organization, because they address the basic organizational choice of the functions for which internal expertise is developed and nurtured and those for which such expertise is purchased. These are basic decisions regarding organizational design. Therefore, decisions concerning outsourcing should not be made because a vendor makes an offer that is too good to refuse or because it is currently faddish to outsource a particular function or service.

Major outsourcing decisions are strategic and should be made after other key choices pertaining to a vision, a mission, core competencies, and key success factors. Although this may seem like a textbookish approach, the fact is that outsourcing a function that might potentially be a core competence or a key success factor, merely because it may be economically desirable to do so in the short run, may result in the unplanned "hollowing" of the organization, thus jeopardizing its raison d'etre. (This notion was first discussed in "The Hollow Corporation," a 1986 *BusinessWeek* report that focused on companies that had outsourced production to the degree they had little or no production base to support the products they marketed.)

Factors in Deciding to Outsource

A wise decision about outsourcing IS depends on having a solid understanding of some fundamental factors, including:

- the overall consequences of any make-or-buy decision
- an explicit multiple-criteria understanding of what constitutes a core competency
- an assessment of whether IS might be a future key success factor, even though it has not been one in the past
- the new skills and attitudes that are required for effective outsourcing
- alternatives to outsourcing

CONSEQUENCES OF A MAKE-OR-BUY DECISION

One simple view of outsourcing is to characterize it as a simple make-or-buy choice. However, the textbook version of the make-or-buy decision is inadequate because it usually views the choice as an isolated one that has no long-term implications. Even in the simple case of the decision to make or buy a part or component, it should never really be a do-whatever-is-cheapest decision, because when an organization chooses to buy it is, to some degree, foreclosing the possibility of having both options in the future.

The reason, of course, is that with every "buy" choice, the capability of "making" in the future is, to some degree, lost. Eventually, in a series of make-or-buy choices, this loss of expertise comes to dominate the decision, and it is always less expensive to buy than to suffer the fixed costs of rebuilding the degraded expertise. Eventually, such rebuilding is not even feasible to do, and the expertise has been forever lost.

The former Secretary of Labor Robert B. Reich had described a situation in which a company's engineers complained that "[the company] thinks it's cheaper to buy rather than build, and it is today. But if we don't make it in-house, we don't gain the experience and knowledge that goes with making it. And then we can't develop a whole range of technologies that are likely to evolve from that component."[1]

WHAT IS A CORE COMPETENCY?

The notion of core competencies is clearly important to outsourcing decisions. The ideas that companies should follow a contrived "hollowing" strategy, in which only core competencies are retained and other capabilities are purchased, is very much in vogue. The identification of IS as a function that is not a core competency is often made casually and in retrospect, when in fact the parameters of what constitutes a core competency should be carefully spelled out and assessed before such a decision is made.

Criteria for Core Competencies

Just because a business is good at something does not necessarily mean that it is a core competency, even though it may have been the basis for considerable competitive advantage in the past. Conversely, just because something has not been of critical importance in the past does not mean that it is not, or might not be, a core competency.

A core competency is a capability that:

- evolved slowly through collective learning and information sharing
- cannot be quickly enhanced through additional large investments
- is synergistic with other capabilities
- cannot be easily imitated or transferred to others
- confers competitive advantage in the perception of customers
- can be a key success factor for the industry (one that historians will use to explain who won and who lost in the marketplace)
- cannot readily be "cashed out" (i.e., one in which investment is irreversible)[2]

A careful look at many organizations that do not typically think of IS as a core competency reveals that IS can be seen to have (or be very close to having) many of these traits. For example, IS often meets the first three criteria, and significant elements of IS usually meet the fourth. IS often has the potential to meet the fifth and sixth criteria as well. Such an assessment should give pause to anyone who wishes to dismiss IS as a bothersome service function for which an outsourcing choice is a no-brainer.

A FUTURE KEY SUCCESS FACTOR

Even though IS may not meet the key success factor criteria from a historical perspective, the critical question is, "Does it have the potential to be of critical importance?"

In an information age, a wise business manager will not be too quick to dismiss the possibility of developing strategic systems those that can create competitive advantage or systems that are competitive necessities those that can match the competition and keep the business in the ball game. Similarly, the potential for using IS to make products or processes more information intensive should be carefully thought through. Information-based innovations in products and processes are some of the most common that are currently being implemented, so it seems unwise to forfeit this opportunity.

Of course, defenders of IS outsourcing will argue that most large organizations do not outsource critical elements of IS such as the development of new applications, so many of these things can still be done even after some IS operations are outsourced. However, this may be too clever a distinction. When it comes to IS expertise the kind that can confer competitive advantage or add value to products or processes using IT there is no way of ensuring that the "right" capabilities are kept and people and the wrong ones are outsourced.

So, outsourcing IS may lead to the loss of a capability that could potentially be a key success factor. This has been demonstrated in many industries that are not information intensive as well as in those that depend on IS.[3]

New Skills and Attitudes Required for Effective Outsourcing

Outsourcing is often viewed as a way of reducing the total administrative and coordination costs within an organization and of avoiding the management headaches associated with IS. However, this may be a simplistic and unrealistic view because outsourcing requires the organization to develop a new set of skills and new ways of managing, which increases other costs and creates new headaches.

Difficulty in Managing Outsourcing Contracts

Executives who believe that they simply sign a contract and walk away from their problems need only look at the U.S. government, which outsources the procurement of everything from soap to complex weapons systems. The federal government's contract management system, which is necessitated by this outsourcing, is a professional discipline in itself one whose best-known manifestations are the purchase of $300 hammers and $800 toilet seats.

Many organizations have several IS outsourcing vendors one for data center operations, one for network administration, one for disaster recovery, for example. Managing a single large, complex outside vendor relationship is difficult; managing several of them amplifies the difficulties.

Lack of Options. Contract changes are a major issue in managing outsourcing. Many government contractors are alleged to buy into contracts with unrealistically low prices, then make a profit on the changes that are invariably required in long-term contracts involving complex systems. So, the government's purchase of overpriced toilet seats and hammers stems partly from the lack of alternative sources that are available to the purchaser after it becomes subject to a long-term contract and from the need to provide fair compensation when changes are made or new requirements are placed on the vendor. The hammer may be something that seemingly should cost only a few dollars because it is similar to one available in any hardware store. But, when a hammer is added to a large weapons systems contract, it often has a special purpose, so (to use an IS analogy) it must be tested so that it does not introduce bugs into the system, and the vendor must be compensated for the extra costs, including overhead, involved in providing it in small quantity.

The Fine Print. In outsourcing contracts, the devil is truly in the details, and careful, detailed management is therefore required. Changes are inevitable in a long-run contract and many cannot be foreseen. However, when many changes that could be foreseen are added to those that could not, contract management can become a nightmare. It is not uncommon for an IS executive to be surprised when the IS vendor bills for software license transfer fees, or when the IS executive finds that no provision has been made for obtaining cost data needed for negotiating contract extensions or enhancements.

Who's a Partner? Of course, vendors attempt to sell outsourcing contracts as "partnerships." Generally, they are no such things! Partnerships require a significant degree of commonality of objectives; outsourcing vendors are primarily motivated by their own profit.

In one highly publicized case, Massachusetts Blue Cross and Blue Shield's (BC/BS) large outsourcing contract was hailed as a model in 1992 in part because of its applications development partnership provisions.[4] However, in January 1994, Blue Cross and Blue Shield was ordered to pay $7 million to employees who had been transferred to the vendor on short notice (some of whom were subsequently terminated). A representative of the vendor is quoted by *InformationWeek* as reacting that the court judgments " ... were against Blue Cross [not against us] and from [our]... perspective were probably justified."[5] Therein lies a lesson both in partnerships and details.

Once IS is outsourced, top management no longer has direct command authority over it. Every special or emergency request becomes the subject of a contact change proposal that must be formalized and negotiated. So, an entirely new set of attitudes and way of managing is required when IS is outsourced.

Alternatives to Outsourcing

Suppose that a manager is considering outsourcing the IS function and that it has already been determined that it is not now, or ever likely to become, a core competence. Then, is not it best to farm out this nettlesome function?

Well, perhaps it is, but IS should be viewed as a window on the world of information and communications technology, which clearly is going to become even more important to everyone. Is it really sensible to not pay attention to this significant function and its associated technologies? Is it reasonable to expect that an organization will adequately keep aware of the latest technological opportunities when it does not have specialists with intimate knowledge of the technologies, or if it has far fewer of them? Hardware and software vendors quickly learn that there is no payoff in calling on those who have outsourced IS. IS executives who once viewed these salespeople as irritants can quickly come to feel that they are out of the loop when it comes to new developments.

The alternatives to outsourcing are not just the status quo, which may well be unsatisfactory. The first to be considered is the partial outsourcing that is done by many large organizations. Many organizations retain applications development in-house, for example. In effect, by doing so they are insourcing new, potentially important systems and outsourcing legacy systems that are necessary but not important to the future of the business.

Other alternatives should include consideration of the same strategies that are currently being employed in other core business activities redesign of the IS function and processes, new IS training programs, IS quality programs, and new incentives such as productivity gain sharing. There is evidence that such efforts can produce results that might represent a significant improvement on the IS status quo.

CONCLUSION

In an era in which most organizations have given up trying to perform all functions, it is reasonable to consider outsourcing rote utility-like systems while retaining the expertise to develop a strategic infrastructure, an information architecture, and a suite of strategic systems. However, this must be done very carefully after consideration has been given to the long-term loss of expertise, a sophisticated notion of core competency, a serious assessment of potential future key success factors, a realistic assessment of the new problems that outsourcing is likely to create, and the alternatives that are available.

Notes

1. R.B. Reich, "Companies Are Cutting Their Hearts Out,"*The New York Times Magazine* (December 19, 1993), pp. 54-55.
2. This list is based on several sources including: P.J.H. Schoemaker,"How to Link Strategic Vision to Core Capabilities" *Sloan Management Review,* (Fall 1992), pp. 67-81;I. Diericky and K. Coll, "Asset Stock Accumulation and Sustainability of Competitive Advantage"*Management Science 35* (1989), pp. 1504-1514.
3. W.R. King, V. Grover and E. Hufnagle, "Using Information and Information Technology for Sustainable Comparative Advantage," *Information and Management,* (1989), pp. 87-93.
4. N. Margolis, "Massachusetts Blue Cross Tries EDS Rx," *Computerworld 26,* no. 4 (January 27, 1992), pp. 1, 131.
5. J.P. McPartlin, "Crossed Up: Ruling in Blue Cross Case Send Pointed Message to Outsourcers and Their Clients," *Information Week* (January 31, 1994), p. 12.

Chapter 27
The Effects of Outsourcing on Information Security

Marie Alner

OUTSOURCING CAN ENCOMPASS A VARIETY OF INFORMATION TECHNOLOGY FUNCTIONS. Any function can be outsourced: systems operations, Transaction Processing, application development and maintenance, network management, and microcomputer integration and maintenance. The decision to outsource depends on a combination of logistical, organizational, and financial considerations.

Historically, outsourcing has been more common in mainframe environments. But as a result of downsizing, companies are increasingly inclined to outsource desktop services, including LAN administration and maintenance.

WHY OUTSOURCE?

The primary motive for considering outsourcing is cost reduction. Long-term outsourcing contracts convert variable costs to fixed costs, and make technology spending more predictable. The tax advantage comes from the ability to deduct the expense of outsourcing fees from current year earnings as opposed to depreciating an internal data processing department's hardware assets over time. Outsourcing agreements can yield capital for cash-strapped organizations if the outsourcer purchases the client's hardware assets. In addition, companies who outsource enjoy cash flow improvements resulting from the transfer of software licenses and personnel to the outsourcer, and the release of obligation from a facility lease and the associated physical plant maintenance costs of a data center.

Outsourcing providers guarantee service and system availability. Their data center facilities are outfitted with redundantly designed systems to avert power and cooling failures and to detect water leakage, smoke, or excessive heat — anything that will adversely affect system continuity. Furthermore, the operations procedures of outsourcing providers — which might include advanced system and communications monitoring tools and specialized professional training — are designed to ensure uninterrupted processing and network availability. Leading-edge data center facilities are costly to operate; the expense can rarely be justified without the economies of scale derived from a shared environment.

In an outsourcing relationship, software and hardware upgrades become the concern of the outsourcer rather than a distraction to senior management. The client no longer deals with day-to-day information system details and can focus instead on business planning. Executives are freed from having to spend hours evaluating technology directions, technology funding plans, and the resulting vendor proposals. The outsourcer should be charged with maintaining service levels for current needs and providing timely and cost-efficient technology solutions in support of the proposed strategic direction.

Hiring and retaining highly trained technology professionals is often cited as an additional incentive to outsource. The core business focus of outsourcing providers is technology. Their personnel are highly informed about emerging technologies and their implementation within specific industries. This level of knowledge is shared by their security professionals as well.

TYPES OF OUTSOURCING ARRANGEMENTS

In an outsourcing arrangement, everything is negotiable. Some of the most common arrangements are:

- Specialty transaction processing only (e.g., payroll and credit card processing including data communications from the data center to the client site
- Systems operations (e.g., operations and maintenance of mainframe hardware and systems software) including data communications from the data center to the client site
- Systems operations and applications development (e.g., operations and maintenance of mainframe hardware and systems software combined with application programming and maintenance) including data communications from the data center to the client site
- LAN hardware and or software administration in a microcomputer environment which may or may not be connected to a mainframe by means of a network
- Any of the preceding combinations plus distributed mini-and microcomputer systems. This is the most complex environment, with mainframes, mini-, and microcomputers all connected via a network

The type of outsourcing arrangement selected directly affects the type of information security issues and concerns that will be encountered. Because communications networks are a key component in all of the previously mentioned arrangements, security and access issues are particularly pertinent.

Given space limitations, this chapter focuses primarily on the second and third options given — that is, systems operations and systems operations and applications development. Some microcomputer and LAN issues are discussed when appropriate because PCs and LANs can compromise mainframe security no matter how well the mainframe itself is secured.

SECURITY STRENGTHS AND WEAKNESSES
OF OUTSOURCING ARRANGEMENTS

There are several advantages to outsourcing arrangements. The outsourcer's information security staff can often provide valuable insight, in a confidential manner, about how other companies handle the same types of security problems.

The outsourcing company's information security administrators and systems programmers specializing in information security can be a valuable asset to the client organization. For example, the outsourcing provider may be able to help the client reengineer access rules to tighten security or to react to regulatory changes. The outsourcer may provide valuable information when your applications programmers perform a database migration or an update that involves internal application security, and may be able to provide product recommendations, thereby saving the client's staff from a lengthy evaluation process.

Aside from the benefits derived from the outsourcer's data center experience and internal resources, clients stand to gain from the overall information security environment. Because outsourcing providers have strict contractual obligations to their clients and must maintain their reputation in the marketplace, their control procedures are usually well documented and enforced.

On the minus side, a shared environment with multiple clients poses more risks than the contained environment of an internal data center. In multiple client sites, LANs, wide area network, dial-up access for multiple clients increases the points of exposure: the risk of third-party employees having access to data; the risk of more than one client sharing direct access storage device or spool, the risks inherent to data transmissions; the risks of sharing a network; and in some cases the risk of sharing central processing unit under one operating system or under separate logical partitions. In addition, other clients may have gateways to the mainframe from LANs and other distributed systems. A small exposure can grow several orders of magnitude larger in an outsourcing environment because of the sharing of resources with the outsourcer's other clients.

These risks are addressed by the outsourcer's physical and logical security procedures. The greatest risk comes from poor upfront planning and poor communications between outsourcer and client.

DIVIDING UP RESPONSIBILITIES

In the new environment, the company's information security becomes a cooperative effort between the client company and the outsourcer. Whereas the outsourcer is the custodian of the data, the client is still the owner.

Planning is of the essence. Great attention must be given to determining which parts of the information security function should be performed by the outsourcing company and which should be handled by the client. Because the client company still owns its data, it should reserve some of its staff to monitor the security work handled by the outsourcer. Therefore, it is not advisable to transfer the entire security staff to the outsourcing company. Although the outsourcer's staff will most likely handle the routine functions of maintaining a secure system, the client's staff must monitor internal compliance with the outsourcer's security policies and procedures as well as internal information security.

The following paragraphs discuss responsibilities for performing specific security functions.

Installation and Maintenance of the Information Security Software. Information security software is an integral part of the operating system. In an environment where the mainframe and its system software are being controlled by the outsourcing company, it would be wise to also have the outsourcer's staff support the information security software. It can be installed and maintained either by the group that installs the operating system or by the outsourcer's information security group.

Access Control and Security Administration. Responsibility for such administration depends on whether the information security function is centralized or decentralized. In a centralized environment, one group of people is primarily responsible for setting up log-on IDs, writing access rules, and ensuring compliance with information security policies and procedures. If information security is currently administered in this manner, it should probably be kept that way.

However, because outsourcers are ultimately responsible for the integrity of the information security databases, they will probably prefer to have their own security staff actually add and delete log-on IDs and write the access rules on the client's behalf. The client's group may be limited to making updates to existing log-on IDs (e.g., resetting passwords and suspending terminated employees). Requests for new log-on IDs or for access rules would be approved by the client's security staff first, then passed to the outsourcer's information security staff for processing. In this manner the outsourcer's information security staff could ensure that the client is not inadvertently creating security exposures.

In a decentralized information security environment, security administrators may be assigned locally to each of the client's departments or divisions. These local administrators set up log-on IDs and write access rules for their area only; they are not able to make changes to log-on IDs or access rules belonging to another department or division.

Centralized control results in a more consistent implementation of information security and its associated policies and procedures. If administering information security centrally is not a viable option for an organization, it is critical that the information security staff monitor the work done by local security administrators to ensure that the integrated security procedures of the client and the outsourcer are implemented consistently throughout the company.

Violation Report Review and Investigation. The outsourcing company should provide the client with the necessary data for violation reports. However, the review and investigation of these violations are probably best handled by the client's own information security staff because they are more likely to know which data is critical. In addition, because the client's security staff is most familiar with internal personnel and operations, they can move more quickly to follow-up on security violations. The outsourcer's information security staff should be available as needed if additional investigation is required to resolve a particular problem.

Relationship of the Outsourcer's Information Security Staff with the Company's Users and Customers. A company that prides itself on its personal relationship with customers probably wants to keep contact with the outsourcer's staff minimal and only at the company's request. The company may also act as a liaison between the outsourcer and customers if contact is required to resolve a problem.

It may also be desirable to handle internal users' contacts with the outsourcer's information security staff in the same manner. Many problems and questions concerning information security are specific to company policies and procedures; these can be better explained by the company's own staff. If the outsourcer is to handle users' information security problems and questions, guidelines should clearly delineate what the outsourcer's staff should handle, whose authorization is required to address routine information security problems, and what types of issues should be referred to the company's own information security staff. A good outsourcing company should insist on clear guidelines so neither the company's internal staff nor its customers feel like they're getting the runaround when trying to resolve security problems.

Responsibility for Information Security Policies and Procedures. The outsourcing company has its own internal information security policies and procedures, as does the client company. Incompatible policies can create problems. Therefore, it is important to check for conflicts in the company's and the outsourcer's information security methodology as early in the process as possible. It is easier to resolve problems early rather than later, after everything is locked in. The outsourcer can provide help in writing or revising company policies and procedures.

Responsibility for Security Awareness Training. Although the company is ultimately responsible for ensuring that its employees receive the proper training, the actual training sessions can easily be turned over to the outsourcing company. The company should ensure that the outsourcer and company are in agreement over class curriculum.

OUTSOURCING SECURITY ISSUES

This section of the chapter addresses several security issues that are specific to the outsourcing environment.

Sharing Computer Resources with Other Clients of the Outsourcer. One of the major functions of the outsourcer's information security group is to ensure that its clients do not compromise each other's processing environment either intentionally or unintentionally. With some outsourcers, several companies may share the outsourcer's computer resources. For example, processing may be run on the same central processing unit; this might be done under separate logical partitions or under the same operating system. If computers are to be shared, the client company should verify that other clients cannot access the company's applications.

With shared direct access storage device and shared tape devices, the outsourcer's other clients may be able to access the company's data, even if processing is not shared. Security software should be implemented to prevent such exposures.

It is very likely that client companies will be sharing a network. There are various ways to implement network security, including several network security products that recently have become available that interface with the mainframe's information security software. The outsourcer's network security methods and software tools should be identified and evaluated. The service level agreement should specify the network security controls desired by the client.

Assurance That the Company Is Not Billed for Another Client's Use of Resources. A charge-back software product can solve this problem. In addition, information security software should be used to ensure that only authorized log-on IDs use cost centers belonging to the company.

Information Security Audit Rights of the Client Company. As noted earlier, the outsourcer should give the client's information security staff the ability to review (and in some cases, update) its log-on IDs and access rules. The outsourcer should also give audit authority for those same log-on IDs and access rules to the client's auditors. It would, however, be counterproductive for the outsourcer to allow all of its clients' auditors to do a full system audit whenever they wish. Instead, the outsourcer should regularly provide clients with the results from full systems audits performed by a mutually agreeable third party.

Outsourcer's Access to Client's Data. To ensure the availability of the client's data, some of the outsourcer's staff need to access the company's data. The challenge is to determine what the outsourcer needs to know and what is the appropriate level of authority for data access.

The outsourcer's internal policies and procedures should be consulted to answer these questions. Is the outsourcer staff required to sign confidentiality agreements? Does the outsourcer have stringent access controls? Is its staff bonded? Are policies and procedures enforced and disciplinary measures clearly stated? Which types of individuals on the outsourcer's staff have powerful privileges and why?

If the company plans to outsource its applications programming to a systems management provider or to a third party, it should ensure that there is a methodology to create test data as opposed to copying current production data into a test file. The application programmers should be prevented from updating production data. There should be an emergency procedure in place to fix production problems in a controlled manner and provide an audit trail of what was done and why.

Determining Ownership of Data and Programs. The client owns its business data; the outsourcer is a mere custodian of that data. But what about the data governing the outsourcing relationship? Who owns the billing information? The performance data? The client should determine which data actually belongs to the company and which data requiring the company's access belongs to the outsourcer. This distinction is important when it comes to writing access rules, because the data owner determines who is allowed access to that data. The distinction between these should be clearly spelled out in the service level agreements.

If applications programming is outsourced, information security should have a prominent place in the development cycle. A test methodology should be in place so that copies of production data are not copied into test files. Appropriate change control procedures should also be in place.

Even ownership of policies and procedures can become an issue. If the outsourcer writes policies and procedures for the client but owns the copyright, the client company cannot change the policies and procedures without approval from the outsourcer. The contract should transfer intellectual property rights and copyrights to the client so the client can update procedures in the future and take them at the end of the outsourcing arrangement.

Data Retention, Destruction, and Backup. Responsibility for data backup should be clearly defined. This decision should take into account the most efficient and cost-effective method of backup.

Outsourcing providers may have automated backup tools that can make the efficiency question easy to answer. As data management becomes more and more automated, it becomes increasingly important for the guidelines regarding data retention, destruction, and backup to be completely documented.

The outsourcer's chargeback rates for data storage are based on the requirements for availability and performance of data sets. Space on a high performance disk drive is substantially more expensive than that on tape. The rates directly affect management's decisions regarding how and when data is backed up and archived and to what type of storage device.

Service level agreements regarding data management should clearly spell out exactly what is required in terms of retention, destruction, backup, and performance. In addition, it should be ensured that the data is protected adequately until destroyed in accordance with the guidelines in the service level agreements.

SECURITY AND GENERAL MANAGEMENT ISSUES

There are some areas for which the information security staff is not usually directly responsible but which must be considered. Several of these issues are discussed in the following paragraphs.

Physical Security. It should be verified that the outsourcer has adequate physical security to meet the client company's needs.

Change Control. The outsourcer should have implemented an adequate change control methodology. The client company should always be informed of any hardware or software changes that could affect it. These types of changes could involve anything from installing a new central processing unit to upgrading the security software. In addition, the client's staff should be given the opportunity to test these changes before they go into production and provide feedback to the outsourcer regarding the test.

Disaster Recovery. The outsourcer should have an adequate disaster recovery plan and a contract with a reputable hot-site vendor that has a configuration that will meet the client company's needs. The hot site should also have a backup plan, and it should have physical security at least comparable to what the outsourcer has at its regular site. It should also be verified that the security software is fully functional when processing at the hot site. The client company's staff should be involved in testing the disaster recovery plan on a regular basis, and the plan should be updated as needs change.

Regulatory Requirements. The outsourcer should be able to handle any special regulatory requirements the client company may have. For example, a bank has to deal with bank regulatory agencies; an investment firm with SEC regulations. The outsourcing company should be made aware of any special requirements and its ability to meet the relevant industry's regulatory demands in a timely fashion verified.

SERVICE LEVEL AGREEMENTS

Service level agreements are critical in the outsourcing business. The client company and the outsourcer must know exactly, in writing, what to expect from each other. The quality of the service level agreements directly affect the quality of the relationship between the client company and the outsourcer.

The outsourcer will probably go out of its way to ensure that the client is satisfied with the agreements. Do not assume anything — if its important, get it in writing. Outsourcing contracts generally are in effect for three to ten years. A lot can happen during that period — people are reassigned to other projects, are promoted, leave the company, or simply forget. Nonetheless, an outsourcer should allow for reasonable interpretation of the service level agreements during the life of the contract.

The information security service level agreement should specify the services expected from the outsourcer's information security staff and what functions will be retained by the client's staff. For example, if the outsourcer is setting up log-on IDs and access rules for the client company, expected turnaround times and accuracy rates should be indicated.

The service level agreement should also specify how emergencies will be handled. Whose authorization is required to fix specific types of problems? Which problems are to be handled by the client's staff and which by the outsourcer's staff? Will there be 24-hour-a-day coverage from the outsourcer's staff or is coverage during normal business hours sufficient?

The agreement should also indicate how special requests will be handled. This includes customizing information security software and implementing interfaces between information security software and applications. Will there be additional cost associated with these special requests? And, what kind of turnaround time is expected on these types of changes?

Preventing Conflicts. It should be verified that other departments of the client company that deal directly with the outsourcer also have written service level agreements and that these agreements do not conflict with those written for information security. For example, consider the consequences of conflicting procedures when a production job abnormally terminates in the middle of the night as a result of a security violation. The information security service level agreement may state that before the outsourcer's staff writes the access rule, they must secure authorization from the client's information security staff to ensure that data is not compromised by inappropriate change control procedures. Concurrently, computer operations may have a service level agreement written with another department in the client company that states that abnormal terminations will be fixed within two hours, regardless of cause or resolution. If the client information security staff could not be reached within the stated period of time, the resolution window would be missed, which would probably result in conflict and finger-pointing the next morning.

The service level agreements should indicate courses of action that can be taken if the agreements are not met. Often, service-level agreements include bonuses for service delivery above stated standards and penalties for substandard service. Only very serious service level agreement breaches allow the contract to be terminated.

It should be remembered that service level agreements are a two-way street. If the client company does not fulfill its end of the service-level agreements, the results can be equally devastating. The client should understand the liability associated with information security breaches by either party, including the limitation of damages. There are legal implications if either company fails to fulfill its obligations; this should be adequately covered in the contract.

In November 1991, new sentencing guidelines from the United States Sentencing Commission took effect. If a company or its employees is involved in criminal activity (which can include breach of information security), the company is now exposed to monetary penalties substantial enough to push the company into bankruptcy and to court-ordered supervision of its future business activities. To protect against such action, both the client and the outsourcer must have effective information security policies and procedures so as to prove in court that both have an effective compliance program in place. Any fines will be substantially lower if it can be shown that an effective program is in place.

CONCLUSION

Because companies outsource their data processing for a variety of reasons or, at some point, at least investigate the possibility of outsourcing, the need for writing thorough service level agreements cannot be stressed strongly enough. It is important that everyone involved, both at the client company and at the outsourcer, knows exactly who is responsible for each function in order to prevent misunderstandings. (Exhibit 27-1 summarizes the responsibilities of the outsourcer and the client.) It is also important to make information security an issue at the beginning (i.e., during the outsourcing selection process) to ensure a successful outcome.

Exhibit 27-1. Outsourcer and client responsibilities.

Outsourcer	Client
• Installs and maintains data security software.	• Defines business needs and identifies data security issues.
• Writes and maintains data center data security policies and procedures.	• Writes and maintains internal data security policies and procedures.
• Quality ensures client's log-on ID structure and access rules.	• Defines structure for log-on IDs and access rules.
• Sets up log-on IDs and access rules according to agreed-on specifications.	• Approves log-on IDs and access rules as implemented.
• Provides data for violation reports.	• Updates log-on IDs.
• Supports client liaison to internal users and customers on as needed.	• Investigates and resolves violation reports.
• Supports client training through technology transfer; may deliver training on contract basis.	• Acts as liaison between outsourcer and internal users and customers.
• Upholds service-level agreements and enforces policies and procedures to protect all clients.	• Arranges or provides data security training for internal users.
• Implements regulatory compliance procedures in a timely fashion.	• Adheres to stated policies and procedures and ensures internal compliance.
	• Provides outsourcer with regulatory requirements.

Index

Index

I

J

K